# The College and University Band

# The College and University Band

An Anthology of Papers from the Conferences of the College Band Directors National Association, 1941–1975

*Compiled by*

**David Whitwell**
*California State University, Northridge*

**Acton Ostling Jr.**
*University of Louisville*

Music Educators National Conference
in cooperation with
the College Band Directors National Association
Reston, Virginia

The text and folios for this book were set in Palatino, a typeface designed by Hermann Zapf and named after Giambattista Palatino, a sixteenth-century calligrapher. Titles were set in Cooper Black Italic, designed by Oswald Bruce Cooper and introduced in 1921 by the American Type Founders Company.

Edited by Duke Johns
Designed by Malcolm E. Bessom
Cover illustration by Joseph Scopin

Copyright © 1977 by Music Educators National Conference
All rights reserved

Library of Congress Catalog Card Number: 77-84482

Printed in the United States of America

Music Educators National Conference
1902 Association Drive
Reston, Virginia 22091

# Foreword

More than three and a half decades ago, a surprising number of us gathered at the Congress Hotel in Chicago in response to William Revelli's call for a meeting on matters of common interest to college and university band directors. What was discussed then has mostly faded from memory, but what was accomplished has not—the permanent establishment of a group that became the College Band Directors National Association.

From its inception, the CBDNA has been led by men of strong persuasions. Yet that leadership has always sought to enlist the opinions of its membership on pertinent topics. More than three decades of such opinion are presented in this anthology, selected from biennial conferences. When the association began to expand in the years immediately after World War II, guest composers, publishers, administrators, and acousticians were invited to present papers at general sessions; some of those are here, too.

This collection is, to me, a fascinating and honest sampling of CBDNA thought and action, and when one pauses to contemplate what has happened since 1941 in politics, science, and education, and within the labyrinth of contemporary musical thought, one cannot help but be amazed and grateful that we are still alive and functioning at the beginning of this third century of the republic.

And we are all part of this functioning, we who have decided to give of our lives to the American college and university band. It is an exciting, vital contribution, one to which I have not always felt myself to be fully equal, perhaps, but one engaging my full and enthusiastic participation nonetheless. I am sure it has been the same for many readers—CBDNA members or otherwise. Sometimes more gifted with hindsight than positive vision, we have plowed our way through to today. But, in all fairness, it must be stated that the bulk of CBDNA leadership has been of the positive variety. The results of its work are both visible and audible in the constantly improving performances of college and university bands everywhere in our country.

The emphasis today is squarely on the music. This fact in no way demeans the articles on administrative, promotional, and functional considerations that fill the bound proceedings of past bienniums. They, too, contributed their weight to the gross, but they may not be as attractive to the general reader as those selected for this volume.

I have studied every work in this collection, not so much to evaluate the thought or the writing as to retrieve the spirit and excitement of their delivery by men I have known all my professional life. The words of many of these brilliant and devoted individuals read even better than they sounded. I can hear Revelli's high-pitched intensity as he warmed to his favorite subject of an international instrumentation, remember Fitzgerald's low but probing profile as he reviewed where we stood on repertory in 1949, and regret that I missed Hugh Henderson's sobering post-directorial conscience-pricker he called "Straws in the Winds." I also missed Mark Hindsley's "Intonation for the Band Conductor." But even without the musical examples or the force of his presence, his words in print bring back the inspiration and insight he could convey to the field.

If anything is missing from this source book, it is any words from the real source himself—Albert Austin Harding. I don't know of any articles or speeches by this shy, powerful man, and perhaps that is how it should remain; I don't know of any articles or speeches by Arturo Toscanini, either, save for a quote of thanks he gave to *Life* magazine on the occasion of the Allied liberation of Italy in 1945. But it was Harding's sometimes blinding example, radiating out of Champaign-Urbana, Illinois, that paved the way for many of the best achievements of college and university bands.

William Revelli realized the debt of gratitude we all owe Harding. His way of expressing it was to get us all together. Thanks and admirations, W. D. R.

FREDERICK FENNELL
UNIVERSITY OF MIAMI

# Preface

The articles in this volume were taken entirely from the proceedings of the conferences of the College Band Directors National Association. They were selected not so much for their literary merit as for their representation of the concerns and ideas that have influenced the college band movement.

Credit for the selection of material should go to a large number of distinguished college band directors—the national and divisional officers of the 1973–75 and 1975–77 bienniums. Special thanks should go to Acton Ostling Jr., national CBDNA secretary-treasurer from 1967 to 1975, who kept this project alive from the time of its inception by Louis Wersen, then president of Music Educators National Conference.

DAVID WHITWELL

# Contents

## Preliminaries

CBDNA Declaration of Principles — xvii

CBDNA Officers — xix

## Part 1
## The Concert Band and Its Music

The University or College Band as a Concert Organization — 5
William D. Revelli/1946

The Band's Service to Music as an Art — 9
Frederick Fennell/1947

The Music of the Concert Band — 13
Bernard Fitzgerald/1949

The Band as a Medium of Musical Expression — 19
Frederick Fennell/1952

The Band's Future Concert Repertoire                                     25
Paul Creston/1960

A Brief Glance Backward in CBDNA's 25th Anniversary Year                 31
Keith Wilson/1966

Band Repertoire from the Tradition of the Professional Bands            35
Harold Bachman/1967

Band Literature Developed by Band Associations                          45
Paul R. Bryan/1967

Avant-Garde Band Literature                                             51
Robert Vagner/1967

Band Music from a Historical Perspective                                59
David Whitwell/1967

The Emerging Band Repertoire                                            63
William A. Schaefer/1967

# Part 2
# The Concert Band and Its Instrumentation

Band Sonorities                                                         71
James Neilson/1950

The Eastman Wind Ensemble                                               79
Frederick Fennell/1952

Report on International Instrumentation                                 85
William D. Revelli/1958

Conference on the Band's Repertoire, Instrumentation, and
    Nomenclature                                                        99
Charles Minelli/1960

# Part 3
# The Marching Band

| | |
|---|---|
| Pertinent Questions Concerning Marching Bands: A Survey<br>Arthur Williams/1958 | 109 |
| The Concert Band Conductor and the Marching Band<br>Mark Hindsley/1960 | 113 |
| Problems, Solutions, and Present Status of Small College Marching Bands<br>Richard Colwell/1960 | 119 |
| Varied and Changing Styles of Halftime Shows: A Survey<br>William D. Cole/1960 | 123 |
| Music Problems in the Marching Band<br>Gale L. Sperry/1961 | 129 |
| The Role of the Marching Band in the College Band Program<br>Paul R. Bryan/1962 | 133 |
| The Future Marching Band<br>Hubert Henderson/1962 | 135 |
| The Marching Band in 1975: A Survey<br>Manley Whitcomb/1962 | 139 |
| Marching Bands and Television Coverage: A Survey<br>George Cavender/1964 | 141 |
| Marching Bands in the View of Music School Deans, Department Heads, and Chairmen of Music Departments: A Survey<br>William Campbell/1964 | 147 |

The Small College Marching Band　　　　　　　　　　151
Glen Yarberry/1967

# Part 4
# Techniques

Problems and Responsibilities of the Guest Conductor　　　157
William D. Revelli/1950

Rehearsal Warmups and Intonation　　　　　　　　　　161
Donald E. McGinnis/1969

Intonation for the Band Conductor　　　　　　　　　　175
Mark Hindsley/1971

# Part 5
# The Profession at Large

The Influence of Contests on University and College Bands　　203
L. Bruce Jones/1950

The American Music Heritage　　　　　　　　　　　　211
Frederick Fennell/1956

The Responsibility of the Musician　　　　　　　　　　219
James Neilson/1958

Straws in the Winds　　　　　　　　　　　　　　　　225
Hubert Henderson/1969

The CBDNA in the Future　　　　　　　　　　　　　233
David Whitwell/1975

# Part 6
# Composers' Analyses of Their Works for Band

Sinfonietta  241
Ingolf Dahl/1964

Meditation  247
Gunther Schuller/1964

Symphonic Requiem  257
Vaclav Nelhybel/1966

Music for Prague 1968  259
Karel Husa/1971

Transitions  267
Henk Badings/1973

# Appendixes

Testimonial to Albert Austin Harding, Honorary Life
 President  275
Frederick Fennell/1958

Citation for William D. Revelli, Honorary Life President  279
Guy M. Duker/1971

Index  281

# CBDNA Declaration of Principles

We affirm our faith in and our devotion to the College Band, which, as a serious and distinctive medium of musical expression, may be of vital service and importance to its members, its institution, and its art.

To its members the College Band, through exemplary practices in organization, training, and presentation, should endeavor to provide effective experiences in musical education, in musical culture, in musical recreation, and in general citizenship.

To its institution the College Band should offer adequate concerts and performances at appropriate functions and ceremonies, in the interests of music culture and entertainment, and for the enhancement of institutional spirit and character.

To music as an art and a profession the College Band should bring increasing artistry, understanding, dignity, and respect, by thorough and independent effort within the band's own immediate sphere, by leadership and sponsorship in the secondary school program, and by cooperation with all other agencies pursuing similar musical goals.

To these ends we, the members of this Association, pledge ourselves to seek individual and collective growth as musicians, as teachers, as conductors, and as administrators.

# CBDNA Officers

1941–45
    President                   William D. Revelli
    Secretary                   Joseph A. Gremelspacher

1946
    President                   Gerald R. Prescott
    Vice President           L. Bruce Jones
    Secretary                   Gerald H. Doty

1947
    President                   Mark H. Hindsley
    Vice President           L. Bruce Jones
    Vice President           John R. Halliday
    Vice President           C. R. Hackney
    Secretary                   Alvin R. Edgar

1948
    President                   Raymond R. Dvorak
    Vice President           Alvin R. Edgar
    Secretary                   L. Bruce Jones

## OFFICERS

**1949**
- President — Alvin R. Edgar
- Vice President — L. Bruce Jones
- Secretary-Treasurer — Daniel L. Martino

**1950**
- President — R. Bernard Fitzgerald
- Vice President — L. Bruce Jones
- Secretary-Treasurer — Joseph A. Gremelspacher

**1951–52**
- President — L. Bruce Jones
- Vice President — Clarence Sawhill
- Secretary-Treasurer — Joseph A. Gremelspacher

**1952–54**
- President — Clarence Sawhill
- Vice President — Hugh McMillen
- Secretary-Treasurer — Charles Minelli

**1954–56**
- President — Hugh McMillen
- Vice President — Frederick Fennell
- Secretary-Treasurer — Charles Minelli

**1956–58**
- President — Frederick Fennell
- Vice President — James Nielson
- Secretary-Treasurer — Charles Minelli

**1958–60**
- President — James Nielson
- Vice President — Frank Piersol
- Secretary-Treasurer — Charles Minelli

**1960–62**
- President — Frank Piersol
- Vice President — Keith Wilson
- Secretary-Treasurer — Charles Minelli

**1962–64**
- President — Keith Wilson
- Vice President — Manley Whitcomb
- Secretary-Treasurer — Charles Minelli

**1964–67**
- President — Manley Whitcomb
- Vice President — James Jorgenson
- Secretary-Treasurer — Guy Duker

**1967–69**
- President — James Jorgenson
- Vice President — Guy Duker
- Secretary-Treasurer — Acton Ostling Jr.

**1969–71**
- President — Guy Duker
- Vice President — Richard Bowles
- Secretary-Treasurer — Acton Ostling Jr.

**1971–73**
- President — Richard Bowles
- Vice President — Karl Holvik
- Secretary-Treasurer — Acton Ostling Jr.

**1973–75**
- President — Karl Holvik
- Vice President — David Whitwell
- Secretary-Treasurer — Acton Ostling Jr.

## 1975–77
    President                        David Whitwell
    Vice President            Frank Battisti
    Secretary-Treasurer     Robert O. Briggs

## 1977–79
    President                        Robert Vagner
    President Elect           Frank Battisti
    Vice President            William P. Foster
    Secretary-Treasurer     Robert O. Briggs

# The Concert Band and Its Music

# PART 1

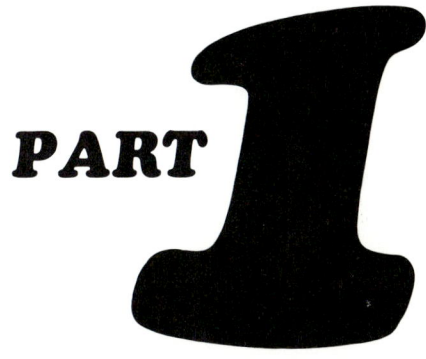

The minutes of the first meeting of the CBDNA in 1941 indicate that the only time given to the concert band and its music was a presentation entitled "The Concert Band's Place in the Curriculum," by Harold Bachman of the University of Chicago. The need for more and better literature was seen primarily from the perspective of helping maintain course credits.

By 1949, considerably more attention had been drawn to the common problem of locating literature. The proceedings of that year's convention published extensive lists and sources of band music in print, manuscript band music (388 titles, of which 179 were original compositions), woodwind ensemble music, and brass ensemble music. This activity has continued, in one form or another, until the present day.

In 1950, CBDNA President Bernard Fitzgerald of the University of Texas began to shift the focus to the conductor's responsibility toward concert band literature, the necessity for his becoming more selective as well as reaching for higher musical standards of performance. The 1950 book of proceedings included a "Bibliography of Recorded Band Music," compiled by Bryce Jordan (who later became president of the University of Texas). It listed 603 items, summarized as follows:

| | |
|---|---|
| Quickstep marches | 61 percent |
| Serious music (a general category that includes all works designated as overture, suite, tone poem, etc.) | 16 percent |
| Patriotic music | 6 percent |
| Concert marches | 5 percent |
| Folk music (straightforward treatment of folk melodies without any developmental treatment) | 4 percent |
| Novelties | 3 percent |
| Waltzes (other than symphonic works such as *Rosenkavalier* waltzes); ensembles and solos (with band accompaniment); descriptive works; opera selections; fanfares | 5 percent |

The composer represented the largest number of times was John Philip Sousa, whose name appeared eighty times.

As college band directors began to concern themselves more with the quality of their literature, there was a natural tendency to look to the publishers as the agents responsible for so much music of doubtful value. As a result publishers' representatives were invited to address the membership. In addition to presenting the economic realities of their business, they tended to pass the responsibility back to the conductor for the quality of published music. For example, Arthur Hauser of Theodore Presser Company, speaking in December 1960, noted:

> Some years ago, when addressing CBDNA on a similar subject, I stated that while publishers must accept responsibility

for printing much so-called "poor" music, educators must accept the greater responsibility, because if they would not buy it, the publishers would not publish it. This situation exists principally because many educators have not had sufficient experience with good music to take the lead in insisting on its use in their schools. We can expect that in time this might be rectified with a stronger emphasis on quality repertoire in the curricula of music education. I believe one would agree that this situation must be corrected if bands are ever to improve their repertoire. Without a deep-seated understanding of good music, whether it is contemporary or from another period, by many more band directors than represented by your fine organization, I fear that your efforts to improve the literature for bands will take more years than any of us have remaining in this short life.

In 1966 the proceedings of the southwest division convention included the findings of a 1963–64 survey by Ray Tross of more than 100 college conductors throughout the United States (this survey became the basis for Tross's doctoral dissertation, *The Present Status of Band and Band Department Ensembles in Higher Education*, at Colorado State College). Tross presented a number of findings about concert bands:

(1) An average of four major band concerts were being programed each year.
(2) The symphonic wind ensemble was making initial efforts to present its own concerts as an organization distinct from the concert band.
(3) More than half of the surveyed institutions presented out-of-town concerts or tours.
(4) Faculty and students were used as concert soloists by 94.1 percent.
(5) Ninety percent indicated programing student compositions.
(6) A large number of conductors favored formal or semifor-

mal attire rather than uniforms for indoor concerts. Of these, 43.2 percent reported using tuxedos, whereas only 30 percent indicated they still used traditional band uniforms.

A majority of the conductors said they were striving to program original and contemporary works. Major works by such American composers as Hindemith, Creston, Persichetti, Nixon, and Giannini were beginning to be programed regularly.

Two hundred and sixty-four concert programs were returned with the questionnaire. Some of the programs lacked a proper balance of literature from different periods. Contemporary and Romantic periods were well represented, the Baroque and Classical periods less so. Gustav Holst and Ralph Vaughan Williams, two pillars of English band music, still remained perennial favorites for a majority of the college band directors.

One hundred and four conductors were asked: "Of the compositions in the past five years you have programed, which do you consider to be the finest and best original band works?" Among the total of 416 compositions listed, the most frequently mentioned were Hindemith's *Symphony for Band*, Giannini's *Symphony for Band*, Persichetti's *Symphony for Band*, Holst's *Suite in E♭* and *Suite in F*, and Milhaud's *Suite Française*.

# The University or College Band as a Concert Organization

William D. Revelli/1946

The university or college concert band exists, first of all, for its students, and next as a concert organization to represent the entire institution in the concert field—that is, to perform artistically for the student body and patrons of the university. Those patrons include students' parents, prospective students, and citizens of the community interested in the university and its music.

The college or university needs good concert organizations to assist in the general cultural development of its students. The band must provide its share of "appreciation" opportunities for nonmusic students as well as for the music students both in and out of the band. I was not trained as a band leader; consequently, I think I am being objective when I describe the band as sometimes the first step in music education and appreciation for many people.

In relationship to the school or department of music within the college or university, the band has an especially significant role to play. It assists in the education of the music major by offering him opportunities for rich concert ensemble experience. The social experience a player has in a band can also be of inestimable value to him throughout life. The band, furthermore, becomes a training ground for advanced students of music theory, composition, and conducting. We do great injustice to the band and to the players in it when we assume that it is the place in which students can learn to play instruments. The private teacher must guide the student in the formation of correct playing habits; it is impossible for the band leader to do this with his large group.

The concert band, as I see it, has no direct relationship to the athletic department except in schools in which the entire band program is financially supported by funds from that department. The concert band does, however, have an indirect relationship to the athletic department by virtue of the fact that the concert band, varsity band, marching band, and pep band often include some of the same players. There must exist a well-worked-out program of artistic and musical cooperation between the concert band and the service bands to avoid conflicts. The concert band, as an organization into which every player strives to gain admittance, must offer a challenge to the players in the service bands, just as the first squad football team offers a challenge to players in the second team.

The educational institution, the music department within it, or the concert band within that, also has a *cultural* relationship to the state, apart from any financial relationship. If the college concert band does not give performances that are artistically and musically worthwhile, who will? It is inconceivable that this particular slice of culture could be left out of the cultural pattern of any community or state. After all, there are very few professional concert bands.

The concert bands in our colleges must be of such a high standard that every young instrumentalist will look forward to the day when he or she can play in one of them. Only then will young people be motivated to pay the price in hard study to arrive at a level of performance that will admit them into a concert organization.

The concert band in the college or university has the responsibility of raising the general level of bands everywhere. It must be an example and an ideal to high school, junior high, and grammar school bands. In areas where this is not the case, splendid high school players give up their music when they enter college. Some are bound to do this anyway, but the mortality rate is much too high for our general cultural good. We must not and need not lose as many players as we do. These people need music throughout their lives and the longer we can keep them in bands, the more their music tastes and education are enriched and the better will be the band's future audience.

Composers in the last two decades have provided high school bands with more and better music. Some of this music can be used by colleges to good advantage, but much of it is not fitted to our students, who in most cases are more mature of mind and spirit than high school players. We band leaders in colleges and universities must devise ways and means of motivating our better composers to give us masterpieces of original music.

More people participate in bands and more people attend band concerts than attend concerts given by other music organizations. The influence of the band, consequently, is extremely great. It reaches many people who otherwise would be very little interested in music. It is our responsibility to entertain these people and to help them acquire a taste for the band and band music. Of greater importance still is the responsibility we have to educate these people to the beauties of fine music in any form.

# The Band's Service to Music as an Art

Frederick Fennell/1947

Our committee believes present instrumentation is adequate for our needs as a medium of serious musical expression. This topic is bound to invite divergent opinion, much of it of high merit and sound musical judgment, and we cannot hope to submit workable outlines that might be remotely acceptable to the whole association. We ask the president to appoint a special committee to study this aspect of our problems and to charge this committee to bring a comprehensive report to the 1948 meeting with specific suggestions for an approved instrumentation for college bands.

The committee feels the existing literature for the college band is insufficient. We recommend each conductor take it upon himself to interest composers known to him, or those he may cultivate, in writing for the wind band.

We recommend the CBDNA investigate the establishment of a clinic for composers, that they may hear a properly constituted and carefully trained band reveal the musical materials with which they must be acquainted if they are to write for the wind band. We suggest the appointment of a select committee to contact composers on behalf of the CBDNA for the purposes of encouraging composition for the band.

The committee believes intelligent and effective transcriptions of music conceived for other mediums should be encouraged rather than scorned. The committee also suggests that the CBDNA compile a central source list of existing original transcriptions and compositions that are in each band's individual library. We grant that for various reasons, mostly economic, certain of these transcriptions of music not in the public domain must remain the exclusive property of the publisher and may be used only by the school making the score and extracting the parts. To the end that we might see the easing of these controls by publishers and individual conductors, the committee hopes that the association will not overlook any opportunity to make these unusual transcriptions available to those who wish to perform them. This source list of music in the public domain might well be the basis of a system of interband library loan, similar to the systems of conventional university libraries.

The committee observes that broadcasting by college bands seems subject to local conditions and controls, and that, save for halftime shows at football games, college bands are not heard on the networks. However, if and when negotiations are resumed or begun between the representatives of music education, the American Federation of Musicians, and the National Association of Broadcasters, the view of the CBDNA—that the college band is a force for the cultural development of American audiences—should be represented during such negotiations. We commend those of our colleagues who are currently broadcasting over local stations and urge their colleagues to encourage them.

Our review of the existing commercial recordings of the band's best literature reveals that there is almost no record of these items. The committee believes there is little the CBDNA can do about it other than to urge commercial firms and labor leaders to rectify this situation. In the event conventional commercial recordings do not materialize, the committee suggests an alternate plan by which the CBDNA might prevail upon educational foundations to underwrite the recording, for educational purposes exclusively, of a representative library of the band's best music.

The musical betterment of college bands rests squarely on the shoulders of the men who conduct them. It is up to the college band director himself to bring about the acceptance of the band as a medium of serious musical expression, and this he can do by preparing himself more thoroughly for his tasks, by presenting literature of the highest available caliber and by being a better musical leader to those who play in college bands.

# The Music of the Concert Band

Bernard Fitzgerald/1949

College and university bands must assume the responsibility for developing the concert band repertory. Since professional bands are almost nonexistent and high school bands usually lack either resources or musical maturity, leadership is therefore in the hands of the colleges and universities. The burden of proof is upon us, the directors. Are we willing to accept the challenge or will we be content with the present status of the concert band? We cannot afford to perpetuate the concert band in the music tradition of the town band of several years ago unless we are willing to accept the musical reputation that was associated with it. Although it may be difficult to accept, we must in all honesty admit that the concert band is still considered a musical stepchild.

The current stage of development of the concert band repertory is crucial. Its condition is comparable to that of an incomplete music composition in which a slow introduction (the late development of bands and band music in contrast to the orchestra) is followed by an allegro (the exposition to basic themes and ideas provided by the bands of Innes, Gilmore, and Sousa). To this point the music form is normal, but the development section that should follow has not materialized. Instead, an increasing accelerando and crescendo has accumulated to a presto on the original themes (this indicates the tremendous growth of school and college bands during recent decades). Now we have reached the bottom of the page, and speaking musically, we are faced with two possible alternatives: (1) writing the coda and being finished as soon as possible, or (2) making a dal segno involving major musical revision, returning to the original allegro, and beginning the development section now!

Are we to continue to be so dependent upon transcriptions of orchestral music, which we must admit can be performed more effectively by an orchestra? While there is no reason to ignore this rich musical heritage, the time has come when we must stop leaning upon the orchestra so heavily, and start developing a repertory of band music by contemporary composers. Richard Franko Goldman is making a valuable contribution through new editions of original band music of the eighteenth and nineteenth centuries, but this music does not exist in sufficient quantity to provide a basic repertory by encouraging contemporary composers to write for the medium. This must mean the enlistment of top-ranking composers to compose original band works representative of their best creative efforts.

The combined efforts of composers and publishers will have little effect in the development of a fine band repertory unless the music is performed! There have been many complaints that publishers do not provide the concert repertory the college concert band needs, but publishers who have undertaken such financial hazards have definite evidence that bands do not want this music in sufficient quantity to warrant the investment. Since this music is not being sold, it is not being performed either. Why? The customary excuses offered are that the music is too difficult or the audience won't like it. A tempered musical judgment must certainly be exercised in respect to both of these items but this should not imply that the present situation must be accepted as inevitable.

It is true that some contemporary band music is so difficult technically that the musical results may not warrant the effort expended in preparing the composition for public performance. Composers need our guidance as to what is suitable for the band so that they can acquire a better understanding of its capacities and limitations. But there are often other reasons that cannot be justifiably excused for not performing contemporary music. In too many instances the performance of new music is likely to be avoided either because it is too much extra work for the director, or because he is unwilling to admit his inability to understand contemporary music or to present it intelligently and effectively.

The familiar and sometimes ironic question, "Are you a musician or a band man?", frequently strikes too close for comfort when the musical artistry of the band is compared with that of the orchestra. Although the band has been handicapped to some extent by inadequate original repertory, the artistic qualities of a band are usually present in proportion to the capacity of the director. We must be willing and eager to increase our music knowledge and stature in every possible way. We must acquire an understanding of new music idioms and ideas so that we will be prepared to interpret the music intelligently. We must adopt a more aggressive and persevering attitude, with a willingness to experiment with scoring, new color effects, and so on, so that the music may receive the most favorable performance possible.

The capacity of audiences and their receptiveness to new music varies greatly throughout the nation, and unfortunately there is no effective formula that can be applied to all communities. It is difficult to accurately estimate audience receptiveness to new music ideas, and—as a last resort—it may be necessary to use the trial and error method. Geographical location, proximity to urban areas, general cultural backgrounds and surroundings, average economic levels, and racial ancestries are all factors that may influence music tastes and standards of performance in a given community. There are relatively few localities in which a program of entirely new band music would be received with enthusiasm (the exceptions would be music centers that have promoted festivals of contemporary music). This condition is due partly to the fact that audiences attending band concerts are more often interested in being entertained than in hearing a program that challenges their listening capacities. The average concertgoer requires some familiar music. An entire concert of new music flavors involves too many new taste sensations, leaving the listener craving something familiar.

It is not enough to adopt the attitude that we ought to include a new composition on the program for the sake of the composer or publisher. We must also be convinced of the merit of the music itself; otherwise it cannot be presented intelligently or in a manner sympathetic to the intentions of the composer. An understanding of contemporary music can be acquired only through a long and sometimes painful exposure to new music (much of it inferior) in order to develop an adequate musical discrimination that can be intelligently applied. Quite naturally, much of the new music being written today will be forgotten in a short time. This is to be expected. Even from the Classical period few composers have survived to today except Haydn, Mozart, and Beethoven. But this does not relieve us of the responsibility of investigating new music personally and of being sufficiently acquainted with contemporary idioms to be able to form intelligent judgments.

Any attempt to influence the tastes of the audience must be exercised carefully and skillfully, in many instances by infiltration over a period of several years. The ultimate goal is to capitalize upon the best repertory of both old and new music, certainly not to abandon the old for the new. The process is bound to be a laborious one involving much sifting of music materials, but it is absolutely necessary if the concert band is to be regarded as a respected medium of musical expression rather than as a miscellaneous group of wind instrumentalists who attempt to perform orchestral music.

The many other services and functions of the band should not be discarded; that would be sacrificing one of the most distinctive features of the band—its versatility. Actually there is no choice in the matter at present, since the public demands pageantry for athletic events. This demand is a result of the band's own emphasis on this function. But directors can present the band in such a way that spectators not only will recognize the versatility of the band but also will be attracted to hear it in concert appearances. While it may not be practical to present a concert at a football game, some special music might be included to emphasize the musical artistry of the band.

The lack of response to the efforts of publishers to make contemporary band music available may result in the curtailment of new publications, since publishers cannot afford to operate at a financial loss. Publishers who invest in the future of the concert band have only one means of gauging the results of their efforts—the sale and performance of their publications. Publishers, composers, and audiences can accomplish very little for the college band without our initiative. To quote one publisher who has been particularly active in issuing new publications for the concert band:

> We are seriously thinking of discontinuing our series of what we have been told are worthy works for band. As publishers, we have a high responsibility and obligation to the music public of our generation. We have tried to carry it out and hope that we have succeeded in some measure. We will continue to do this in those fields of music where the people concerned are ready to accept it. To put it bluntly, the band medium has proven that it is not yet ready.

Think it over! The indictment is serious. Is our Declaration of Principles merely a statement made for public consumption and intended to convey the impression of excellent intentions? Or are we really sincere and willing to accept the obligations and responsibilities that are essential to the realization of this Declaration? The public is very band-conscious and we must prove both the sincerity of our intentions and our determination to achieve them. The time is now. Tomorrow may be too late.

# The Band as a Medium of Musical Expression

Frederick Fennell/1952

Just what is the band's own immediate sphere? Currently, it has only one functional sphere indigenous to itself—that of playing out-of-doors on foot where other ensembles, which lack its mobility and acoustical projection, cannot function. In this element its supremacy remains unchallenged.

Its natural resources take the band into the street, onto the gridiron, into athletic arenas, to outdoor bandstands and concert shells. Beyond these services the wind band's purposes remain obscure, in spite of the vast number of books and articles currently endeavoring to define them. The unique efforts of several organizations, found in large colleges and universities, which perform difficult musical feats with enviable instrumental virtuosity, do not yet constitute a clear definition of the place of the so-called wind concert band in American musical life.

The existence of the outdoor band has never suffered in this way. It provides, better than any other ensemble of music instruments, a workable medium of sound and cadence, supplies adequate color, and permits mobility for public events held in the open air. For these services it is as completely equipped as any music ensemble in existence. It is for this express purpose that it was conceived and, in turn, developed by the military of early nineteenth-century Europe. Just why the American military and public at large adopted the European plan en masse, without attempting to shape the band to their own needs, has never seemed quite clear, aside from the irrepressible instinct to ape our brothers across the Atlantic.

The outdoor band has a distinguished music literature to which the composers of almost every occidental culture have contributed generously and without persuasion. This band has the acoustical fabric required for the accomplishment of its purposes. This band has a standardized instrumentation, which admits of no instrument that has not proved itself suitable to these purposes. This band has organization in the extreme, it has distinguished leadership, and it exists and functions with unbelievable success in almost every community of the Western world. But this is the band that almost every college and high school supervisor of music is anxious to pass on to an assistant, or better still, to eliminate from his activities entirely in favor of an ensemble that has not found that place in the hearts and minds of the American people so long desired for it by its thousands of ardent supporters. It appears to be axiomatic, therefore, that this second sphere of the band's influence, though it be arrived at by default, is exclusively an educational one.

By whatever means, and regardless of the methods by which they were achieved, almost every educational institution in America, be it private, public, or parochial, has some sort of band. Community-sponsored concert bands are increasing in the Midwest, but the professional band, existing outside the educational institution—that ensemble that was so vital a part of American concert life at the beginning of this century and that expired so suddenly with the advent of radio—seems to be quite dead at this writing.

Our high school and college bands hold in their very being a vast responsibility to the music education of the youth of our country. It is no overstatement to say that an appalling majority of the youth of America who are engaged in instrumental activity will never play in any ensemble but a band. They deserve the best available leadership.

This leadership must review its resources, its abilities and techniques, with a personal discipline in musicianship that is practically nonexistent in educational conducting of today. This leadership must be honest with itself about the uncertain position the band holds in the musical life of America. If this leadership is truly concerned about the future of the band in America, it need only look to itself for any lasting musical contribution. We who stand each week before a gathering of modestly inquisitive and often exceedingly capable performers hold in the palm of our hand and the recoil of our downbeat the musical future of America. Frankly, we are not yet equal to the task. Conducting is the greatest responsibility to be held by a single person in the whole field of musical art. Conducting is rehearsing, for it is in the rehearsal that we must endeavor to achieve the complete artistic experience that is the honest performance of good music. Our study and performance of the masterpieces of music composition can become the most practical synthesis of what we glibly call "the fine arts." Rehearsals offer magnificent opportunities for the functional study of languages; they allow us the study of the practical application of the arts of design, architecture, poetry, and drama, and of the sciences of acoustics and psychology. Rehearsals offer opportunities for the study of the history of musical art and performance such as are not to be found in any lecture hall. Rehearsals should be the laboratory in which a student's lectures and exercises in the theory and structure of music are confirmed in living performances.

We must awaken in our players a curiosity about music. We must strive to make ourselves and our players cognizant of its beauty, of its necessity in our lives. We must bring all our forces to bear upon the awareness that the years they spend in college, playing music as a hobby or in preparation for a career as a teacher or player, are the most valuable and formative of their musical lives. That when, for instance, they have played the "Prelude" and "Liebestod" from *Tristan und Isolde* in the band a half tone lower than its original key, they have lost nothing, provided, of course, they hear the beauties of the Tristan chord in any key; and provided they will listen to an orchestral performance of the score and perhaps even hear the opera on records or see a performance in the flesh and thus realize that the beauties of *Tristan* are theirs for as long as they live, not alone for the years of school or the hours spent in rehearsal. Then, perhaps, we may have fulfilled some measure of the band's educational obligations to music as an art.

We who train the college and university band conductors of today and tomorrow must prepare them more thoroughly for their tasks, placing the greatest emphasis upon the development of their musicianship and musical integrity as leaders of people. Their work often takes them to communities where they alone, with the bands they are hired to build or maintain, are the sole purveyors of live music in that area. We must send them to their posts with the full awareness of their responsibilities to the art of music, not with the erroneous (though shockingly prevalent) belief that they have to make the world safe from the orchestra.

A new type of conductor should emerge. He must be a conductor with fanatical devotion to his art, with unlimited capacities for work, for study, and with the all-too-absent critical faculty that is granted to the Toscaninis and Koussevitzkys. The question might be raised as to when a man in the average American college can find time to be a Toscanini. He must grow into that state by perpetual industry, by intelligent study, and by persistent immersion in the problems and beauties of all the arts. Arturo Toscanini didn't just happen; he is the result of a lifetime of work, without which his genius for leadership in general and the conducting of music in particular might scarcely have achieved a modicum of its present greatness.

And our new band conductor, who is to achieve the purposes of the educational sphere of the band's influence, will not find much help in his search for the conductor's knowledge in average graduate courses. They will help, to be sure, but no degree in music education or outside it has thus far produced the conductor for whom this article begs. Perhaps it is because we conductors are expecting some university or music school to educate us, when we ignore, each day of our lives, the greatest opportunities in centuries to educate ourselves with easily obtainable books and scores on every conceivable facet of music.

Those who aspire to conduct bands must know how black is

the past and much of the present history of bands in America. The decades of charlatanism, the decades of perhaps inspired but incompetent leadership, the often vulgar and usually unmusical direction that has dogged the band since its inception, have left their brands.

The history of lasting music mediums is written indelibly in the literature that has been composed for them. No book or thesis has yet expressed their history with greater clarity. The history of the wind band must not be ignored. The only way to a new and more distinguished history lies exclusively in the hands of those who now conduct and those who will one day direct the musical destinies of the college band. When college band conductors are musicians equal to their responsibilities, and when their bands are accordingly equal to their tasks, the world's best composers may yet provide the band with the literature it never has had, but can only be secured through the musical transformation that the band's influence alone can achieve.

# The Band's Future Concert Repertoire

Paul Creston/1960

Anything that has to do with the future belongs to the realm of prophecy, and since I am most assuredly not a prophet, I usually avoid the issue. But I have chosen to consider only what the band's future repertoire should be and not what it will be. This is not the realm of prophecy but rather that of aspiration, hope, or dream.

Let me clarify my topic. I am concerned with music composed originally and especially for the band, not with arrangements or transcriptions; with music of a caliber appropriate to a concert hall and not to a football field or a parade. In other words, I am concerned with music for a specific medium, a specific place, a specific audience, and a specific time. If this music conforms to the capabilities and virtues of the instrument or instruments employed, it will fulfill the first requirement: the medium. If it results in a well-constructed, coherent, expressive, and significant piece of music, it will fulfill the other three requirements, for it will be suitable to an important gathering place, address itself to a musically intelligent audience, and, because of its lasting values, project itself well into the future.

Why are band directors so concerned with original concert music? For the same reason that concert saxophonists are interested in original music for the saxophone, and harmonica players are interested in original music for the harmonica. It seems that when an instrument is taken from the home, the beer tavern, the night club, or the boy scout camp, and is brought to the concert stage, it has been accepted by respectable society; it has arrived. I do not wish to imply that these other places should not have those instruments or that such music should not exist. There is a time, a place, and an audience for every type of music, and I do not look down on any so long as it is good music, so long as it fulfills its particular function and is true to its form. But there certainly is an importance attached to music that is directed toward a musically intelligent audience gathered to listen to significant music per se, and that is not performed as a background to conversation or merely to fill embarrassing silence. So as it is perfectly natural for a concert saxophonist to want to elevate his instrument to the level of the concert hall, it is perfectly reasonable for a band director to strive to present his music on the same stage as a symphony orchestra.

The matter of bringing the band to the concert stage may not seem such a problem to many people. But there are obstacles in the path. There is a common prejudice against anything that is not the status quo. The general music public is accustomed to vocal recitals, piano recitals, violin recitals, and orchestral concerts. To a lesser degree, it has accepted cello and harp recitals. But how often does it hear a saxophone recital or a band concert at Carnegie Hall, Symphony Hall, Northrop Auditorium, or any other important concert hall? It often assumes that the instrument is not worthy of such hallowed ground. I have been asked many times, "What made you write for the saxophone?" My answer always is that I like the sound of the instrument and that it has certain virtues and beauties that I want to demonstrate and exploit. The response usually is that surely the saxophone is not as lovely as the violin. I reply by asking, "Have you heard the saxophone in the hands of a great artist like Marcel Mule, Vincent Abato, or Al Gallodoro? Furthermore, what sounds can be more excruciatingly painful than those of a violin in the hands of an untalented beginner?" As one pioneering concert saxophonist once told his audience, "There must be a lot of good music in the saxophone because it has never come out."

The band is in the same category as the saxophone in that it has been a neglected instrument. For many years I have received appeals in support of and for championing various neglected instruments. My *Concertino for Marimba and Orchestra* was the very first composition in serious form written for that instrument. My *Suite, Sonata,* and *Concerto for Saxophone* were among the first compositions written for that instrument, as were my *Fantasy for Trombone and Orchestra* and my *Concerto for Accordion and Orchestra*. So I have a sympathetic understanding of the problem of building a concert repertoire for the band.

The first obstacle to be overcome is the general public's disinterest in the band as a concert medium. It must be shown that the band is a beautiful instrument: expressive, flexible, colorful, and powerful. This must be proven to the public by developing ensembles of technically proficient and musically intelligent players. Fortunately, this first obstacle has been wonderfully overcome in this country by many superlative college bands; so the first step in creating a demand for original band music has been achieved. The greatest conducting thrills in my life have not been with any symphony orchestra but with the National Intercollegiate Band and the band of the University of Michigan, to name only two.

However, the problem is not merely in the demand but in the supply of original band music, though the latter could not exist without the former. This shortage is the second and most important obstacle to bringing the band to the concert stage. How do we alleviate it? The first step, of necessity, is transcriptions. I am neither for nor against transcriptions in general, because there are certain types of music that sound equally well for various media. Much music was written in the 16th century for voices *or* viols. We know the many magnificent transcriptions Bach completed of his music and that of other composers, and the glorious orchestrations Ravel created of his own piano pieces. But on the other hand, there is a type of music so indigenous to the instrument for which it was written that any transcription, no matter how clever, is a travesty, a desecration. To present the band in its true light, it must have its own, original, specifically created literature.

If one wants an original play one does not ask an actor to write it; one goes to a playwright. Similarly, if one wants original music for a particular instrument, one does not go to the instrumentalist but to the composer. This seems like a simple procedure, but there are impediments. Obviously, a band director will ask for a worthy and significant composer. Such a composer will most likely be one who has proved his worth—a mature and established composer. What can one offer such a composer in return for months of creative toil? A commission, or, to express it in the vernacular, money. And not $50 or $100 or even $500, but $1,000 and up.

Until recently the composer usually has been offered only the promise of publication and performances by major college bands. One might think that publication is indirectly a form of financial remuneration, but perish the thought. Even if a pop tune were involved, the pennies that trickle in from the sale of sheet music would hardly fill a piggy bank, so you can imagine what little can be squeezed out of a serious piece of music.

If you can offer your composer a substantial commission fee plus a continuing return from performances, he will be most pleased to deliver a significant composition to help build the literature of the band. Every person who must work for a livelihood, whether he be an artist or artisan, professional or tradesman, desires and deserves to earn that livelihood through that work for which he is best fitted and best trained. And the composer, no less than the plumber or electrician, has bills to meet and mouths to feed.

The band's future concert repertoire should consist principally, and perhaps most completely, of music written originally and specifically for the band. This original music should be written by internationally established, first-rate composers. I do not mean that no other composers should write for the band (it is not my intention to stifle creative expression anywhere at any time) but I do mean that only the cream of the crop should find its way to the concert stage. The cause of concert band music is not helped in the least by inflicting inept, insignificant, and dull tripe upon an audience.

What type of music is most needed in the band repertoire? When I was asked to write my first band piece, *Legend*, I was given two important rules: it must last no more than six minutes and it must end loudly. Of course I was given other rules, too: no solos for this or that instrument, sparing use of these instruments, and so on. Those rules I broke with the greatest pleasure and with gratifying results. I did adhere, however, to the six minutes and the loud ending. The same adviser made a statement at a meeting to the effect that one could not expect a composer to write for an ensemble that was not definitely standardized because it imposed too many limitations. I disputed this statement. Every composer who is worth his salt always has worked within limitations and with successful results, whether it be for a string quartet, a wind quintet, or any combination or any number of instruments.

I am convinced that the band has come a long way since 1942, the year I composed *Legend*. What it needs now, more than ever, is not six minutes of music in order not to tire the audience or a loud ending to give the cue for applause. It needs compositions of major proportions: twelve-minute overtures and tone poems, twenty-minute suites, and thirty-minute symphonies. It needs the tonal colors of combinations of instruments. It needs the presentation and development of vital and significant musical ideas in the framework of large and important forms. We have the composers, in America as well as Europe, who can produce such music. We have the bands in our colleges that can do it full justice and perform it magnificently. What are we waiting for?

# A Brief Glance Backward in CBDNA's 25th Anniversary Year

Keith Wilson/1966

What were college bands like and what music did they play before the CBDNA came into being?

In 1934, I registered as a freshman at the University of Illinois. My home was in Fort Collins, Colorado; so why had Illinois been the college of my choice? The reasons were simple. I had decided to make music my career, the high school band I played in was the most important musical group I had experienced, and I was well aware that A. Austin Harding's University of Illinois band was the best college band in the country. It was at the University of Illinois that the first band clinics were presented, and during the Thirties those annual affairs attracted hundreds of band directors, publishers, and composers from all over the country. Harding had been the pioneer in developing the symphonic band. In his band of well over a hundred there were complete and balanced choirs of single and double reeds and conical and cylindrical brass. However, most of the music it performed consisted of transcriptions of orchestra literature, surprisingly little of it was published, and what was Harding edited thoroughly to conform with the instrumentation he used. Everyone is aware of the countless transcriptions of major orchestra works that Harding made during his lifetime. He did not hesitate to cut around sections that didn't transcribe effectively for band, and he saw no wrong in playing excerpts from a long and complicated work. His objective was to play music that was of high quality, and to prove that a band could be an effective and expressive musical ensemble. His ultimate goal was to entice major composers to write for band as they wrote for orchestra or any other medium. At that time very little had been written for band by major composers, except for the Holst and Vaughan Williams works that now are classics in our repertory.

Even though the symphonic band in the Thirties had little literature of quality of its own to play, it had beyond all doubt become an important and influential performing vehicle in the musical life of the country, especially in our educational institutions. By 1941, excellent high school bands flourished in all parts of the country, and a considerable number of college bands were challenging Illinois' claim as "the greatest." Publishers now provided F as well as E♭ horn parts, even for marches; alto and bass clarinet parts had become standard; and it was not too unusual to find printed English horn and contrabass clarinet parts. Arrangers such as Erik Leidzen and Lucien Cailliet were providing transcriptions that were vast improvements over those made for twenty-five-piece park bands that had made up the bulk of the band's repertory, but the list of major composers who had added to the band repertory had increased hardly at all.

Unfortunately, an event occurred in December 1941 that caused the postponement of the CBDNA's embryonic plans, and most college bands, if not forced to cease operations entirely, seriously curtailed their activities during the next four years. Nevertheless, a dedicated nucleus of charter members kept the CBDNA alive, and when colleges were able to resume normal operations, the CBDNA was ready to go into action.

The area in which I feel the CBDNA has made its greatest contributions is that of the band's music. This contribution is not limited by any means to the work of the Original Compositions Committee. The discussions stimulated by the Instrumentation Committee and the lecture-demonstrations given by several composers and arrangers concerning scoring techniques have greatly influenced the sound bands now produce. The vast difference in the sound of contemporary band scores and those of some decades ago was clearly demonstrated to me and members of the Yale band recently. The sponsor of a concert we were to give requested a particular nineteenth-century overture from the standard orchestra repertory. The available arrangement originally was published at the turn of the century, and even though it now has "new parts added for modern bands," the sound was unbelievable. We hadn't gone far when many players started laughing, and it was all we could do to finish the piece. When we did, several asked whether I was seriously considering playing anything that sounded like that. The next day I called the sponsor to tell him we could not honor his request, and fortunately he accepted my suggested substitution.

I was, of course, contending with a condensed score that contained such explicit indications as "brass added," "woodwinds," "clarinets," "drums," and so on. It brought to mind the many heated discussions between band conductors and publishers at early meetings of the CBDNA on the appalling scarcity of full scores. No small part of the difficulty in convincing publishers of the necessity of full scores was the unfortunate fact that some band conductors would not buy the full score even when it was available. Now most conductors and publishers realize efficient rehearsals and effective performances are greatly hampered when the conductor does not know what each player is supposed to be playing. As a result, the vast majority of worthwhile publications now have a full score.

The Committee on Published Band Music examines hundreds of new releases every year, and keeps an up-to-date list of music it considers worthy of performance. The Committee on Solos with Manuscript Accompaniment has compiled an imposing list of works, most of them arrangements by CBDNA members, which is available to and popular with members.

The most phenomenal difference in music available for band today and in pre-CBDNA times is, of course, in the quantity and quality of that written directly for the medium. In my opinion the efforts of the Original Compositions Committee have had more influence than the efforts of all other forces combined. This influence extends far beyond the confines of the CBDNA, because a large segment of the entire music profession is now aware that band conductors want a literature of their own, and that the modern band is a serious performing medium playing an increasingly important part in our musical life. Any informed band conductor can now make up interesting programs consisting primarily of original band music if he so desires, and some of our colleagues maintain we should play only such music, an assertion that would have been considered fantastic and impossible twenty-five years ago.

At the national meeting in 1962, after considerable discussion, it was decided that the time had come when the CBDNA should commission a major composer to write a piece for band. Some divisions of the organization had already found means for granting commissions, and certainly quite a number of individual members had managed to find funds for this purpose, but the national organization had not ventured into this area before. I trust that most of the CBDNA membership shares my view that this first commission was highly successful, and that in Aaron Copland's *Emblems* we have a genuinely significant new work in our repertory.

# Band Repertoire from the Tradition of the Professional Bands

Harold Bachman/1967

Although I am constantly being referred to as one of the "older men" of the band business, I actually am a relative newcomer to the American band scene. I was born just twenty-two days before the death of Patrick Gilmore in St. Louis, Missouri, on September 24, 1892. Two days after Gilmore's death, John Philip Sousa, who had resigned from the United States Marine Corps to organize his own professional band, gave his first concert with this band in Plainfield, New Jersey. The opening number on this concert was a piece called *Voice of the Departed Soul* by Patrick Gilmore, played as a memorial to the great bandmaster.

Incidentally, those who think that the idea of the small band, now so often referred to as the wind ensemble, is of recent origin, would do well to examine the instrumentation of Sousa's first band of forty-eight pieces.* It is quite similar to that of many of the wind ensembles that have become so popular in college circles.

I was a little young to have played with Gilmore. By the time I

---

*Editor's note: Some disagreement exists concerning the size of Sousa's original band. Richard Franko Goldman believes the band included forty-nine members, and an 1893 St. Louis photograph supports him. Paul E. Bierley, however, contends that only forty-six players worked with Sousa until 1896.

had achieved enough prominence and skill to have qualified for the Sousa Band I was fully embarked on a career as conductor of my own professional band. Much to my regret, I never played under Sousa's baton. But I did have the satisfaction of seeing many young musicians who started their professional careers with the Bachman Million Dollar Band become important members of Sousa's Band, and a number of the veteran members of his band played with me during the winter seasons in Florida in the 1920s. I met Sousa on several occasions and think I can discuss the literature of his band and his ideas of programing with some personal knowledge.

But the man best qualified to discuss the literature of the bands of the past is Richard Goldman. He has done this so thoroughly and well in his three books, *The Band's Music, The Concert Band*, and *The Wind Band*, that I find it difficult to broach the subject without referring to him. I freely credit him with being the source of many of the comments I make.

The bands of Arthur Pryor, Frederick Innes, Bohumir Kryl, Alessandro Liberati, Giuseppe Creatore, Patrick Conway, and my own Million Dollar Band, which operated with some success during the twilight of the Gilmore, Sousa, and Goldman era, were all commercial organizations. Their success depended on the ability to secure profitable bookings and please their audiences. Some called this ability "showmanship." I prefer to think of it simply as using good judgment in choosing literature and in programing it.

I note that in the criteria used in selecting outstanding original compositions for band, the CBDNA uses the term "audience appeal." These directors were skilled in selecting program material that had "audience appeal." This does not mean that the programs were cheap and trivial. But they were geared to the music tastes of their times.

On September 23, 1892, the day before his death, Patrick Gilmore opened his concert at Exposition Hall in St. Louis with the overture to *Tannhäuser* by Richard Wagner. This concert, which proved to be his final one, also included selections by Handel, Weber, and Liszt. At that time a band performance of the *Tannhäuser* Overture was about as progressive as the performance of a work by Nelhybel is today.

The principal numbers on the program of all these commercial bands were the same, and they were not much different from those played on the programs of the symphony orchestras of that period. The early programs of the Sousa Band contained many of the same numbers that were played by the Theodore Thomas Orchestra in Chicago. And I am sure that Victor Herbert programed many of the same numbers he had played with the Twenty-Second Regiment Band in New York (the old Gilmore Band) after he assumed leadership of the Pittsburgh Symphony Orchestra. The band directors of that period believed that the function of the concert band was to give concerts. For the concerts to be successful there had to be audiences and to attract audiences the music had to appeal to the basic facets of musical interest.

An examination of band concert programs over the past seventy-five years reveals that they contained some music that had only temporary popularity. But even the earliest of them contained selections that are still played by bands, are still enjoyed by audiences at band concerts, and have certainly earned the right to be considered part of the permanent repertory of any concert band.

For fifty years the Goldman Band of New York has successfully presented many of the best selections from the repertoire of the older bands and at the same time pioneered in the movement of band literature. The literature has been greatly enriched by the transcriptions of standard works created for the Goldman Band. Henry Cowell has been quoted as saying, "that it is now possible to offer a program of fine art music of great variety and interest, all written expressly for the band by famous living composers, is very largely due to the efforts, influence, and persuasiveness of Dr. Goldman."

Other successful professional bands, such as the Leonard Smith Band in Detroit and the Long Beach Municipal Band, as well as service bands in Washington and in stations throughout the world, follow a similar pattern of programing. All have developed programs that present both new and old music and that appeal to a variety of music tastes.

What of this literature belongs in the permanent repertoire of the concert band? I would answer by saying, "A good deal of it."

First of all are the marches. This literature definitely belongs to the band and sounds best when played by bands. In the marches of Sousa, Goldman, Karl King, Henry Filmore, R. B. Hall, Russell Alexander, and many of the fine European composers, we have one of the richest sources of good band literature, which should be in the permanent repertory of every band. Rehearsed carefully and played with style and expression, these marches are worthy of a place on the most serious concert band programs.

A list of my favorite marches would be like naming a favorite child or grandchild. When asked which is my favorite march by John Philip Sousa, I usually reply that it is the one I have played most recently. It is a great thrill to rediscover and perform one of the old marches that has not been played frequently. I note that a university band and one of the Washington service bands recently programed *The Boys of the Old Brigade* by Paris Chambers. This is just one of hundreds of musical gems in this category that have been neglected by bands in recent years.

Each director should do a little research and prepare his own list of old marches. As a start he might acquaint himself with some of the fine marches by Victor Herbert and D. W. Reeves. He will find such research a rewarding experience that will add numbers of distinction to his concert programs.

Some may be concerned with the idea that bands should appeal to a more sophisticated musical audience. I have never heard a competent music critic comment unfavorably on a fine performance of a good band march, even though some of them were less favorably impressed by performances of longer, more pretentious works.

Another category of music from the literature of the Gilmore, Sousa, Goldman, and Pryor era is that of instrumental solos. Much of this literature certainly belongs in the permanent repertoire of the concert band. Many of the engagements of the old commercial bands were out of doors and in places like parks and fairs where it was difficult to sustain the attention of listeners to highly refined selections of considerable length. Consequently, many of the solos were for cornets, trombones, and other instruments of brilliance and carrying power. Each soloist usually carried his own book containing the accompaniments for the solos in his repertory. These were short, brilliant showpieces for the instrument, often written by the performer himself.

The concertos for the various instruments by masters of the eighteenth and early nineteenth centuries were largely neglected by the directors of the commercial bands. College bandmasters, with superbly talented players and with the opportunity to present concerts in well-constructed auditoriums before knowledgeable audiences, have an opportunity not only to preserve some of the best of the solo literature from the older bands, but to improve on what they did by presenting more of the complete concertos for various instruments. Band accompaniments for some of these will have to be arranged, but this, too, can be a rewarding experience.

Another category of music featured in band concerts from the days of Gilmore to the present is overtures. Early Gilmore concerts featured overtures by Suppé, Rossini, Weber, Flotow, Bellini, Verdi, and others. One of Gilmore's major contributions was a respectable library of band transcriptions of many of the works of famous composers that had not previously been available in American band editions. Much of the Gilmore library was published and became a staple part of the repertoire of American concert bands.

I was recently informed by Ken Walker of Carl Fischer, Inc., that the old Gilmore Library editions in their catalog are entirely out of print. Of course many of the numbers have been reissued in more modern arrangements. But if you can find some of the old Gilmore Library editions of standard works, you will be surprised how close the instrumentation is to what we now think of as "symphonic band" editions.

These overtures represent a rich source of literature worthy of a place in the permanent repertory of a concert band. In fact, some of them are now almost exclusive to the band repertoire because they are so seldom performed by orchestras. They fall between the type of music performed by major symphony orchestras and that broadcast by typical radio or television concert orchestras. In this twilight zone lies much excellent music. In addition to overtures, we find concert suites, excerpts from forgotten or seldom performed operas, rhapsodies, concert waltzes, dances, tone poems, and other gems by important composers from Handel onward, which come nearly as much within the exclusive province of the concert band as do marches, cornet and trombone solos, and original symphonic band compositions.

How often would we hear the overtures of Franz von Suppé if they were not played by bands? Last year I programed the *Raymond* Overture by Ambroise Thomas at a summer music camp. I was surprised to learn that none of the high school students and only a few of the young band directors had played this overture. We have a tendency to dismiss pieces like these as old war horses, but we forget that generations of students have grown up without ever having played *The Beautiful Galatea, Orpheus, Norma, Zampa, Semiramide*, and other overtures in that class. These players will thrill to them as we did when we first played them, and listeners, who have not heard them for a long time, may greet an occasional performance as they would greet an old and dear friend after a long separation.

Rather than submit lists of specific numbers played by the old concert bands that should have a permanent place in a band library, I have tried to suggest categories of such material that are worthy of consideration. Although the concert band library must contain music that will appeal to a wide range of music interests, it should reflect the personal tastes of the director. I suspect a modern concert band library could get along well enough without *The Race of London* by Riviere, which appeared on an early Gilmore Band concert program, or *The Wets and the Drys*, which was performed on the 1926 tour of the Sousa Band; but I can't imagine any concert band library being complete without good arrangements of the overtures to Gomes' *Il Guarany* or Wagner's *Rienzi*, some of the other excellent transcriptions of overtures and scenes from the Wagnerian operas, some waltzes by Johann Strauss, the tone poem *Finlandia* by Sibelius, the *1812 Overture*, and some of the Bach transcriptions, which are so well adapted to band.

The descriptive fantasy *Death of Custer*, which I first played with Kryl's band in 1914 and which later was a feature number on some of the Bachman concerts before and shortly after World War I, has been lost from our library for a long time. Frankly, it is not greatly missed. But I would consider my library incomplete without copies of the *Egyptian Ballet* by Luigini, the *Phèdre* Overture by Massenet, the *Oberon* Overture by Weber, and the *Second Hungarian Rhapsody* by Liszt.

These are just a few of the many selections that have achieved permanence by appearing on band programs from the days of Gilmore on and that have preserved the same freshness and interest to players and audiences that they had in earlier days. Much of this literature will, of course, be in the form of transcriptions for the modern concert band. Goldman, Harding, Bainum, McAllister, Maddy, Grabel, O'Neil, Dvorak, Falcone, Buys, Revelli, Hindsley, and Prescott are the names of a few of the men who took the lead in pointing out the need for new arrangements of standard works better suited to the instrumentation of large symphonic bands. Several of these men made notable contributions with their own transcriptions.

One of the early purposes of the American Bandmasters Association was to encourage publishers and arrangers to meet this need. Progressive music publishers risked large sums of money by scrapping old editions and publishing new and more expensive ones required by the larger bands. They enlisted the talents of skilled and sensitive arrangers like Lucien Cailliet and Erik Leidzen. The results are that the bands of today have superior arrangements of many of the standard works that were performed by the old bands.

At a recent state clinic one of the most successful composers of serious original music for band was asked if he thought the time would ever come when bands would no longer play transcriptions. His reply was that he hoped not. Some of the reasons he advanced were as follows: (1) Much of the world's finest music is only available for band in the form of transcriptions and some of it lends itself very well to arrangement for band. (2) Many musicians receive their most vital musical experiences from playing in bands and they should not be barred from playing great music because it is not played by the exact instrumentation for which it was written. (3) Many bands reach a segment of the listening audience that might never hear the music in its original form. (4) Many of the transcriptions for band are good ones and some even improve the total effect of the music over the arrangement for which it was originally written.

In the choice of transcriptions for the permanent band library, as in the choice of other material, the director must use judgment and musical discrimination. Some of the overtures, for example, are available in several different arrangements. Choosing between them to find the one best suited to his band is a challenging problem for the director. In solving this problem he will become well acquainted with the overtures and improve his general musicianship.

Incidentally, if you do not find some of the older arrangements in the Fischer, Chappell, and Boosey-Hawkes Journal editions satisfactory for the large symphonic bands, try them with your smaller wind ensemble units. Few of the older arrangers had in mind bands of 100 pieces or more. Some of the Safranek, Lake, Winterbottom, and Godfrey arrangements are ideally suited to the smaller instrumental groups.

In the words of Manley Whitcomb, CBDNA president, "Let us seek to broaden the repertoire of the concert band in all directions." Some band directors tend to be interested only in that which is new in band music. The real test to apply is what is good, whether it be new or old, whether it be in the form of a transcription or something composed for the concert band as we know it today. As one who has devoted his life to the band profession, I look forward with anticipation and confidence to exciting new horizons in the expansion of music in which band music will play a more important role than ever before in the cultural life of the nation.

## Typical Gilmore Band Programs

Selected from a collection presented by Arthur Ford to the American Bandmasters Association Research Center, McKeldin Library, University of Maryland, College Park, Maryland.

The following may have been a tour program. No date or place is listed.

| | |
|---|---|
| Overture—*Semiramide* | Rossini |
| Piccolo Solo—*Polka Brilliante* | De Carlo |
| Nocturne Religiose—*Monastery Bells* | Wely |
| Aria—*Vanne Vanne* | Meyerbeer |
| Lillian Norton | |

Intermission

| | |
|---|---|
| Overture—*William Tell* | Rossini |
| Cornet Solo—*Leviathan Polka* | Levy |
| Walter Emerson | |
| Air—*Oh Had I Jubal's Lyre* | Handel |
| Lillian Norton | |
| Saxophone Solo—*Fantasie Norma* | Bellini |
| E. A. Lefebre | |
| March Potpourri—*A Day with the Irish Brigade* | Kappetz |

Following are the programs for the last concerts conducted by Patrick S. Gilmore.

Exhibition Music Hall
St. Louis, Missouri
Friday evening, September 23, 1892

First Concert 7-8

| | |
|---|---|
| Overture—*Triumphale* | Rubenstein |
| *Träumerei* | Schumann |
| Grand Duet from *Norma* for clarinet and oboe | Bellini |

Messrs. Stockigt and De Chiarri

| | |
|---|---|
| *Scènes Pittoresque* | Massenet |
| Bass Aria—*Rocked in the Cradle of the Deep* | Knight |

(First time, baritones and euphoniums,<br>Second time, bass instruments in unison.)

| | |
|---|---|
| Finale to *Ariele* | Bach |

Second Concert 9-10

| | |
|---|---|
| Overture—*Tannhäuser* | Wagner |
| *Largo* | Handel |
| Allegro Appassionate from the celebrated *Concertstück*, Opus 47 | Weber |
| Old German Air—*Ein Vogel* | Siegfried Ochs |
| Poème Symphonique—*Hungaria* | Liszt |
| March—*Bay State Commandery* | Burrell |

Introducing "Adeste Fideles"

# Band Literature Developed by Band Associations

Paul R. Bryan/1967

The emerging repertoire is the most important of the many problems that must be considered by the conductors of our college bands. Has a body of literature been developed in the last twenty-five years, and what agencies have been responsible? Is there a developing tradition and is there an emerging literature worthy of inclusion in the permanent repertoire of the college band?

The college bands' unique role, in both the field of music and the world of bands, must be taken into account when one considers problems of programing. The general public expects to be entertained in a manner competitive to a Broadway musical review. Athletic associations, which spawned and sponsor us, believe our function is to aid and abet their activities, which are almost completely entertainment-oriented. Our upper-level administrators are pretty well cued in to our publicity values, especially at athletic events, but are generally not aware of other potentialities, since not many band directors seem to become college presidents. Even music administrators are frequently preoccupied, unaware, or unsympathetic—possibly as a reflection of their own personal backgrounds, the attitudes of their superiors, or the attitudes of their more immediate colleagues.

The college band director is also subject to other pressures. He is usually contending almost single-handedly with a complex situation involving multifarious pieces of complicated equipment and personalities. He feels that his financial support is geared to his ability to attract widespread attention and approbation, and that the surest way to success is through the assistance of high-pressure public media such as newspapers and television. On the other hand, his artistic sensitivities, innate intelligence, and sophisticated training naturally rebel against devoting so much energy for such aesthetically unsatisfactory results. Furthermore, these same sensitivities, plus the attitudes of his professional colleagues, force him to a recognition of the low level he occupies on the musical totem pole. Thus, he is forced into a dichotomy in which his artistic impulses are at war with the fundamental human desire for support and public recognition. He has merely to suggest the need for new uniforms, but is forced to fight for a Heckel bassoon! And even when he succeeds in getting the bassoon, his best player would rather play it in the orchestra if he were forced to make a choice. Perhaps there isn't even a capable bassoon player on campus—a decided influence upon the choice of literature! At any rate, almost all external influences strongly encourage the performance of uncomplicated and entertainment-geared music—a remarkable attitude in this day of cultural explosion.

The unique position of the college band puts its leader in the fortunate position of being able to control its destiny—maybe. It is possible to perform the most challenging literature to which we can reasonably aspire and at the same time fulfill our entertainment function. I have yet to hear that a band conductor was fired because his audiences were small. No college president worth his salt interprets the success of his English, history, or philosophy departments on the basis of public response.

There are compelling reasons why we must seek and perform the "worthy" literature. In the first place, our students must have the opportunity and exposure, whether they are to be professionals or enlightened amateurs. Secondly, the extent of our participation in the highest cultural institutions in the land will, in the long run, be relative to what we add to the intellectual milieu in which we function. This point again raises the question of our ability to control our own destinies, because I believe that we must justify our existence as intellectual participants or most of us will cease to exist.

History shows there are few musical absolutes. Masterpieces of one period are later forgotten and judgments of even the most astute critics frequently prove unsound. In other words, each of us will decide for himself as to the quality of the literature he chooses. No man can eschew his background and natural abilities. He can, however, keep his ears and mind open, and thereby avoid atrophy. We might not agree in all instances about the worthiness of individual compositions to be included in the emerging body of literature, but we must agree on the necessity of encouraging the concept that the band is a medium of musical expression worthy of the best efforts by the finest composers.

A mere scansion of the programs I have saved in the last ten years reveals literally hundreds of new works and a constant increase in their numbers. The majority are by talented young composers who have not yet established themselves in the music world. Perhaps the most helpful agency in this regard has been the Ford Foundation, whose composers-in-the-schools program has been of tremendous encouragement to all and has resulted in some excellent works for all media.

A most encouraging sign is the appearance of more compositions by mature, established composers who have decided that perhaps the band offers a congenial medium of expression. Almost all these works have resulted from a financial arrangement whereby the composer was guaranteed a sum of money to write a certain kind of piece. This so-called commissioning process has always been basic to the production of the creative arts. As a matter of fact, I believe the term even can be interpreted to include any situation whereby an artist is given external encouragement. Depending on his mood, financial condition, and so on, many a composer has responded because of the prospect of publication, the promise to extract parts from the score, or even the assurance that a performance will be given. It is my impression, however, that almost all recent works by "established" composers have resulted from commissions that promised a fee as well as the extraction of parts and an assured performance.

Although I have not prepared a complete list of commissioning agencies, a casual search suggests that the band associations' efforts are almost insignificant in comparison to the accomplishments of many individuals and the groups they represent.

The real pioneer seems to have been Edwin Franko Goldman, whose early commissions probably were the basic inspiration to many. The relationship between him, the League of Composers, and the Goldman Band in encouraging composers to write for band is not clear to me, but there is no doubt of the importance of all three. That Richard Franko Goldman has continued the process is tremendously beneficial to us all. Probably many are unaware of the younger Goldman's unique position in the music world. He is at once the conductor of one of the few professional bands in this country and a topflight scholar who writes for the most respected musicological journals of the world. Although he is not responsible for the destinies of a particular college band, his books and other manifestations of understanding and interest in college band problems make it clear that we should seek his advice and aid more than we do.

A complete list would include more than forty commissioning agencies. The champion seems to be the Ithaca High School Band, whose director, Frank Battisti, has placed twenty-two commissions at last count. Theirs has been a high-quality as well as high-quantity achievement—the result of the finest possible kind of leadership.

Several band associations, notably the CBDNA and the ABA, have been influential, and it would be legitimate to consider their competitions part of the commissioning concept. The band fraternities, especially Kappa Kappa Psi, have provided several commissions. A major source of encouragement has been provided by CBDNA member colleges and universities, at least twelve of which have commissioned one or several important works. The efforts of Ithaca High School have been abetted by several other localized secondary school groups. Major composers such as Hindemith, Holst, and Milhaud have responded to the plea of military bands, and Stravinsky has written for the Barnum and Bailey circus. Publishers like G. Schirmer, Leeds, and Marks have been willing to take a chance in a very risky business. A few pieces even have been called forth by government agencies to help celebrate special occasions. May there be more of them!

The greatest recent impetus has come from educational institutions or through their influence and encouragement. I feel sure my list could easily be expanded at least half when a more thorough study is made.

The conclusion about the emerging repertoire is, therefore, that there is a tradition whereby composers are actively encouraged to write for band and that it is in a healthy and advancing stage of development. I find it very encouraging to see the increasing gap between the number of works I would like to play and the amount of rehearsal time and performance opportunities required to present them.

Unfortunately, however, there are a few discouraging aspects. There has been an almost frantic search for new works. Perhaps this is a reflection of the Madison Avenue-inspired cult of "newness." The resulting unanswered question: how do we have a repertoire when we give repeat performances of so few of our works?

With very few exceptions, the pieces that achieve the best sales are quite conservative in idiom. I fear also that some very fine works are languishing unheard because we are not inured to the rental concept. Symphony orchestras spend much money renting music, even though they possess large libraries and a tremendous literature to draw from.

Because of our position as leaders of college bands, we must be willing to extend outselves beyond the seeming demands of our jobs. Although few of us are forced by our superiors to do more than tread musical water, we must get into the pounding surf! Whether we are protecting the future of the band, developing artists and appreciators of the future, or fulfilling and satisfying our own artistic potentialities, we must realize that it all depends on us as individuals. For better or worse, we are the professionals and developers of our highest standards. There are no giants to guide us—there are mostly scoffers, or worse yet, those who would ignore us. Our efforts will determine whether great composers will take us seriously or not. Not our technical proficiency but the makeup of our serious programs will persuade our colleagues in the music world to recognize us as peers. The real challenge is music—not the band in the neighboring school. We must challenge ourselves and our students to the utmost of our ability. Only by considering ourselves primarily as artists rather than showmen, as musicians rather than band directors, can we properly fulfill our mission.

# Avant-Garde Band Literature

Robert Vagner/1967

We have many discrepancies in our terminology for music written since 1900: specifically, the terms modern music, contemporary music, twentieth-century music, new music, and avant-garde music. I see programs of "contemporary" music listing pieces by Debussy (who died in 1918), a composition written in 1906 by Anton Webern, and a number written by a living composer in 1965. One may be easily fooled by these terms, or one may be amazed by the differences in style of much of the so-called new music. For example, in that wonderful edition of the Selmer *Bandwagon* of November 1965, we note that Schoenberg's *Five Pieces for Orchestra* was composed before a number of well-known pieces, yet it is still considered a modern piece by many. Or you might see a program with Alban Berg's 1913 *Four Pieces for Clarinet* followed by a Hovhaness piece written in 1960. Which one is modern, contemporary, or new?

Perhaps it would be easiest to call avant-garde music "experimental music," but this doesn't fit either. We can go back into history and find there were almost always musicians who were experimenting, shocking, and alarming the populace and even the intellectuals of our Western culture. Charles Ives' father was a band conductor ridiculed for his experimentation. For example, he would make young Charles sing in one key while he accompanied him in another. These experiments had a profound effect on Charles Ives, and one has only to look at the score of his *Fourth Symphony* and wonder why we consider some of the things happening today avant-garde. Beethoven was considered a foolish man because of his innovations, and we all know that Stravinsky had his day as a really shocking avant-gardist in the early twentieth century. *Pierrot Lunaire* is still somewhat disturbing after over fifty years. It is said to be *the* event of modern music. Edgard Varèse said, "There is no avant-garde; there are only people who are a little late."

The latest avant-garde movement started around 1950. Neo-Classicism was dying out by the end of World War II, and composers were looking for a new mode of expression. In France, Olivier Messiaen and Pierre Schaeffer led a new movement with a younger generation of French and German composers. In Germany, a number of composers followed the path set by Anton Webern, who had not left Nazi Germany and Austria before the war. In the United States, Varèse already had written music that seemed to fit the prevailing philosophy of creative effort—that of developing a new sound world that could exist on its own without any of the rhetoric or humanistic values of the past.

One phase of this new activity was called the post-Webern movement. In this writing most of the tones and sounds were totally organized with mathematical precision. This music, however, did not seem much different than Webern's music. In fact, it was difficult to tell whether a piece had been written by Webern in 1920 or an Italian in 1960.

Electronic music was an extension of this movement. In this music, the performer was eliminated. The composer could control all phases of his music, and "freeze" the performance forever, like an artist who has painted a picture. The interest in this activity grew rapidly in a short period of time. Electronic music studios opened almost everywhere. But the interest in this phase of contemporary music seems to be lagging. The staggering amount of work necessary to turn out a piece was too much, and the idea of an audience going to a concert hall to hear two or three loud speakers just didn't catch on. However, the concept of using electronic sounds or taped sounds with other instruments or with performers on the stage seems to be a direction that has some merit. Gunther Schuller's highly rated opera *The Visitation*, performed for the first time in 1966 in Germany, used some electronic sounds that illuminated the performance on stage. In 1964, *Interpolations* by Arthur Jordan was performed by the University of Houston band. This piece was performed in a circular auditorium, with the band onstage coordinating live sounds with prerecorded taped sounds emanating from three speakers.

A reaction against the formalism and organization of post-Webern and electronic music set in around 1960. The concepts of chance and indeterminacy in music were championed by the American John Cage. The performer was brought back—in fact, his status was elevated by making him a creator. He had some choice in the way a performance was shaped and designed. He even was asked to improvise at times. This kind of chance music or indeterminate music involves certain fixed elements of improvisation and choice.

Jazz, of course, also is based on the technique of improvisation and it seems to have grown in stature in the postwar world. Musicians and writers now speak of it as an art, not just a skill. One French writer even goes so far as to say that jazz is the only living phase of music, and all other creative efforts since Debussy are total failures.

What avant-garde music do we have for wind instruments? There is an unlimited amount of new avant-garde music available for smaller ensemble combinations using wind and percussion instruments. In fact, without them, there would be very few significant new works available. The twentieth century is a wind instrument century and wind instrument performers have gained much prestige, particularly in the last fifteen years. The tuba player, the percussion player, and the saxophone player are rated equal to the violinist and the pianist in much of our new music.

A strange paradox exists with this rather sudden emergence of the wind instrument in avant-garde music. A new composition for alto saxophone and soprano voice by Jerome Rosen recently was performed with other twentieth century music on a special program for a regional meeting of musicologists at the University of Oregon. This unusual work turned out to be one of the most successful numbers on the program, which included works by Poulenc and Schoenberg. But a number of those musicologists would be the first to criticize anyone for studying and playing the saxophone seriously.

The wind instrument also has come of age as a solo instrument during the postwar period. In Western Europe, I would guess, there are at least as many successful solo flutists as there are pianists and violinists. A number of these flutists are using avant-garde music in their repertory. In 1966, a trombonist made a sensational debut as a soloist in Oakland, California. The major part of his program consisted of avant-garde works written for him. Solo percussionists and small wind and brass ensembles are also booked on the concert circuits, performing the latest works from Europe and the United States.

The contemporary ensemble of today varies in size from two to twenty players, and many are patterned after the International Contemporary Ensemble of Europe, which performs at the School of New Music in Darmstadt, Germany, and at numerous festivals all over Europe. This ensemble is flexible in that a composer may write for any combination of available instruments. The approximate basic ensemble consists of flute, oboe, clarinet, bass clarinet, bassoon, trumpet, trombone, horn, a string quartet, two keyboard players, and two percussion players. It provides most of the available instrumental colors, and the core of sound and texture for most pieces written for it naturally leans heavily on wind and percussion instruments. There is a substantial body of first-rate music that can be performed by this ensemble by adding or subtracting a few instruments and/or voices when needed.

Another significant factor in the present advancement of new music is the availability of grants from both private and public funds for the arts. At the University of Chicago, $4,000 grants are available to players for performing new and experimental music. The University of Iowa has a grant for the performance of new music. A pianist on the faculty at Portland State College in Oregon just received a grant to take avant-garde music to the hinterlands of Oregon.

What about the future of the large ensembles—the symphony orchestra and the band?

There are some musicians, and Leonard Bernstein is one, who believe the large symphony orchestra is possibly doomed. They feel the time will come in the not-too-distant future when the symphony orchestra will cease to exist, unless it is nurtured with some vital new music and a concert public that is willing and able to accept this music. This pessimism also could apply to bands. Nevertheless, there are several directions of creative effort that seem to be encouraging for the large ensemble. Krzysztof Penderecki has written a piece called *Threnody for the Victims of Hiroshima* that uses many striking effects with a mass sound unit. Each string player plays a separate note or effect within a unified rhythm structure. This piece may have started a trend, as there have been a number of other pieces written in this style. I am quite surprised that no one has written a band piece using some of these techniques. Gunther Schuller comes close to it in his *Meditation*, but his strict use of serial technique seems to predominate in this work. Other experimental works use several groups within a large ensemble, spaced at different parts of a concert hall or stage, with the possibility of using more than one conductor.

We also find some symphony orchestras venturing into the realm of the avant-garde. The Chicago Symphony Orchestra, the Concertgebouw Orchestra in Amsterdam, the San Francisco Symphony, and the Buffalo Philharmonic are among those that have programed series of new music concerts.

What band works do we have from the recent avant-garde activity? Very little. *Interpolations* in 1964 was perhaps the first successful venture. Morton Gould entered a new sound world with *Prisms* in 1963. Barney Childs wrote a chance piece in 1965 for the Ithaca, New York high school band called *Six Events for Fifty-Eight Players*. Hale Smith has a published work for high school band called *Take a Chance*. Just recently, on the Davis campus of the University of California, a piece called *The Word* by Stanley Lunetta was given its premiere. It is a "theatre piece" for band, with two conductors, actors, electronic tape, and projectors. George Rochberg wrote *Apocalyptica* for the Montclair College band in 1965. This work calls for fourteen percussion players and has some unique instrumental effects, though Rochberg might be apprehensive about placing it in the category of avant-garde. *Apocalyptica* also is one of the few band works that has been written up in the *Musical Quarterly*. It was given a refreshing and sensitive review.

The time is ripe for the acceptance of the band medium by all of our composers, if we are willing to experiment a little. I have not found a composer who was not interested in writing for the band. We must, of course, give some freedom to the composer in the choice of instrumentation. We cannot insist that the instrumentation be a static and frozen imitation of the nineteenth-century symphony orchestra.

Today there is a healthy feeling that much of the avant-garde activity since 1950 has been good for music. George Rochberg says, "We have now a rich vocabulary to choose from and we should see some really first-rate works being written today and tomorrow." To state this forcefully, let me quote Billy Jim Layton:

> Not for a moment should it be thought that the solution lies simply in a return to the style or unchanging content of one of the greatest classical ages of the past. It is elementary that a tradition which is not constantly enriched by the suffusion of new elements soon degenerates into a sterile ritual. One of the greatest mistakes made by composers of the recent past is their facile assumption that style is all that really matters. But we must guard against the equally fatuous notion that there is a simple, one to one relationship between style and meaning, that for instance, tonality equals morality, or serialism equals science. There is not the slightest reason to reject any particular technical device, electronic means, chance methods, anything, merely because it was invented or employed for aesthetic ends with which we are not much in sympathy. The true liberal will accept whatever, in his judgment, is useful and necessary to him, either of the past or of the present. What really matters is whether he has a firm hold upon his aesthetic goal, consequently permitting these

technical procedures to find their place in a total scheme which has flexibility and strength.[1]

Now let me quote Charles Ives:

The hope of all music, of the future, of the past, to say nothing of the present, will not be with the partialist who raves about an ultra modern opera (if there is such a thing), but despises Schubert, or with the party man who viciously takes the opposite assumption, nor will it lie in any cult or any idiom or in any artist or any composer. "All things in their variety are of one essence and are limited only by themselves." The future of music may not be entirely with music itself, but rather in the way it makes itself a part with—in the way it encourages and extends, rather than limits, the aspirations and ideals of the people, the finer things that humanity does and dreams of; or to put it the other way around, what music is and is to be may lie somewhere in the belief of an unknown philosopher of a half century ago who said, "How can there be any bad music? All music is from Heaven. If there is anything bad in it, I put it there by my implications and limitations. Nature builds the mountain and meadows and man puts in the fences and labels."[2]

Band conductors and teachers already have helped create a healthy environment for the acceptance of the new in music. The last third of the twentieth century should be challenging and exciting to all of us.

---

[1]Billy Jim Layton, "The New Liberalism," *Perspectives of New Music*, Vol. 3, No. 2 (Spring/Summer 1965).
[2]Charles Ives, "Conductor's Notes to Fourth Symphony." © Copyright 1965 Associated Music Publishers, Inc. New York. Reprinted by permission.

# Band Music from a Historical Perspective

David Whitwell/1967

There is a vast body of eighteenth- and nineteenth-century literature that exists for large wind ensemble or wind band. Only a few random specimens from this body of literature are now available. No one has been able to study enough of the unpublished music to be able to judge the relative worth of what we do have. For example, I published a short work for chorus and band by the late eighteenth-century Frenchman Charles Catel. It was simply a manuscript I found that seemed to be worth performing. I do know that works for chorus and band exist in great numbers from the French period, not the least of which is Gossec's *Te Deum* for voices and 300 wind instruments. Until we can see most of these works we shall never know if the little piece I published is representative of the best or the worst of them.

The reasons we do not know this body of music today, and the reasons we should, are all related to the social position of the band itself. In the eighteenth and nineteenth centuries the wind band was primarily functional and not a medium for artistic expression. The nonfunctional artistic works we have were written sometimes on commission, such as Gounod's *Symphony*, but more often simply out of the composer's own interest.

The first basic change in the traditionally functional role of the wind band was personified in Sousa. With Sousa the band became a vehicle for entertainment, and vastly popular at that. Entertainment as a goal was very important to Sousa, and not only from a financial standpoint. He once wrote that he believed entertainment was "of more real value to the world than technical education in music appreciation." By "technical education in music appreciation" he meant the appreciation of orchestral music. More to the point, in comparing himself with Theodore Thomas, conductor of the Chicago Symphony, Sousa wrote in his autobiography: "He performed Wagner, Liszt, and Tchaikowsky in the belief he was educating his public; I performed Wagner, Liszt, and Tchaikowsky with the hope that I was entertaining my public." Whatever Sousa's contribution to bands, or however popular he made them, he did not succeed in moving bands into the mainstream of music culture.

Twentieth-century bands in the United States, Europe, and South America are best characterized by their adoption of orchestral repertoire in transcribed form. The long period during which we primarily performed transcriptions produced one far-reaching detriment. It placed us in an artistic competition that we can never win—the band versus the orchestra. This curious association has led to a situation in which a public school will tend to support either a band or an orchestra, rather than both as it should. It even has extended our vocabulary with such ludicrous terms as "bandistration" to fill a gap seemingly created by the term "orchestration." More important, we have been sidetracked to a position where neither the public nor scholars view us in relation to our own history. In this century books dealing with music history, orchestration, and aesthetics have virtually left us out. I challenge anyone to find a standard undergraduate music history text that deals with the history of wind instruments or their music, however briefly. I challenge anyone to find a music encyclopedia that does justice to such a man as Sax, a figure of considerable influence on music of the nineteenth century. And yet, are not the same encyclopedias filled to overflowing with accounts of insignificant singers and court musicians of the past centuries?

We can begin to reestablish our heritage by performing some of the music written for wind band and wind ensembles during the past two centuries. Perhaps it should be staged more emphatically. Perhaps it is vital that we give our future band conductors, who I assume are among the ranks of our college bands, the historical background they will not otherwise receive in college.

There is a body of eighteenth- and nineteenth-century wind music that I believe should form a part of our repertoire. But before such an addition to the repertoire of a large number of conductors is possible, some important problems must be studied.

First, what role shall this music play in the traditional university band program? The very need for collective thought in this area is implicit in the titles we see on programs. We have wind symphonies, wind orchestras, wind sinfoniettas, chamber bands, chamber winds, in addition to regimental bands, concert bands, and symphonic bands. Why cannot the word "band" include all the wind band music from Johann Christian Bach to Nelhybel? Why cannot the band be a flexible medium, changing according to the requirements of the composition? I realize I am suggesting a death blow to any future attempts at creating a so-called standardized instrumentation, but this concept has never worked and there are fundamental artistic and nationalistic reasons why it never will work. Since composers have primarily been the object of our search for a standard instrumentation, I might suggest that the best way to give confidence to prospective composers of wind music is to demonstrate our confidence in past composers of wind music.

Second, we must locate this body of music. In what museums does it exist? Who in this country has copies—and of what? Who will lend them out for performance? Who is interested in publishing the best of them?

Third, what are the best solutions regarding obsolete wind instruments? In addition, what solutions are best in balancing modern horns and clarinets in the performance of music written for eighteenth-century horns and clarinets?

Fourth, we must make information available on eighteenth- and early nineteenth-century rhythm and ornamentation traditions, as well as editorial practices.

These obstacles and more stand in our way. Fortunately, some are studying these very problems, but duplication and waste of valuable time occurs. Considering the decade or so that the wind ensemble movement has been in progress and considering the large number of colleges that maintain some sort of smaller wind group, I find it curious that the CBDNA has not done more in this area. In order to facilitate the performance of this body of eighteenth- and nineteenth-century music, in order to bring into clearer focus the relationship of current bands and music history itself, I call upon our next president to appoint a standing committee on the wind ensemble.

Such a committee would face an enormous task—a task requiring, in time, the help of all wind conductors. But let us begin. We have nothing further to gain in performing a borrowed repertoire; we have everything to gain in redefining our position in light of a two-century-old tradition. Let us give old works new performances and let us describe new works according to how they reflect or break old traditions.

# The Emerging Band Repertoire

William A. Schaefer/1967

If I were asked which two people have influenced band music most significantly, my answer would be Marconi and Edison. As respective fathers of radio and the phonograph, they have had a profound effect on music. The use of their inventions has created in large measure a knowledgeable and discriminating public.

Not long ago, the band brought to a large segment of the American public the only instrumental music it ever heard. Lacking any basis for comparison, any critical evaluation of what was played or the manner in which it was played was not possible. However, all instrumental performances are now held up for comparison to the finest instrumental groups in the world.

This audience sophistication places an increased responsibility in standards of performance on the conductor. It also relieves him of the obligation of programing music not ideally suited to his group, since there is ample opportunity for both the listener and the performer to have all the contact with music of their choice that they might wish.

Band directors frequently envy the extensive literature of the symphony orchestra. One could wish that the musical giants of the past had left a greater legacy of band music than they did. However, the orchestra conductor must follow much stricter programing traditions and customs than those faced by the college band director.

The typical orchestra concert consists of an overture and two major works, traditionally a symphony and a concerto. The audience expects and gets at least one work by a major symphonic composer. This is both a privilege and an obligation. Furthermore, the orchestra conductor is aware that a soloist, especially a pianist or violinist, creates a greater demand for tickets than an all-orchestra program—even when the concerto is by Chopin, who used the orchestra insignificantly. How rare are the solo appearances of wind instruments with major orchestras!

The bulk of orchestral fare is traditional literature of the Classical period, Romantic era, and early twentieth century. Very little music by American composers is played, and new works are very sparingly presented. For example, in a full season in 1965–66, the Los Angeles Philharmonic Orchestra presented two new works, while the University of Southern California Symphonic Band premiered five major new works and programed a host of other works written within the last twenty years. In other words, the composer must woo the orchestra conductor in hopes of obtaining performances of his works, whereas the enterprising band conductor seeks the composer out. This strategy is producing a great number of works for band.

One obvious additional comparison of orchestra and band literature is that of length of works. The band has very few works of major proportions that are readily available for performance.

Orchestra conductors never have restricted themselves to music that is commercially profitable to publish. They always have been accustomed to renting music for performance to augment the published literature they hold in their own libraries. Publishers are in the business to make money and thus must print what they feel to be marketable. Alas, the large quantity of poor published band material reflects the tastes of those who purchase and use it. The overhead on short, easy music is low and the returns great. Thus we find publishers reluctant to publish major works that are long and difficult and thus performed by fewer groups. Ingolf Dahl's magnificent *Sinfonietta*, conducted by the composer at the CBDNA's national convention in Tempe, is an example of a work that has yet to be published for these reasons. Yet there still have been many performances, each involving a personal arrangement between the composer and the performer.

So to upgrade our literature, we must use unpublished editions. We must understand that costs of rental exceed costs of purchased materials of comparable length. We must continue to assist composers and performers by compiling lists, by encouraging publishers to publish more difficult works, by performing works that are inconvenient to obtain—perhaps even by going into the rental or publishing business ourselves. Approximately half of all the music the University of Southern California band plays is unpublished, and we are renting two or more works per concert. Our next concert includes Gunther Schuller's *Symphony for Brass and Percussion* and the Stravinsky *Concerto for Piano and Winds*, two works of major stature available only through rental.

The subject of transcriptions looms in the back of our minds during every consideration of literature. Should we once and for all eliminate all but original wind music from our repertoire? Can we afford to yet? What is the attitude of other musicians toward music performed in a medium other than that for which it was first conceived?

The orchestra's use of transcriptions is much more limited than ours, but I am willing to forgive them for borrowing Handel's *Royal Fireworks Music* from the wind literature, for it sounds so very well. Indeed, isn't the main criterion that it sound well for the group performing? Composers often have transcribed their own works or works of other composers, or requested that their works be rescored for new media. Mozart, for example, wrote a *Fantasia in F* for clock organ on commission. Later he set it for organ and piano with four hands. The four-hand setting is perhaps the best known; indeed, who would ever hear it on a clock organ?

My question regarding the performance of a transcription is, "Would the composer's appearance at the concert embarrass us?" Shostakovich was most enthusiastic upon hearing a band performance of his Ninth Symphony during a visit to Los Angeles a few years ago. Is it not possible that some works sound even better in a different medium than the original? What about Ravel's setting for orchestra of Mussorgsky's *Pictures at an Exhibition*, or Leidzen's for band?

Several years ago, when I was band director at Carnegie Tech, a visiting professor of piano, Massimo Bogianchino, was planning a recital. We discovered in a discussion over lunch that both of us planned to include *Pictures* on our next program. He had never heard an American band, and from the interest created in our discussion attended the rehearsal later the same day. At our next chance meeting he said, "By the way, I am not playing the Mussorgsky on my recital, nor for that matter ever again." When I asked why, he replied that the band achieved in the "Great Gate at Kiev" what he had sought and been unable to obtain from the piano.

We should be concerned that we play a reasonable balance between the music of the past and present, for the growth of those students whose principal music-making is in the band. We also must seek works of real substance. We must not, in the name of playing only original music for band, resort to music of second-rate composers, nor the second-rate works of first-rate composers. Each of the masters wrote works that were discarded by orchestra performers. The luxury of the orchestra is not that it has works of Haydn to include in its repertoire, but so many to throw away.

I have heard it said that the mid-twentieth century may be remembered as the period in which composers discovered the percussion and audiences learned to regret it. In balancing a program, we must avoid the overemphasis on percussion characteristic of many contemporary band works.

In programing old band works, editing to adjust them to our present groups is a relatively easy matter. Elimination of precautionary doubling—such as the saxophones with the horns—and a use of bassoon and bass clarinet in place of baritone and tuba with the woodwind choir are very helpful. Returning to the original percussion parts, if transcribed from orchestra, provides additional clarity, as does the reduction of woodwinds used when the original involved orchestral woodwinds. Where bass clarinet parts have been provided by rubber stamping a tenor saxophone part, it is a basic consideration of writing for band that when the bass clarinet and tenor saxophone have the same part, one of them is wrong. Not all older editions can or should be still performed, but many of them are worth salvaging.

Composers who write for the band may be concerned over the unpredictable instrumentation. But what guarantee did Brahms have that his symphonies would never be played except by an orchestra of ideal proportions? He would be quite surprised to see the trumpet used by an American orchestra, for its is quite unlike the instrument he had in mind. Our trumpet is still called a "jazz trumpet" in Europe.

By the way, we can perform a real service for composers and arrangers by sending them programs when we perform music they have written. So armed, they have a better chance of persuading publishers to publish additional works.

A group of symphonic proportions that imitates a small improvisational group is at a great disadvantage. A symphony orchestra is also at a disadvantage playing music for the string quartet. An elephant gives a very poor imitation of a flea. Serious concerts should not contain these commercial pieces. But elements of jazz appearing in serious compositions appropriately conceived for a concert group are certainly welcome in the repertoire.

To summarize, the band's literature is drawn from original music of the twentieth century, both published and unpublished; from original music of the past, much of it yet to be uncovered and made available; and from transcriptions from other media—until such time as the literature grows to include sufficient works to minimize the use of other sources. I have no doubt that this will come about, for we are moving rapidly in that direction.

To borrow Lincoln's famous phrase, I hold these truths to be self-evident: (1) All music performed in concerts should be musically worthwhile. (2) It should fit the group performing it. (3) Music should not be repeated during a student's continuing participation in a school organization. (4) Commercial music does not belong in the context of a serious concert. (5) Though the audience is important, those the conductor faces while conducting are much more so.

# The Concert Band and Its Instrumentation

# PART

During the early years of the CBDNA, no subject received so thorough a discussion as the attempt to agree on a standardized instrumentation. This debate, it should be mentioned, was echoed in other professional organizations such as the American School Band Directors Association and the American Bandmasters Association, and received considerable support from publishers.

The climax of this debate, insofar as the large band was concerned, came in 1960 when President James Neilson called a special two-day conference on the subject in New York. Participants in the conference included past presidents of the CBDNA, distinguished composers, and leading publishers.

The expectation was that this conference would serve as a catalyst and finally produce a consensus. As Neilson expressed it:

> Publishers, composers, manufacturers, and conductors are all impatient for progress in this area, for out of the confusion of existing differences both here and abroad must some day

emerge the final pattern of an instrumentation which, like that of the orchestra, will compel great musicians to write for our medium. It is my hope that out of the deliberations of this convention a significant step in this direction will be taken.

As it turned out, the conference seems to have had the opposite effect. Although an attempt to revive the discussion occurred at the 1967 national convention, after 1960 the topic never again seemed so urgent to the membership. President Wilson, speaking in 1966, spoke of this ironic outcome:

> The resulting band of seventy-two pieces had not only never existed, but not a single piece of music had ever been written for it, and to my knowledge not one conductor to this day adopted this "ideal" instrumentation. Frustration and failure for the committee? Not to my mind. On the contrary, it proved about as conclusively as possible that a rigid standard instrumentation was not only impossible but completely undesirable. As a consequence, band scores today, at least an increasing number of them, original works and transcriptions alike, are much more varied and interesting, simply because the composer or arranger is not shackled by an imposed instrumentation, but instead he can feel free to write for an instrumentation that will present his musical ideas the most effectively.

We have included in this section the historic paper that appeared in the 1952 book of proceedings announcing the formation of the Eastman Wind Ensemble. While Frederick Fennell's original purpose was as much to explore a wider literature, the smaller instrumentation became a symbol of a new philosophy.

# Band Sonorities

James Neilson/1950

The symphonic band as an ensemble for the performance of serious music has come of age. More composers of merit are being drawn to it as a medium through which they may express themselves. But if the development of the symphonic band is to proceed in a normal fashion, there are pertinent problems to discuss and clarify. Chief among these is the need to define the sound of the band in terms of its overall sonority. Two questions thus confront the composer and the conductor: (1) what sonorities and timbres should predominate in the symphonic band, and (2) what techniques must be developed to make these sonorities possible. The way in which these questions are answered probably will decide the future of the symphonic band.

The first question has two possible answers, and present-day bands are being developed according to the specific way in which individual conductors answer it. One large group of conductors believes that the woodwind sonority (saxophones included) should predominate. To these persons, the brass instruments (horns excepted) make only a secondary contribution to sonority. With many excellent bands being trained in this fashion, it becomes possible to evaluate performances in terms of these sonorities:

(1) A general smoothness and suavity of tone with a consequent lack of vivid tonal color.
(2) Performances within reduced dynamic levels. There are no immense climaxes of finely spun pianissimos, although the latter may be an empathic reaction due to the absence of vividly brilliant, contrasting passages. One might well liken these performances to those of an a cappella choir singing with a "covered" tone.
(3) A lack of brilliance in tutti passages, due to the fact that since the brass instruments must play at a reduced dynamic level, they are unable to contribute properly to the ensemble tone. A brilliant brass tone cannot be achieved at these levels.
(4) Because the brass section always must use legato tonguing, there is a lack of the percussive quality in the tone necessary in attaining certain functional attributes of performance on brass instruments. These attributes produce qualified subito effects at every dynamic level.
(5) A total sound pleasant to hear, yet lacking in exuberant vitality.
(6) A certain affinity to music written by impressionistic composers and to transcriptions from the orchestra repertory.

Bands portraying sonorities in this fashion achieve a seemingly smoother quality of ensemble tone in two ways: (1) by reducing the quantity of the brass tone well below the maximum dynamic levels possible in the woodwind section (this plan is adopted by the majority of bands playing in this style), and (2) by increasing proportionately the number of woodwinds. Research by Hugh McMillen and Cecil Effinger at the University of Colorado seems to indicate some such arrangement for instrumentation as that used by the symphony orchestra, with the woodwinds in a ratio of 2 ½ or 3 to 1. In a band of eighty performers there would be eleven first, eleven second, and eleven third clarinets (capable of further subdivision), seven bass clarinets, fifteen other woodwinds, and twenty-five brass and percussion. In such instrumentation, no position seems to fit the timbre peculiar to the tone of the saxophone. It is too early to analyze objectively the results of the experiments.

However, some of the weaknesses inherent to the proposed new instrumentation are as follows:

(1) With the proportionate number of brass players reduced, the resultant sonority would eliminate much of the brightness of the composite tone in the ensemble tutti.
(2) Because of the prevailingly weak sonorities in the throat tones of the clarinets, a portion of the composite tone (from $E'$ to $A\flat'$) would be very weak. The better composers and arrangers of band music make much use of the secondary brass in reinforcing this part of the ensemble sonority in vertical alignment.
(3) In the proposed instrumentation, the solo line possibilities of the entire clarinet family would be sacrificed in the interest of basic woodwind sonority.
(4) It would be necessary to make extensive use of the string bass, with a probable ratio to the brass band of 2 to 1, thereby greatly reducing the breadth and dignity of the brass bass sonority in the ensemble tutti.
(5) It would be necessary to rearrange entirely most band music in current use, since this music would not fit the proposed instrumentation. Bass and alto clarinet parts and the secondary brass parts would need to undergo extensive revision. The upper clarinet parts would need revising to allow them to function as the first and second violins do in the orchestra. The proposed instrumentation would, however, enhance band transcriptions of music written originally for the symphony orchestra.

In contemporary bands where woodwind sonority is allowed to predominate, much music cannot be played in style and there seems to be an inability to function as a unit while playing music written specially for band by Holst, Vaughan Williams, Milhaud, Stravinsky, Copland, Creston, and others. One hears bands of this type play exquisite performances of, say, the Unfinished Symphony, followed by the *Rienzi* Overture, played in exactly the same manner. This is not a logical procedure, but one finds such glaring discrepancies.

In the second school of thought, the prevailing sonority is allowed to develop according to each type of instrumentation, with the brass instruments making a vital contribution to the total sonority at every prevailing dynamic level. When sonorities are developed in this fashion, first-chair players in each section are permitted to assume solo status, offering composers a large range of tonal color. Contributions to the total sonority are made by both the secondary woodwind and secondary brass. The ratio of brass and percussion instruments to woodwinds is usually put at 1 to 1¼—in a band of eighty-one players, forty-five woodwinds and thirty-six brass and percussion. There are some bands where the ratio is 1 to 1½, with the difference in the clarinet section.

The advantages of the homogeneous tone developed by ensembles of this type seem to be:

(1) A vital and exuberant ensemble tone in which the secondary brass speak with clarity, adding incisiveness to the ensemble sonority.
(2) A resonant bass tone providing a solid tonal foundation.
(3) The possibility of extending the dynamic range to both ends of the dynamic scale.
(4) The possibility of using a variety of solo tone against a rich tapestry of accompanying sound. When a reasonably thought-out dynamic scheme is provided, a wide variety of tonal possibilities are made available to the composer. Many band performances fail to realize full potential because the conductor is not aware that balance is achieved and maintained through the considered use of dynamic perspectives.
(5) The possibility that the symphonic band may properly function in every area for which music has been written for its use.
(6) The maintenance of the virile and masculine quality of ensemble tone that is the heritage of the symphonic band. It is this unique tonal quality that sets the band apart from all other ensembles.

Many superior conductors demand this type of sonority from their bands. Performances at their hands do not lack for clarity, precision, delicacy when needed, or a tonal sheen of many colors. Indeed these positive attributes are coupled to a brightness and overall tonal and dynamic perspective, so that the experience of hearing these bands becomes a pleasure long to be remembered. The brass section, while never overbearing, is allowed freedom of expression and in the ensemble tutti may develop its sonority to the full extent. Performances are vital, alive, and tonally opulent. They are brightly conceived and executed expositions of the best in music, in direct contrast to the rather somber performances of bands using other techniques.

There is no way by which the symphonic band can produce precisely the tonal sheen of the symphony orchestra. The multiplied overtones of open strings in free and sympathetic vibration have no counterpart in the symphonic band. The transparency of tone thus afforded is uniquely the exclusive possession of the orchestra. This fact makes it imperative to keep the brightness of tonal texture that can be supplied to the band only through its brass section. Much is said about modern composers not understanding the symphonic band, due to a lack of specific information concerning its timbres and sonorities. This is difficult to believe, since music written for band by Holst, Vaughan Williams, Milhaud, Resphigi, Copland, Creston, and others reveals no conscious striving after effect. These composers show the same intuitive sense for tonal color as in their major orchestral works. I note that Creston, Milhaud, Copland, Harris, and other moderns are able to balance dissonance in the same careful and precise tonal relationships in works written for both band and orchestra. Here, indeed, is proof that the symphonic band has come of age.

The techniques that must be used in order to develop either basic sonority largely concern the brass section. In bands where sonorities center in the woodwind section, brass players must be masters of legato tonguing. The failure of many bands to develop a true woodwind sonority is due to the inability of the brass section to master legato. When the basic sonority is in the woodwinds, the brass section must forego the marcato approach at all times. Staccato passages must be played lightly and without sudden attack. Such effects as sforzando, forte-piano, accents, and so on, depend upon the woodwinds for their precise articulation. Since the brass section must play at a constantly reduced dynamic level, it is necessary for its members to be able to support tone with the utmost restraint. In the ensemble sonority, sudden dynamic effects are produced by an accurate balancing of instrumentation, with a consequent weighing of tonal values. With unlimited rehearsal time and boundless patience, sudden dynamic effects can be produced precisely by developing the basic woodwind sonority; however, since the brass players must avoid the marcato approach, too many of the sudden dynamic changes cannot be produced.

With all articulation subordinate to that produced by the woodwinds, and with all other sonorities glowing with lesser light, the brass bass must speak with a greatly reduced urgency. Indeed, often it will be unable to play within the narrow dynamic range allotted it. It therefore becomes an adjunct not necessary to successful band performance, its place usurped by the string bass. This could be a blessing in disguise for many bands I have heard, but surely the elimination of the noble tone produced by the tubas is not the answer to the problem of achieving smoother sonorities. In bands using the basic woodwind sonority, the sonorous possibilities of the brass section would be more fully developed through the addition of such instruments as fluegelhorns and upright E♭ and B♭ tenors.

In bands where the ensemble sonority permits the brass section to make a valid contribution, brass players must become masters of every conceivable style of tonguing, able at will to control the action of the diaphragm in supporting tone, to control the speed of the release of the tongue, and to provide the proper size of opening for the release of breath. The lack of brass performers able to do so causes many conductors to insist upon the basic woodwind sonority, or to fail in projecting the basic sonority inherent to full ensemble tone. In conducting performances where the basic sonority is a homogeneous whole, it often becomes necessary to reduce the weight of the brass tone by reducing the instrumentation. Conductors must not be opposed to this interpretive device, since at the highest level of symphonic band performance a correct balance of timbres is often achieved in this fashion. Of course, it is always necessary to edit the scoring to suit the specific needs of each individual band. Since these alterations are minor, they do not profoundly affect the ensemble sonority.

Which type of band is best? For me, the brass section must be allowed to contribute the values of its timbre to the ensemble sonority. I do not imply I find performances by bands using other techniques to be wanting in musicianship. But the tonal character of the symphonic band has been solidified. I believe composers already have sensed the unique tonal quality of these bands and presently are well able to write in the band idiom. We should consider the symphonic band to have "arrived." We should cease our apologies and demand for the symphonic band its just rights from composers, from audiences, and from conductors who so often misuse it.

# The Eastman Wind Ensemble

Frederick Fennell/1952

The development of wind playing has been one of this country's greatest contributions to music performance in the first half of the twentieth century. We have unleashed a force for music-making that is perhaps unparalleled in the whole history of musical art. The whole symphony orchestra, the opera and chamber orchestra, the dance band, the studio and recording orchestra, the entertainment and theatre orchestra, and the band in its multifarious delineations—all these ensembles utilize wind instruments.

Each of these instrumental assemblies has a function in American musical life which will doubtless be transformed with the inexorable progress of time. But it is not likely that they will disappear if the great music of the past and present is to be recreated in the future.

The many ensembles listed above represent a vast industry and mass preoccupation with techniques in sound. It may seem presumptuous to propose the development of still another kind of ensemble, but I believe there is a place and function for one.

Editor's note: This paper first appeared in the September 1952 issue of the *Music Journal*. Copyright © 1952 by *Music Journal*. Used by permission.

I urge our schools of music, our colleges and universities, our community and professional musical societies (including those which maintain our symphony orchestras) to develop wind ensembles. The purposes can perhaps best be revealed by outlining the plans which we have for such a project at the Eastman School of Music this fall.

Any effort on its behalf must be based upon the assumption that this renascence of wind playing will continue indefinitely and the hope that the current renewal of interest in string study will continue unabated.

We propose combinations of from nine to thirty-four instruments for the list below of standard wind, brass, percussion, and keyboard instruments, which can be found in almost any high school in America.

**Woodwinds**
Two flutes and piccolo and/or alto flute
Two oboes and English horn
Two bassoons and contrabassoon
One E♭ clarinet
Eight B♭ clarinets, or A clarinets divided in any manner desired, or fewer in number if so desired
One E♭ alto clarinet
One B♭ bass clarinet
Choir of saxophones—two alto E♭, tenor B♭, baritone E♭

**Brass**
Three cornets in B♭
Two trumpts in B♭ or five trumpets in B♭
Four horns
Two euphoniums (bass clef)
Three trombones
One E♭ tuba
One or two BB♭ tubas
One string bass

**Other instruments if desired**
Percussion
Harp
Celeste
Piano
Organ
Harpsichord
Solo string instruments
Choral forces

Within this "maximum" instrumentation, which shall carry no label other than that of wind ensemble, it is possible to perform, with but few exceptions, all of the great music written for wind instruments dating from the sixteenth century through the years to the *Symphony in B♭* (1951) by Paul Hindemith. This is an imposing amount of music. Much of it was written in the sixteenth, seventeenth, and eighteenth centuries, utilizes small choral forces, and is as beautiful as it is unknown. This segment of the literature is crowned by the vast amount of music which Mozart wrote for the winds of his day—music which should be studied and which is seldom performed.

We have established the above instrumentation as a point of departure, fixing no limitation other than that there should be no doubling of parts save where sonority in the score shall so indicate. Within this assembly of wind-brass-percussion sonorities exists a reed ensemble, a brass ensemble, a reed-brass ensemble, a reed-brass-percussion ensemble, and almost limitless combinations of all three groups, in both large and small instrumentations.

Concerts will consist of one-third music for reeds, one-third for the brass, and one-third for the reed, brass, and percussion combination. The field of transcription is well covered elsewhere so we shall confine our activity principally to original music of high artistic standards. Following is a program which we presented as this plan took shape in 1951:

| | |
|---|---|
| *Ricercare for Wind Instruments* (1559) | Adrian Willaert (1480–1562) |
| *Canzon XXVI (Bergamasca) for Five Instruments* | Samuel Scheidt (1587–1654) |
| Motet: *Tui Sunt Coeli* for Eight-Voice Double Brass Choir | Orlando Di Lasso (1532–1594) |
| *Sonate pian' e forte; Canzon Noni Toni a. 12* from *Sacrae Symphoniae* (1597) | Giovanni Gabrieli (1557–1612) |
| *Suite No. 2 for Brass* (Turmmusik) | Johann Pezel (1639–1694) |
| *Three Equale for Four Trombones* (1812) | Ludwig Beethoven (1770–1827) |
| *Serenade No. 10 in B♭ for Winds* | Wolfgang A. Mozart (1756–1791) |
| "Angels" from *Men and Angels* for multiple brass choir | Carl Ruggles (1876– *) |
| *Symphonies for Wind Instruments in Memory of Claude Debussy* (1920) | Igor Stravinsky (1882– **) |

This program argues strongly against the old complaint leveled against wind instruments that there is no music written for them which is of sufficient interest to make anyone care to hear it performed. But since progress in all music is dependent more upon composers than upon players, the Eastman School will hold one annual symposium of music which is yet to be written for the wind ensemble.

When Dr. Howard Hanson established his symposiums of new orchestral music by American composers, he began with the simple logic and vision that a composer should have a laboratory in which to test the products of his creative instincts and mental processes. This has been a great contribution to the development of some five hundred American composers. The wind ensemble program will serve a similar purpose.

It has been suggested that other schools and community music societies investigate the possibilities of the wind ensemble. The average student in our schools of music desires more training and experience than current conditions can offer. His contact with the music of the sixteenth, seventeenth, and eighteenth centuries is

*Died in 1971
**Died in 1971

practically nil as are his experiences with the best music of the twentieth century. This is as though our universities gave courses for instructors in drama but included no plays written before 1700 (Shakespeare and Euripides) or after 1900 (Shaw and O'Neill). Whether we like it or not there is an increasing number of our students who are not interested in the band and I do not doubt that those who are noncommital on the matter are weary of being the fifteenth cornet or the twenty-fourth clarinet. Wind ensembles above the level of the wind quintet would serve our prospective teachers and performers in a variety of ways.

For the community musical society, the wind program would be important on both the amateur and professional levels. For the sometime proficient wind player who now plies another vocation, such organized opportunities to play for his own pleasure as well as for the enjoyment of others might prove to be an attractive outlet, one through which this person might see some return on his past investment of time and money. Such wind groups could meet privately and might even contribute something toward the much needed return of music-making to the homes of the American people. To the professional player they offer opportunities limited only by the vision of management and the equipment and curiosity of the musical director. Even if the principal conductors of our major and minor symphonies were not interested in this work it would afford an excellent opportunity for their pop-and-children's-concert-happy assistant and associates to make a further significant contribution to musical society. I believe many of our fine professional players would respond with enthusiasm to such an organized opportunity to vary their otherwise routine existence, dominated as it must be by concert formulas and other managerial conventions.

The *Wall Street Journal* states that more money is spent annually in America on what it calls "high brow" music than on baseball, so it would seem that the audience is ready for the wind ensemble. Music publishers are always ready for anything that will move their stock. Composers constantly seek wider acceptance by the public and the performer, and the country is densely populated by young men with a burning passion to conduct.

It seems that the time has come to furnish the wind instruments with a decent home of their own, unmortgaged by the limitations and traditions of other properties in which they have resided so long. We are going to try to provide one such home in Rochester.

# Report on International Instrumentation

William D. Revelli/1958

For more than a century, bands as they are known today have existed in every civilized nation of the world. In some countries, such as Italy, France, Belgium, Germany, and England, wind bands, especially those of military instrumentation and function, have been in existence for more than two hundred years.

Yet in spite of the band's mature span of existence, it remains grossly neglected as a serious medium of musical expression. The band's lack of artistic growth can be attributed to the fact that it has failed both to achieve a fixed instrumentation and to develop a repertoire that can be performed by bands throughout the world.

The instrumentation situation will remain static so long as each nation persists in maintaining its own theories. Not until the music leaders, composers, arrangers, conductors, and publishers of the world cooperate to design an international band instrumentation will the band achieve its proper status. The problem is not so difficult as it would appear. There are some similarities from country to country—the German instrumentation being akin to that of England, and France's to that of Italy and Belgium.

In America, the development of a standardized band instrumentation was given some consideration years ago when the high school band program was inaugurated. The American Bandmasters Association, more than two decades ago, designed an instrumentation that was expected to standardize the concert band's instrumentation. Although it undoubtedly contributed to the band's present instrumental balance, each band and its conductor maintained a distinct and separate instrumentation.

Bands are usually entitled "marching band," "parade band," "football band," or "gridiron band" when performing out-of-doors and "concert band," "symphonic band," or "symphony band" when performing indoors—although the same personnel may perform at the football game on Saturday afternoon and on the auditorium stage the following evening.

In recent years, some of Europe's most important publishers—Ricordi of Milan, Leduc of Paris, Boosey & Hawkes of London—have published works for American bands. Unfortunately, the works are often merely augmented arrangements from the original band score, rather than a score conceived specifically for American instrumentation. The mere addition of instruments or cross-cueing is hardly the solution to the problem. Only a specific, fixed instrumentation can achieve the desired effect.

Some conductors and publishers believe the musicianship of bandsmen is more important than the number and type of their instruments. However, if international band instrumentation is approved, the bands of various nations will be able to interchange their repertoire and thus substantially improve their individual and collective musicianship. Quality of performance, though important, is nevertheless secondary to making an international band library available to every bandsman throughout the world.

When the repertoire of the bands of America, England, continental Europe, and Mexico is scored so that all bands of these nations can perform the music without change of instrumentation, performance standards are certain to improve immeasurably. The committees now at work on this important project have succeeded in interesting several important composers in scoring serious band works on an international instrumentation basis.

In its current form, American instrumentation is patterned after the English, except that larger woodwind sections are maintained, in keeping with the larger bands of France and Italy. However, we do not include the saxhorn family, so effective in tone color and range. American bands make efficient use of the saxophone family, with the exception of the soprano saxophone, which, as employed by the French and Italian bands, has proved to be most valuable in every element of balance, tone color, and sonority; likewise, the E♭ soprano clarinet is used sparingly in America, but employed to excellent advantage by the bands of Italy and France.

The alto and bass clarinets have become a part of the instrumentation of almost every American band, but since they usually double the saxophones or brass, they are devoid of individuality and merely add weight and thickness to the band's general effect. This situation applies to the bassoons, contrabass clarinets, and tenor-voiced woodwinds.

The problem, then, is not solely one of instrumentation, but also of scoring and usage. It is here that the bands of Italy and France excel, since there is to be found no doubling of voices, and cross-cueing is practically nonexistent. The Italians and French do not agree that a composition can be effectively scored for bands of different instrumentations and sizes.

The time is long overdue for reforms in band scoring, particularly for our American bands. Every conductor, teacher, composer, school of music, publisher, and standardizing agency of this country should promote the development of a specific international band instrumentation that would include the best aspects of each nation's instrumentation and scoring. When this is accomplished, the band as a serious medium of musical expression will make its finest cultural contribution.

In summarizing the principal differences of instrumentation as it now exists between countries, we find the following:

(1) The oboe is included in the band's score by all countries.

(2) The bassoon is fundamental in the English and German military bands, but in France, Italy, and the United States, the saxophone frequently supplants the bassoon or at least doubles its voicing.

(3) The bass clarinet has become accepted internationally as a desirable and valuable voice. Even our school bands have for years

included the bass clarinet in their instrumentation. Unfortunately, arrangers and composers frequently double its voice with that of the saxophones, bassoons, and euphoniums, and it loses its identity, becoming a voice of the full ensemble sound rather than one of individual quality.

(4) The alto clarinet has yet to realize its true value and function in our modern band. Although it is usually included in the band's instrumentation, in practice it is grossly neglected, and composers and arrangers have as yet failed to realize the true potential of this rich and beautiful voice. In the Italian and French bands the bass and alto clarinets have been accorded far greater care and attention, and hence they have made an important contribution to the band's balance, color, and sonority. In all scoring for bands of these countries, we find the bass and alto clarinets performing many solo passages as well as assisting in the harmonic and rhythmic passages, while in America the alto and bass clarinets are usually confined to supporting the lower brasses and woodwinds.

(5) The most drastic variance of instrumentation is found in the saxhorn family. France first adopted the complete family of saxhorns more than fifty years ago and has maintained them since. Thus, the bands of France possess two contrasting timbres within the brass section. The trumpets and trombones provide a bright, brilliant brass quality, while the saxhorns produce a mellow, sweet, and soft texture. Italy, for the most part, is in accord with the French tradition and has followed the French instrumentation of the saxhorn family. In addition, it has added the E♭ alto and B♭ bass trumpets. German bands employ the soprano and tenor saxhorns, but prefer the alto cornet to the alto saxhorn. The E♭ trumpet, an important voice in German scoring, combines with the alto cornet and other low brass voices to give the German band its full and dry but unusually powerful effect. The English use only the baritone and bass of the saxhorn family. Much like the brass sections of American bands, the English employ only one group of brasses: cornets, horns, trombones, euphonium, and tuba. As a rule, English bands rarely use trumpets; thus they do not possess the brilliant, bright, often harsh quality characteristic of bands that use a large number of trumpets and small bore trombones.

The problem of balance can never be resolved until the balance of instrumentation is perfected. The proportion between reeds and brasses, plus the type and family of woodwinds and brasses to be employed, ultimately will determine the success or failure of achieving perfect balance.

Currently, the situation is as follows: Germany advocates one-third woodwinds. France and Italy recommend one-half woodwinds, including saxophones. English bands are approximately one-half woodwinds. America recommends two-thirds woodwinds for concert bands, with the reverse for military or gridiron and parades.

The French and Italian bands maintain two separate and complete brass sections; hence, woodwind sections must be augmented in order to properly balance the instrumentation.

The German instrumentation of one-third woodwinds is effective only for out-of-doors concerts, parades, and military functions. This instrumentation is perhaps the most obsolete and undesirable of all.

The criteria for proper instrumentation should be the achievement of proper balance between woodwinds and brasses. In view of the relative tonal weights of flutes, clarinets, oboes, bassoons, and other instruments of the woodwind family, as compared to the relative tonal weights of trumpets, cornets, trombones, euphoniums, and tubas, the necessity is obvious for an abundance rather than a scarcity of woodwinds.

The woodwinds should and, if properly balanced, can provide sufficient sonority, color, and dynamic contrast so as to be audible at all times, even in the most delicate passages. The brasses, if properly balanced, will provide for blend, additional sonority, tone color, and contrast without subduing or covering the woodwinds.

To summarize, the scoring for the American band is based on its fundamental quintet: soprano, tenor, bass, and contrabass voices, with the woodwinds divided into first B♭ clarinet, second B♭ clarinet, third B♭ clarinet, alto clarinet, and bass clarinet or bassoon.

In England, the same voicing prevails, except that fourth and fifth voices are supplied by the bassoon and/or bass clarinet, respectively. In Germany, the fourth and fifth parts are taken by first and second bassoons.

French and Italian bands use a mixture of clarinets with saxophone. Those of Belgium, Holland, and Spain use approximately the same instrumentation as the larger French bands, except that the saxophone is used only sparingly. The fundamental quintet is thus basically the same, with saxophones considered indispensable only in France and Italy.

Through continental Europe, and particularly in Belgium, France, and Italy, brass instruments have been designated to supply added sonority and color contrast, and occasionally are given solo passages. Four families have been developed employing bright and mellow brasses. This combination provides an excellent opportunity for the achievement of instrumental ensemble and solo effects that are otherwise impossible. In America, England, and Germany, no extensive use of the brasses as contrasting voices is to be found. Too frequently, trumpets and trombones are restricted to accentuating the rhythm or supporting and intensifying the harmonic line.

In Germany, the small E♭ cornet and the alto cornet supplement the soprano cornet, tenor horn, and baritone. Trumpets are usually in E♭. Soprano saxhorns at times replace the cornets, although in most instances the cornet family prevails.

As a whole, the English follow the Germans in their use of brasses, except that English bands have a smaller section. The usual instrumentation calls for three cornets, two horns, three trombones, one euphonium, and three tubas—a composite of the four basic families. In England, the cornet is the solo voice; trumpets are a rarity.

In America, the B♭ cornets, trumpets, and fluegelhorns are usually included, and although some composers feebly attempt to restrict these instruments to their true function, too infrequently we find the score cross-cued and doubled; hence, contrast and clarity are totally lost. Flutes, oboes, and bassoons are often restricted to their orchestral counterparts; however, an encouraging trend to larger flute sections is underway.

A common fallacy of American scoring is doubling the alto saxophone, alto clarinet, and third B♭ clarinet. We also frequently find the tenor saxophone doubling for the bass clarinet, euphonium, and bassoon.

In Germany, instrumentation and scoring seem erratic. The basic quintet is missing in most of the small units. Clarinets are restricted to soprano and alto and do not possess the necessary range to fill the gap usually provided by the saxophones or bassoons. To offset this deficiency, the German bands frequently employ a tenor horn (brass) and a euphonium. While these instruments provide the compass of range of first and second bassoon, they prove to be heavy and inflexible, and usually subdue the woodwinds.

In Italy, scoring for the small band follows the small German band format. As a result, the small Italian band found in almost every village contains a predominance of brass. The scoring, however, is made with this reduced instrumentation in mind; hence, the general effect is usually musically satisfactory. Instrumentation and scoring methods are similar to the French bands. However, Italian bands possess more brass, and balance of the large scores presents a problem. In France, we find the most desirable instrumentation and scoring. With but a few revisions, the French plan could be adapted by America, Italy, Belgium, Holland, Spain, and possibly Germany.

The major problems are with the saxophones. In France they are indispensable to all voices except the soprano. Since alto and bass clarinets are not essentials, further importance is given to the saxophone family throughout France. Clarinets are considered the "first and second violins" of the band, but fail to provide sufficient sonority to stand alone. But since the saxophones are given such importance, brasses are reserved for their proper function—namely, that of providing contrast, sonority, and climaxes.

The wide divergence of national band instrumentations presents barriers that no composer can surmount, should he desire to compose a work intended for all bands of all countries. As a result, he is inclined to either write and score for only the bands of his country, or not compose for band at all. As long as nationalistic band instrumentation and scoring prevail, composers of repute will refrain from composing for band and the repertoire will remain static.

For seventy-five years, little consideration was given to the study or development of an international instrumentation. However, in June 1948 and April 1949, conferences were held in Geneva for the purpose of discussing the unification of the scoring of the band's music. A report of the meetings was presented to the UNESCO Preparatory Commission for Music.

In January 1950, UNESCO unanimously approved the Comité Internationale pour la Musique Instrumentale (CIMI), the International Committee for Instrumental Music. The objectives and aims of this organization follow:

(1) To give new impetus to instrumental music in all its forms and principally to music destined for bands (military, concert, and brass bands).

(2) To standardize the organization of bands in view of conferring upon them an aesthetic quality to elevate them to the level of orchestras of universal character.

(3) To simplify and regulate the writing that is appropriate to the band.

(4) To pursue the technical studies necessary to perfect the work undertaken (pedagogical works, instrumental, encyclopedia, repertory, and journals).

(5) To assure a renaissance of programs by the creation of original works, the establishment of a large current exchange of instrumental compositions for band, the limitation of transcriptions, and the publication of directives as an aid toward the elaboration and elevation of programs.

(6) To facilitate by all means in its power the printing, publication, distribution, and registration under all forms, present and future, of music works written according to the rules set by the association.

(7) To assure the cooperation of existing international organizations in the domain of worthy societies of music with a view toward obtaining the greatest possible distribution of knowledge of the principles passed by the CIMI.

(8) To lead and encourage these ensembles, as well as the man-

ufacturers of instruments, to admit the resolutions passed in the Congress of the CIMI and to put these into practice as soon as possible.

(9) To prepare and organize meetings, congresses, clinics, concerts, and public manifestations in the framework of the movement.

The American Bandmasters Association has embodied in its objectives most of the aims of the CIMI. Since its existence, the American Bandmasters Association has fostered the movement for better bands and band music in America. It is now coordinating efforts with the CIMI to bring about an international instrumentation and universal agreement on bands and band music.

CIMI President Arthur Prevost of Brussels and his committee requested that I prepare a proposed international instrumentation for presentation at the next CIMI meeting. The CBDNA also appointed me to act as its representative for this project.

Following is the instrumentation recommended in September 1958 for presentation to the CIMI:

2 C piccolo (interchangeable with flute)
4 1st flute
4 2nd flute (interchangeable with alto flute)
1 1st oboe
1 2nd oboe
1 English horn (interchangeable with oboe)
2 1st bassoon
2 2nd bassoon (one interchangeable with contrabassoon)
1 contrabassoon (interchangeable with bassoon)
2 E♭ soprano clarinet
6 1st B♭ soprano clarinet
8 2nd B♭ soprano clarinet
8 3rd B♭ soprano clarinet
4 E♭ alto clarinet
4 B♭ bass clarinet
1 E♭ contrabass clarinet
1 BB♭ contrabass clarinet
1 B♭ soprano saxophone
1 1st E♭ alto saxophone

1 2nd alto saxophone
1 1st B♭ tenor saxophone
1 2nd tenor saxophone
1 E♭ baritone saxophone
1 B♭ bass saxophone
2 E♭ soprano cornet
2 1st B♭ soprano cornet
2 2nd B♭ soprano cornet
2 3rd B♭ soprano cornet
1 1st B♭ trumpet
1 2nd B♭ trumpet
2 B♭ fluegelhorn (interchangeable with cornet)
2 1st horn in F
2 2nd horn in F
2 3rd horn in F
2 4th horn in F
2 1st trombone in B♭
2 2nd trombone in B♭
1 bass trombone
2 baritone (saxhorn)
2 euphonium
2 E♭ tuba
2 BB♭ tuba
2 string bass
1 timpani
2 concert drums
1 bass drum
1 cymbals (accessories: triangle, castanet, tambourine, and so on)
<u>1</u> mallet (interchangeable with accessories)
100 Total

This recommended instrumentation is capable of achieving all the artistic effects possible from the practical range of wind instruments.

## The Woodwinds

The large flute section provides for the high register and, with assistance when necessary from the piccolo and E♭ clarinet, we have ample sonority, brilliance, and projection. In addition, the timbre of the B♭ soprano clarinets when playing in unison in the upper register with the flutes will become more mellow and less strident in quality. The flute, being more flexible and fluent than the clarinet, also will enhance the band's technical proficiency, particularly in rapid passages in the upper register, as well as in trills and ornamentations.

Contemporary band scoring places too much emphasis upon the solo and first B♭ clarinets. Too frequently they are required to perform extremely difficult passages that are out of range and technically ungrateful. The flute, on the other hand, is more flexible and capable of greater fluency, and if employed in sufficient numbers, can be more valuable and effective than the clarinet in such passages. Current trends call for larger flute sections; once composers recognize the value of the larger flute section, the B♭ soprano clarinet will assume its proper status in the concert band.

The E♭ soprano clarinet is grossly neglected in America, although it is an indispensable voice in all European bands. In recommending two E♭ clarinets for our proposed instrumentation, we expect they will assist in establishing additional range, brilliance, and sonority beyond that of the B♭ soprano clarinet.

The two oboes and two bassoons have proved their indispensability in America and abroad. They provide the double reed quartet, which contrasts with other woodwinds by performing extended or short solo passages. Band scoring for these instruments has improved recently, and the double reed quartet is gaining a proper place in the band's instrumentation.

The division of the B♭ soprano clarinets into three parts provides for complete harmony and range. With the addition of the four E♭ alto clarinets, the four B♭ bass clarinets, and the E♭ and BB♭ contrabass clarinets, we have the complete range, variety of tone color, and sonority necessary to reproduce any music score.

The flexibility of the E♭ contrabass clarinet enables it to perform passages that are ineffective and frequently impossible when performed by the tuba. The contrabass clarinets, baritone and bass saxophones, and string bass prove to be much more effective in rapid and soft passages than the bass voices of the brass family, which are inclined to be ponderous, sluggish, and inflexible.

By employing the complete clarinet family from the E♭ soprano clarinet to the BB♭ contrabass, plus the complete saxophone family from the B♭ soprano to the B♭ bass, we are able to inject a wide variety of new tone colors, flexibility, fluency, and sonority.

**The Brasses**

The suggested instrumentation employs both the mellow and bright brasses found in the Italian, French, and Belgian bands, with the exception of the alto and bass trumpets, which are covered in range by the fluegelhorn, baritone, and euphonium.

The mellow brasses include the B♭ cornet, horn, baritone, euphonium, and fluegelhorn, while the bright brasses consist of the E♭ cornet, B♭ trumpet, and trombone. The tuba, of course, is basic to either color. The mellow brasses, in addition to providing a mellow and soft timbre, also function as soloists, particularly the horn, B♭ cornet, fluegelhorn, and euphonium.

The bright brasses are used more sparingly. For example, the trumpets are employed only as supporting voices in developing crescendos, climaxes, and percussive effects; they are also most effective in performing fanfares or passages of brilliant, stirring character. On the other hand, the B♭ cornet is ideally suited to the performance of melodies and passages calling for a dolce quality.

The French, Belgian, and Italian bands have long employed cornets and trumpets in this manner. Unfortunately, in America, the policy of mixing cornets and trumpets has resulted in gross misuse of these instruments; they do not produce a unified quality within the sections, but rather a heterogeneous sound that tends to weaken and distort the inherent quality of each. The trumpet, of smaller bore and more cylindrical, naturally possesses a more brilliant, bright, and intense quality. The cornet, larger of bore, conical in design, and more mellow in quality, is the logical soprano brass voice for melodic, legato, expressive performance.

The E♭ cornet readily can adapt itself to either the mellow or bright brasses, although it is perhaps more effective as the soprano of the bright brass. Unfortunately, this instrument is not commonly found in American bands, though it plays an important part in all of the European and British bands. It adds materially to the range of the brass family, is flexible and facile, and possesses power, brilliance, and projection. It also can carry a melodic line with beautiful expressiveness. It is perhaps the most versatile of the brasses.

The fluegelhorn is another instrument of beauty, color, and power. Contralto in quality, it is most effective when performing passages of melodic style and character. It is also effective as a supporting voice to the brasses, especially with the second and third cornets. While it should be used sparingly, it can contribute to the color and sonority of the brasses and as a solo voice possesses a quality that cannot be duplicated by any other brass instruments. It may well be described as the English horn of the brass family.

The trombones have been reduced to five. This reduction does not adversely affect the final result, because we are able to maintain the complete compass, color, and harmonic voicing that could be accomplished with a larger section. By including a complete choir of saxophones, euphoniums, and baritones, we have not sacrificed any range.

The remaining sections are quite standardized throughout the world, except perhaps for the inclusion of the string bass, which is rapidly gaining acceptance. For certain effects, it is indispensable. In short, crisp, pizzicato passages, it can be a valuable support to the low woodwinds. It can substitute for the tuba in passages that are too rapid or awkward. Its individual tone quality is also essential in passages that require a light, fluent style.

Although the recommended instrumentation requires a membership of one hundred bandsmen, just as does the complete personnel of the modern symphony orchestra, the personnel can be reduced without impairing musical quality. For example, if one should wish to maintain a band with sixty members, one could do so without loss of any instrument, by employing the following instrumentation:

4 flute (one interchangeable with piccolo)
2 oboe
2 bassoon
1 E♭ soprano clarinet
4 1st B♭ soprano clarinet

4 2nd B♭ soprano clarinet
4 3rd B♭ soprano clarinet
2 E♭ alto clarinet
2 B♭ bass clarinet
1 E♭ contrabass clarinet
1 BB♭ contrabass clarinet
1 B♭ soprano saxophone
2 E♭ alto saxophone
1 B♭ tenor saxophone
1 E♭ baritone saxophone
1 B♭ bass saxophone
1 E♭ soprano cornet
2 1st B♭ soprano cornet
1 2nd B♭ soprano cornet
1 3rd B♭ soprano cornet
1 1st B♭ trumpet
1 2nd B♭ trumpet
1 B♭ fluegelhorn
4 horn
3 B♭ tenor trombone
1 bass trombone
1 baritone
1 euphonium
1 E♭ tuba
2 BB♭ tuba
1 string bass
1 timpani
1 bass drum
2 concert drum
<u>1</u> traps (accessories)
60 Total

    The only obvious differences between the two bands would be those of sonority, dynamic range, and size. The balance and completeness of instrumentation would be equally effective, providing the playing abilities of the band of sixty members was comparable to that of the 100-member band.

# Conference on the Band's Repertoire, Instrumentation, and Nomenclature

Charles Minelli/1960

The 1960 CBDNA special conference on band repertoire, instrumentation, and nomenclature was attended by William D. Revelli, James Neilson, and R. Bernard Fitzgerald, representing the CBDNA; Paul Creston, Vincent Persichetti, Morton Gould, Philip Lang, Vittorio Giannini, composers; and Benjamin V. Grasso, Ralph Satz, and Alfred Reed, representing publishers. The current CBDNA secretary-treasurer, Charles Minelli, prepared this summary.

The discussion began with a sample survey of instrumentations of high school, college, and university bands, complete with charts, presented by President Neilson.

Considering the instruments in the order in which they appear in the score, the participants expressed amazement at the abundance of flutes. Directors present stated they had eight to twelve flutes in their bands, with more available if they cared to use them. The composers felt this number of flutes was out of proportion to their function, particularly when there are seldom more than two parts (voices) written for these instruments (excluding piccolos). All felt the D♭ piccolo was passé and only the C instrument should be recommended.

Satisfaction was expressed regarding the representation of oboes, English horns, and bassoons. It was agreed that two oboes, one English horn, and two bassoons were adequate. Some suggested the second oboe player double on English horn.

The contrabassoon was discussed at length in an effort to decide if it had a rightful place in the band. The consensus was that due to its expense and scarcity, the contrabassoon should not be recommended as a band instrument. This decision was supported by Morton Gould, who spoke from his broad experience in orchestral writing. It was his opinion that this instrument was almost inaudible except in solo passages and, particularly in band, would make only a minute contribution both in weight of tone and tone color.

All participants felt that, as presently instrumentated, the band was weak in bass voices, not so much in weight of tone (because the volume of tubas is sufficient) as in agility and tone color. For example, the orchestra offers both a string and brass bass, plus the additional choice and color of bassoon and bass clarinet, each having more agility than the band tuba. It may be argued that the band includes both bassoons and bass clarinets, but, in their present proportion to the other reeds and brasses, the volume of tone is insufficient for a true bass voice.

The clarinet family was discussed at great length. There are many conceptions of the functions of the clarinets in the band, individually and as a group. Alfred Reed expounded his view that the clarinet family is the core of the band, and offered as comparison the strings of the orchestra.

President Neilson's charts indicated a sufficient quantity of B♭ clarinets, with parts reasonably well-balanced. There was immediate opinion that clarinets should be divided into two parts, first and second, instead of the usual first, second, and third. Participants felt the traditional writing for the band as a trio ensemble (three clarinet parts, three trumpet parts, and three trombone parts) was a hindrance and invited unnecessary three-part writing to accommodate the third players. With the dual division, three parts, when desired, can be achieved by dividing the first part, and four by dividing both parts.

The charts indicated a strong liking for bass clarinets but showed a sparse representation of E♭ alto clarinets. All composers admitted slighting this instrument due to its small representation, but they felt the instrument was essential for a complete voicing of the clarinet family, and would come in for its share of good writing if it were present in proportion to the rest of the section. The directors were warm in their praise of the latest models, which speak easily throughout the entire compass of the instrument.

Despite its scattered representation in the survey, all felt the E♭ soprano clarinet was essential and that perhaps more than one was necessary. Furthermore, participants felt the superabundance of flutes in no way obviates the need for the E♭ clarinet. This instrument has an entirely different function in the band and offers a distinctive tone color.

Another glance at the charts and supplementary figures showed an astonishingly widespread use of the contrabass clarinet at both high school and college levels. Enthusiasm over this brightening picture was dampened by the information that both E♭ and B♭ instruments are in general usage. The directors compared the merits of both these instruments and concluded that in spite of the desirable extended lower register of the B♭, it is weak in the upper range. Here the E♭ is excellent, and all agreed to this instrument as the better contrabass clarinet voice.

Saxophones, though plentiful, are not always balanced as a section. It is probably for this reason that they receive subordinate treatment in band scoring and are relegated to lower woodwind cues, horn doubling, and so on. The panelists felt that properly balanced saxophones would make a brilliant contribution to the band, both as a section and individually. There was strong feeling for the soprano saxophone, and it was recommended that in place of the usual quartet of two altos, a tenor, and baritone, the balance should be one of each—soprano, alto, tenor, and baritone saxophones, with a recommendation for the bass saxophone as an instrument of great agility, weight of tone, and warm tone color. The quartet is now a quintet.

The cornets evoked the most animated, even heated, exchange of ideas. The cornets are generally too numerous in proportion to the other instruments in the band and too little attention is paid to distinctions between cornets and trumpets. The composers participating deplored the usual practice of doubling cornet parts, as this ruins the desired balance, in dynamics and tone, of the score. Specific indications, such as solo, solos, one stand only, and so on, seem powerless to check this torrent of sound, and strict adherence to the scored number of players is desired.

Panelists noted that most writers avoid high brass writing. This may be due to the uncertainty of amateur performance, which creates dubious intonation and exaggerates the soprano brass quality. The E♭ cornet was offered as a solution and was enthusiastically accepted. This instrument has the desired range, along with a floating quality of tone free from pinch and strain. References were made to the use of this instrument by French and Italian bands, by Salvation Army bands, and in film scoring, television, and Broadway musicals, where its use is increasing.

Generally, horns are a well-balanced section and any doubling is done evenly, with two players on a part. However, the composers did not like large horn sections, feeling that four players are adequate—although an assistant on the first stand may be desired.

Trombones and euphoniums suffer from the same doubling of parts as the cornets, but not to the same extent. It was suggested that there be no more players than voices (parts) and that the section include a bass trombone.

The BB♭ tuba is the only desirable brass bass, and there are usually too many of these in the band. Participants felt that an adequate representation of bass and contrabass clarinets, plus the bass saxophone, gives a writer a new choice of light and heavy bass voices of contrasting tone color.

The percussion instruments came in for only a short discussion, since adequate players are usually available. Two parts will suffice: one for timpani and one for bass and snare drum, mallet instruments, and accessories. This part should be in multiple staves, with a sufficient number of copies.

The second day began with a discussion of the size limits and balance of the ensemble. Each panelist was invited to project instrumentations for forty and sixty players, and the results were charted for comparison. The unanimity of these processes and final totals was astounding; the variance was approximately four to six percent.

The next order of procedure was the collective construction of the "ideal" band when all instruments are available and in any quantity desired. The results were as follows:

| | |
|---|---|
| 1 piccolo (C) | One part for piccolo |
| 6 flute | Two or three parts |
| 2 oboe | First and second parts |
| 1 English horn | Possibly an oboe player doubling |
| 2 bassoon | First and second parts |
| 1 E♭ clarinet | |
| 18 B♭ clarinet | First and second parts |
| 6 E♭ alto clarinet | |
| 3 B♭ bass clarinet | |
| 2 E♭ contrabass clarinet | |
| 1 B♭ soprano saxophone | Straight soprano |
| 1 E♭ alto saxophone | |
| 1 B♭ tenor saxophone | |
| 1 E♭ baritone saxophone | |
| 1 B♭ bass saxophone | |
| 1 E♭ cornet | |
| 3 B♭ cornet | Two parts, three voices |
| 3 B♭ trumpet | Two parts, three voices |
| 4 horn | Four parts |
| 3 trombone | Two parts, three voices |
| 1 bass trombone | |
| 3 euphonium | One or more voices |
| 3 BB♭ tuba | One part |
| 5 percussion | Two parts |
| 73 Total | |

# The Marching Band

# PART 3

The marching band has been a topic of fundamental interest from the very first meeting of the CBDNA in 1941. Indeed, the first topic on the agenda was "military reviews." Motion picture films of the Wisconsin, Michigan, and Illinois marching bands were shown and two specific problem areas were singled out: high drop-out rates (half of the forty men present had experienced a fifty percent drop per year) and radio neglect of halftime shows.

After World War II, conductors began to reevaluate the marching band's image. In his 1948 inaugural CBDNA presidential address, Ray Dvorak commented on a postwar addition to the college band:

> Far too much of a "sports spirit" holds sway in the curious phenomenon of the scantily clad, weirdly gyrating "drum majorettes," whose antics seem calculated to hold a medium of good music down to circus level. Imagine a Toscanini orchestra ushered forth upon the platform by a drum majorette!

In 1950, Hugh McMillen of the University of Colorado

distributed the results of an extensive survey regarding the status of credit for the marching band. He reported that 77 percent of the institutions offered credit through the music department and nearly 80 percent on an all-college basis. Only 26 percent of the institutions allowed the marching band to be substituted for physical education requirements and 8.7 percent for ROTC. The survey reported that more than 67 percent of the marching bands rehearsed five or more hours per week.

By 1950, the general question of ethics had aroused interest. Daniel Martino of Indiana University presented "A Sanity Code for the College Marching Band," which included the following ideals:

(1) To present carefully prepared gridiron music performances.
(2) To strive for the highest standards of gridiron music/marching performance.
(3) To seek improvement in the intonation of the marching band.
(4) To study instrumentations and line-ups for improving general field performances.
(5) To encourage careful and well-prepared renditions of the national anthem.
(6) To discourage uncontrolled, unmusical, loud playing.
(7) To consider the inclusion of at least one reasonable concertized work at each performance.
(8) To strive for a cadence that is reasonable and considerate of music, talent, and instrumentation.
(9) To follow ethical professional practices in relation to visiting bands and band conductors.
(10) To encourage a type and style of marching considerate of the nature, music, talents, and skills of the marching band.
(11) To seek for better and more efficient rehearsal techniques.
(12) To consider the proportionate relationship between the performance time and the available rehearsal time.

(13) To encourage by consistent exemplary practices the finest in music/marching performances among the secondary school band conductors in the immediate sphere of influence.

(14) To cooperate in the respective conferences with all other conductors having similar goals.

Surveys continued to be a popular feature of CBDNA conventions and several of the more revealing ones are included here.

# Pertinent Questions Concerning Marching Bands: A Survey

Arthur Williams/1958

(1) What is your answer to the comment: "The trouble with your football band is that no one cares whether you play fine-sounding music; the band must look sharp, execute maneuvers with precision, and entertain the crowd?"
True: 39 percent
Untrue: 61 percent

(2) Do the better trained freshmen wind and percussion players in your college show (a) keen interest in your football band, (b) lack of interest, or (c) some interest?
Keen interest: 38 percent
Lack of interest: 21 percent
Some interest: 41 percent

Editor's note: In 1958 Arthur Williams sent a questionnaire on marching bands to 271 CBDNA college band directors, through the offices of The Instrumentalist magazine. The Instrumentalist published the results of early returns in its December 1958 and January 1959 issues, with further installments in April 1959, June 1959, and January 1960. The results reprinted here duplicate those submitted by Williams to the CBDNA Committee on Public Relations in December 1958, based on 137 respondents.

(3) If female band players are available, should they be used in the marching band?
Yes: 70 percent
No: 30 percent

(4) What are your more troublesome problems in making the transition from your football band to the winter concert band?
No problems: 23 percent
Tone problems: 39 percent
Instrumentation problems: 18 percent
Other problems: 20 percent

(5) Do you favor using valved brasses instead of the slide trombones for marching purposes?
Favor: 22 percent
Not favor: 78 percent

(6) To what extent does the athletic department at your school support your marching band?
None: 44 percent
Some: 45 percent
Considerable: 11 percent

(7) What musical values do marching band members gain from the marching band?
None: 20 percent
Few: 9 percent
Endurance, projection of tones, breath support, and so on: 13 percent
Rhythmic training: 13 percent
Timing and precision: 12 percent
Acquaintance with march styles, good arrangements, improved sight-reading, and so on: 12½ percent
Other values such as confidence, playing under fire and at wide distances, flexibility, experience for M.Ed., and so on: 18½ percent

(8) What nonmusical values do they gain from this participation?
None: 3 percent
Cooperation: 6 percent
Discipline: 13 percent
Esprit de corps: 11 percent
Exercise: 9 percent
Physical coordination: 8 percent
Pride in achievement—campus recognition, appearance before large groups of people, and so on: 8 percent
Service to school: 4 percent
Showmanship: 5 percent
Social values: 9 percent
Teamwork: 7 percent
Others, such as fun, PE credit, confidence, emotional release, M.Ed. training, and so on: 15 percent

(9) On the basis of abilities or lack of abilities of your entering freshmen, what suggestions do you have for high school band directors?
More stress on fundamentals (including rhythm, dynamics, intonation, technics, fingerings, and so on): 29 percent
Teach musicianship (including nuance, styles, precision, and so on): 18 percent
Stress more sight-reading, including manuscript parts: 9 percent
Stress tone production and tone quality: 6 percent
Less stress on marching maneuvers and "tricks": 5 percent
Strive to use more concert-type music: 5 percent
Stress values of continuing playing in college and adult life: 7 percent
Other factors such as less exploitation, avoidance of "played out" feeling, keeping an open-minded attitude, and on on: 17 percent

(10) If it actually made no difference to your school or community whether or not you fronted your band with girl majorettes, baton twirlers, flag swingers, pompom girls, and so on, what would you prefer?
Favor use of girl majorettes and so on: 52 percent
Prefer no use of girl majorettes and so on: 48 percent

(11) What is your reaction to having two bands, one for all outdoor appearances, including all marching and football appearances, and another strictly concert band? Would this be possible at your school?
Like the idea of two separate bands: 38 percent
Not possible at my school yet: 33 percent
Prefer one all-purpose band only: 18½ percent
Now have two separate bands as a part of our program: 10½ percent

# The Concert Band Conductor and the Marching Band

Mark Hindsley/1960

The school and college marching band is a wonderful and unique institution. After a rather slow start it practically exploded on the American scene. It has assumed a position of importance in school and community life.

As an exceptional example of this importance, I can cite a recent experience as adjudicator of a neighboring state high school marching band contest, a contest entered by almost 100 bands and viewed by some 10,000 people, with the winning band receiving a trophy just as big as that awarded the state championship basketball team.

The college band, regardless of its own traditions and inclinations, inherits a membership and a considerable public quite thoroughly imbued with the marching band idea. In such circumstances, the marching band can be a great positive or negative force in music education and a great credit or discredit to our schools and colleges and communities.

Today's band directors may be divided into three "political

---

Editor's note: Reprinted from *The Instrumentalist* (September 1961, pp. 70-73), © The Instrumentalist Co. (1961). Used by permission of The Instrumentalist Co.

camps" regarding marching. In the center camp are those who believe in and have retained basically the traditional marching of military units and music that is generally appropriate to such marching. They see the band in a rational and conservative perspective, as a musical organization first and a marching organization second, and they develop in the band the best elements of both music and marching.

Those of us who consider ourselves in this center group see other groups both left and right. To us, those on the left have distorted the marching of the band and debased its music. Their performances would seem more appropriate in a night club than on a campus.

On the right we see those who, either because of their disgust with the trend on the left, or because they are feeling the rapidly rising musical and social stature of the concert band and see an opportunity to have something to look down upon, wish to have as little as possible to do with the marching band, and they are willing to abdicate their responsibilities for it.

These are perhaps extreme statements or overly simplified statements of the center, left, and right positions and practices. They nevertheless point up the range of our divergences and controversies, and they explain the concern held by many of us over the effect of the marching band on the total school band picture.

It is natural and proper that we, as band directors, should consider ourselves first as concert band conductors. If we stop there, however, and do not assume or provide for the role and obligations of the marching band director, we cannot be truly and adequately living up to our responsibilities for service of the band "to its members, its institution, and its art."

On the other hand, if we neglect the concert band to the overemphasis of the marching band, or if we stray afar from musical and marching standards, we are helping to defeat our own professed goals and discarding our proposed principles. The concert and marching functions of the band are compatible, and when placed in proper perspective and relationship each will favorably serve the other.

It is somewhat paradoxical that some of our problems are the result of the great progress of our bands, and with that progress an increase in their versatility. Not too long ago the general concept of a band was that of a musical organization of lower caste, made up largely of brass and percussion instruments, capable of making music of a boisterous type for boisterous and gala outdoor occasions, and for leading military and civic parades. The stereotyped march form was its signature, and representative of all music classed as *band music*. When it attempted performances of music outside this class it was considered a transgressor.

At least the "senior" members among us who have lived with bands all our lives know what progress has been made in the refinement of the band, in the elevation of its musical standards, and in its popular evaluation. We know of the bands in the professional, military, college, and school fields that have kept the standards continually rising and that have been responsible for the growth in interest, enjoyment, and participation in bands. Most people have always liked to hear bands play, but now they have become accustomed to hearing bands on occasions and in settings of greater variety.

The versatility and progress of the band in the direction of playing a better class of music has not in any sense reduced its effectiveness for the occasions where bands traditionally have furnished the music and the pageantry. In fact, the variety of music played, the development of instrumentation and the vast technical and artistic improvement of bands have made them far more effective for pageantry than ever before. School and college bands, with their unlimited youthful vigor, have taken the lead in creating out-of-doors musical and marching spectacles that have inspired throngs throughout the country.

Many are the instances when great crowds have stood in silence as a band played, impressed with emotions of loyalty, reverence, love, or pride; when they have been aroused to competitive enthusiasm; when they have laughed heartily at a cleverly humorous stunt; many times still when they have only watched and listened with appreciation and interest, entertained and content. It is within the power of the marching band to do all these things, not only to entertain, but in entertaining to develop a spirit and an atmosphere in accord with the occasion and the times.

School bands are recognized as leaders of school spirit. It may well be that the spirit of the band becomes the spirit of the school. Bands are also leaders of community and national spirit. At least one recent president has expressed himself publicly concerning the value of bands on the national scene. My commanding general in World War II was quoted as saying, with particular reference to bands, "Music is the backbone of morale."

Granted that the marching band plays an important part in entertaining the public and in pointing up its spirit, are these considerations vital in evaluating the role of the school marching band? Certainly they are, from the standpoint of both service and public relations.

Public relationship is a fortunate relationship for the school band. While the marching performances themselves are perhaps very limited in their musical and educational values, the circumstances that make possible these performances—and, more important, the circumstances that are made possible by these performances—combine to create situations favorable for a high level of musical development of the concert band.

Bands could not have found such a prominent position in public attention, in the first place, without a few bands having attained a degree of musicianship and marching ability; and in the second place, the resulting public attention has made possible administrative and financial support that has permitted the musical side of the band to rise to unprecedented heights.

The limelight of marching band performance has exerted a magnetic influence on school youth, an influence perhaps stronger than that of the music itself. The desire to belong to such an organization and to share in its experiences has brought to the threshold of music education countless numbers of youngsters whose interest in music and bands otherwise might have been passive, if not entirely absent. And though the marching band itself may not rate so high musically, what normally goes on in the training of the marching band, and what goes on musically before, during, and after the training of the marching band, afford the possibilities of tremendous contributions to musical and educational development. This assumes that the marching band does not completely dominate the band's program, but is fitted into the program in a sensible and balanced manner, leaving room for musical growth.

The marching band that is an outgrowth of a sound musical program brings credit to itself if its performances are on a sufficiently high plane, musically and otherwise. These performances should capitalize on the attractiveness of the music-marching combination, the human maneuvers and formations on the field, with the association of musical ideas. By its appearances the band takes on a certain character, and suggests the character of the institution it represents. If the marching and playing are mediocre and the program content is of low conception, the band and music education are discredited.

If by its own acts and by those of certain "appendages" to the organization, the entertainment, musical, and emotional values are cheap, the band itself is cheap, and its cheapness reflects on and is a reflection of its institution and its community.

The elements of a marching band performance that are stressed are what give it its character and standing. If good marches and good music of popular nature are stressed, the band has a certain character. If jazz, swing, and rock-'n-roll are stressed, the band has character of another kind. If twirling and majorettes are stressed, they contribute to the band's character. If a marching band features dancing, this becomes a part of the total character. It is apparent that all of these elements are considered appropriate by varying numbers of individuals among us. Whether they are or not, it is perhaps their relative emphasis that determines the public impression of the band, and the band's own impression of itself.

Near the beginning of this article I described three hypothetical marching band "political camps," left, right, and center. If there are any of my readers in the group on the left, those whom I have charged with distortion of marching and debasement of music, let me say that we have a cultural responsibility that transcends our musical responsibility, and a moral responsibility that transcends both—moral not necessarily in the sense of prudishness but moral in the sense of genuine rightness and wrongness, moral in the sense of the dignity of education.

For those catering to the sensational and the sensual because they say the public demands it, let me say that I know of bands that seldom march at a tempo of more than 120, who seldom make a formation on the field, who do not dance or use majorettes or play jazz, who are as popularly received as are bands of opposite tendencies. We ourselves are the principal creators of public demand in our own field, and in nearly every case we are doing what we want to do rather than what we think or say we are forced to do.

If there are any readers who are in the group on the right, whom I have classified as wishing to wash their hands of the marching band, let me say that although your musical idealism may be admirable, an ivory tower may not really be necessary or advisable for the abundant fruition of wind music. Let me further suggest that you consider whether your ambitions and destinies, both as musicians and as persons, and both for yourselves and your bands, cannot be served better in the broad and complete concept of the school band as both a concert and marching band, dedicated to the highest possible musical, cultural, educational, and service standards.

# Problems, Solutions, and Present Status of Small College Marching Bands

Richard Colwell/1960

The following information was obtained by a questionnaire answered by 131 schools. It portrays the director of the small college band as usually pessimistic and the director of the large college band as optimistic, and suggests some possible solutions for common problems.

The "small college band" was determined by the size of the band and not by the size of the school. There are small bands in large schools. The University of Rhode Island band numbers only twenty-eight players. In general, small bands are in places that have small football attendance. I chose seventy players and under as "small." Some schools with many bands have duplication in all members while others have no duplication, so I looked for band programs with seventy different individuals. Of the 131 returns, seventy-three colleges were in the small class with an average enrollment of fifty, while fifty-eight colleges fell in the large class with an average enrollment of 105. The division was sharp.

Four of the small bands played to crowds of more than 10,000, nine of these schools had crowds of less than 1,000, and the average for the small college was 3,000. In the large band category ten bands played to crowds of less than 3,000, but the average was 25,050.

This ranged from 200 for one school with a ninety-piece band to Michigan's 100,000. The band size thus was relatively consistent with the size of football audiences.

The biggest colleges used all-male personnel. The breakdown for other large schools was 80 percent male, while the smaller schools averaged 64 percent male. Music majors in marching bands accounted for 36 percent in the large schools and 35 percent in the smaller ones. Large and small bands reported the quality of their musicians to be "fair."

Certainly the directors of the small college bands were more opposed to marching bands than the directors of large college bands. They probably see the problems as insurmountable, and this dislike surfaced in the questionnaire. At least six schools reported they had no marching band or football team, and most of their reports were marked "hurrah!" Only 40 percent of the small band leaders felt the crowd is interested in the football band, while 65 percent of the large band directors believed the audience is favorable toward what they are doing. Many of the small college directors reported that only 2 percent to 10 percent of their audiences are interested in halftime shows.

Regardless of size, most directors felt limited more by time than by any other factor. Money is apparently not a great problem; most football bands reporting were well supported. Numerical size of the band was a common complaint, even if the band was around 100 in size. Large school directors said a good show was possible with a little band, but small school directors didn't agree. Bleacher height was a factor in thirty-six of the schools reporting.

Only six schools did not have radio coverage of the games. Forty of the schools also had some television coverage of their shows during the season. No apparent significance was attached to whether games were played at night or in the daytime.

Most small college band leaders (fifty-four out of seventy-three) felt they were compared with big schools, and fifty-two of this number had an administration or audience that wanted elaborate halftime shows. Only two thirds of the large school band directors felt the comparison or demand for elaborate halftimes.

There was great variation in number of hours of rehearsal time.

Small schools reported practice about three hours per week, with a range from one to ten hours. Large schools averaged about five and a half hours per week, with a range from three to twelve hours.

Trips made little difference, according to results of the questionnaire. Nine small schools didn't make any, while most made one or two a year, with only a few schools making all away games. Half of the large bands made one trip, and one third played for three or more away games.

Twenty-seven small schools had a Band Day, and seventeen of these furnished meals or more. Forty-three of the big colleges had a Band Day, with twenty-three giving meals or more. Travel, accommodations, and money were sometimes provided.

Most schools still used baton twirlers, but it appears that small schools were taking the lead in eliminating them. They used fewer twirlers, and twenty-seven had eliminated them entirely. Only thirteen big schools had done so.

As for maintaining grade averages for trips, large and small colleges alike were divided. If band was a course for credit, nothing was required beyond fulfilling the necessary band obligations. Many students needed only to maintain an average high enough to stay in school, while scholastic probation ruled out participation. Half the bands in each classification of college had this regulation.

Twenty-five of the small band directors felt there is growing interest in halftime shows. Twenty-five saw no change, and eight reported less interest. In the big colleges, thirty-five felt interest was greater, eighteen saw no change, and three reported audiences becoming less interested.

The budgets for football bands were surprisingly hefty. No one spent less than 100 dollars for music and props, and most spent from three to five hundred dollars, regardless of the size of school. If travel expenses were included in the budget, small schools spent from two to three thousand dollars, and large colleges four to six thousand dollars.

The responses of small and large college band directors differed as to whether their band members liked football band. Small colleges were evenly divided; twenty-six said yes and twenty-seven said no. In the big schools, however, fifty-two said yes and only four said no. A question also was posed as to whether any students liked football band better than concert band. Forty-one small college directors said no and only eight replied yes. In the large college category, thirty-two answered yes, while twenty-four said no. We are either deliberately removing a lot of people from band after marching season is over, or they are dropping out because they do not like concert band. This discrepancy shows up in enrollment figures, especially in middle-sized schools. For those schools that gave figures, at least 20 percent of the students quit after marching season.

Another question on the survey asked whether band directors would like to have a CBDNA central library available for football shows and idea exchange. Eighty-two replied yes, most of them enthusiastically. Twenty said no. Practically all schools used specially arranged music.

Suggestions offered by the respondents included more recognition, more scholarships, and credit for band members. Small college band directors said they would like to stop competing with big school bands. They would like to develop a style of their own, do what they can do well, and convince the audience that they are different from a big college band. Many felt we need to get down to work, stop complaining, and recognize the football band as a musical organization. Large schools where ROTC credit is given for band have an advantage that contributes to the large number of men in their organizations. The very large schools, with 10 to 20 percent female membership, would lose as many as fifty to one hundred band members if compulsory ROTC were dropped. Another problem noted by many respondents was the predominance of freshmen and sophomores in college bands. Upperclassmen usually were required to be in band because they were music majors. Many schools reported no seniors and very few juniors in the band.

# Varied and Changing Styles of Halftime Shows: A Survey

William D. Cole/1960

Six percent of the directors in this survey had bands of forty members; 3 percent had bands of 175 or more; 14 percent had sixty to sixty-five members; 11 percent had eighty-five; an additional 11 percent had ninety-six; and another 10 percent had seventy-five. Thirty-four percent of the directors felt the ideal band should range from ninety-six to 110 members; 23 percent would like to have 110 to 130 members; only 6 percent wanted more than 130 players. Yet 66 percent of the directors preferred larger bands than they presently have; 12 percent preferred fewer members, while 22 percent wanted their bands to remain the same size.

Thirty-five percent of the bands reported female membership between 20 percent and 35 percent; 20 percent had no women; 20 percent had 35 to 50 percent women in the organization; 7 percent reported over 50 percent women; and 18 percent had less than 15 percent.

Seventeen percent of the colleges had a marching band director separate from the director of concert band and the remaining 83 percent had concert band, pep and dance band, ROTC band, and so on, in addition to marching band. Eighteen percent had full-time faculty assistants; 83 percent had none. Similarly, 87 percent an-

The survey also asked about "trends coming about that affect the style of shows being performed." It seems that "precision marching" is the "trend," according to 35 percent of the band directors who answered this question. Another 13 percent felt the trend is toward girls' drill or dance units; 6 percent thought the trend is to devote more time to acquiring a good, full concert sound on the field; and 5 percent felt "extravaganzas" are the trend. However, 43 percent of the directors gave no answer at all.

The next question asked, "Are marching band shows being (a) deemphasized, (b) emphasized, or (c) neither, in your area?" The results produced the following percentages: deemphasize—14 percent; emphasize—25 percent; neither—61 percent.

Even though 37 percent of the band directors felt props were not "worthwhile," 77 percent used them occasionally, 20 percent never used them and only 3 percent used them extensively. In comparison to past seasons, 65 percent of the directors used props about the same, 25 percent used them less, and 10 percent used them more. These percentages indicated a slight decline in the use of props over past seasons.

Only 12 percent of the bands had speeded up their cadence over the past years and 17 percent had slowed down; the remainder were maintaining the same tempo. However, the majority of the bands, regardless of whether they slowed down, speeded up, or remained the same, favored a variation of tempos. The average tempo for all bands was approximately 144. The lowest tempo was 60 and the highest 320. In general the spread in variation of tempo was from 100 to 180.

The 22½-inch pace, or eight steps to five yards, was by far the most popular marching pace. Ninety percent of all the bands represented in the questionnaire used it. The remaining 10 percent used the thirty-inch step, or six to five; nearly all of them marched a cadence of 132 or less. Still, three bands using the faster cadence, 160, preferred the longer thirty-inch pace.

The directors' methods of charting a band show, like the length of step, were generally universal. Eighty-six percent of the bands gave formation charts to each bandsman; 8 percent gave the charts only to the squad leaders or, in one case, to the right guides; only 6 percent used no charts at all. One band director made a master chart that was posted for each bandsman to copy his position in every formation. Thirty-nine percent of the directors indicated that the size of the formation spacing interval depended upon the size of the band and the formation. Many directors, of course, checked more than one interval, depending upon its use in a vertical or horizontal line. The thirty-inch and forty-five-inch intervals are slightly more in use for charting (35 percent) than the sixty-four-inch interval (26 percent). Many directors said they "never give it a thought" and move their bandsmen around until the formation looks good from the stands.

When asked what procedure they preferred in moving from one formation to the next, 30 percent of the directors indicated they used two or more methods in moving. The "scatter" and "evolution" methods were most popular, with movement by ranks being used by 20 percent of the bands. Here again, many of the directors stated that the moving procedure depends upon the bandsman's position in the previous formation.

Thirty-seven percent of the bands used (or as some directors facetiously indicated, tried to use) a high marching step, 31.5 percent used a normal military-style step, and 31.5 percent favored variety in the style of marching step. The trend was to use variety; several directors mentioned they used variety only recently and liked it, or planned to use it this season.

The last question regarding use of company front and block band formation for entrances revealed a definite trend over the past seasons. Seventy-seven percent of the bands were using company front entrances for their pregame and/or halftime entrances. Asked if they varied this entrance during the season, 55 percent of the directors said they favored some variation from game to game, while the remaining 45 percent said they kept the entrance the same over the season. The majority, however, indicated they did not use the same entrance for both pregame and halftime.

The reader can undoubtedly come to his own conclusions about the questionnaire. Attempts to field a good marching band are alive and well. The oustanding marching bands are not produced by accident, but through the well-planned efforts of the director, his staff, and assistants. There is a constant effort to put variety into the performances with the accent on sound, precision, and eye appeal.

# Music Problems
in the Marching Band

Gale L. Sperry/1961

I want to consider the marching band as a service organization, and make no serious attempt to identify the physical and musical values a band member may realize from his participation.

**Instrumentation**

It is hardly necessary to stress the point that it is the power instruments—percussion and directional brasses—that are heard most readily in an outdoor performance. One should not preclude the use of lighter instruments in the football marching band, however. Even though the strength of the band rests with the power instruments, a broader and more characteristic sound will result from the use of more reeds. A typical lineup of a 130-piece football marching band might show the following representation of instruments:

- 20 trombones
- 10 baritones
- 10 alto horns or mellophoniums
- 10 alto saxophones
- 10 percussionists (1 bass drum, 1 cymbal, 4 snare drums, 4 tenor drums)

10 sousaphones
10 tenor saxophones
20 clarinets
30 cornets and trumpets

Any players added to this instrumentation would be reeds, notably piccolos and clarinets. Addition of greater numbers of brasses would result in no appreciable increase in the body of sound, although a corresponding increase in the number of reeds would materially improve both the quality and body of sound.

Let us assume that we have three ninety-minute rehearsals and a brief Saturday morning run-through before a show. A good rule of thumb might be to plan to be able to play continuously through the entire show after forty-five minutes, or certainly no more than one hour, of rehearsal.

If the music is to be well-played with only an hour devoted exclusively to its preparation, we shall have to be realistic in our choice of music. In general, we need to perform less difficult music outdoors than we could manage satisfactorily on the concert stage. Furthermore, there can be no rehearsal time wasted in explanations as to the show's continuity; that is, from what piece of music do we play what part and in what order? No, all of this must be done before the director calls his first rehearsal. The observation may be made here that it is our duty as directors to avoid any waste of a band member's time. Thorough planning of every detail will enable a band to do a more difficult show with less rehearsal time.

A basic rehearsal plan might take this form:

Wednesday: The first 90-minute rehearsal would include a maximum of one hour's music rehearsal, culminating in a taped recording of the music. The final half hour would be spent "walking through" the formations and routines of the show with no music.

Thursday: Meeting directly on the field with instruments, for the first forty-five minutes the band would routinize itself on the show's movements, using the tape-recorded music over the public address system. The show would be put together for the first time with actual playing before this rehearsal ends.

Friday: Continual drill with attention to specific maneuver and music problems.

Saturday: One-hour run-through of the entire show to establish continuity and proper pacing in conjunction with the actual PA script.

**Selection and presentation of music**

Our responsibility to our profession and to the band itself as a medium of cultural expression demands that we play the finest music we can—consistent always with the limitations imposed upon us by the need to perform outdoors. A serious limitation may be the type of audience for whom we are performing. Little music education of an audience is possible if the only abiding interest is their enthusiasm for a sport—whether it be athletic or liquid. Even then, however, good judgment can be exercised in choosing fine music that is appropriate to the sports occasion and that will fit in with the spectators' enthusiasm for the game.

A show featuring precision drill will be enhanced by martial music in keeping with the maneuvers. A pageant that relies heavily upon the ability of the audience to recognize the "picture" you are forming will need to be aided by music whose title can be recognized immediately by the majority of the audience. Too heavy a reliance on spectators' musical sophistication will result in some mighty dead spots.

In general, special scoring of music will result in a more effective presentation. The entire musical continuity, however, should be written out completely—whether or not special arrangements or published versions are used. Hours of student rehearsal time may be avoided by complete planning of the musical continuity—including a final copy of each member's particular part, with all maneuver instructions written in.

If you score your own music, you can obviate many of the difficulties of a published version. A deficiency in your particular instrumentation or a need to write a certain melody at a very fast tempo cannot usually be dealt with in a published arrangement, although occasionally you may find a published version every bit as satisfactory as one of your own. In any case, you must write the publisher for permission before tampering with any arrangement. If you do intend to write for your own band, here are several specific suggestions:

(1) Trumpets and trombones may be used together as a four-part choir with good results. That is, first trumpets and first trombones may be assigned the melody with second trumpets on one harmony note and second trombones on another harmony note.

(2) Alto saxophones and horns make a good section for countermelody or additional divisi harmony. To this group may be added the tenor saxophones and baritones.

(3) In case the alto and tenor saxophones are used with the horns on a countermelody, it may be advisable to use the baritones in octaves, with the sousaphones on a typical bass line.

(4) Rhythm parts are generally the solo responsibility of the percussion section.

(5) Clarinets and piccolos may be used on the melody or on harmony or countermelody, although usually not alone but in conjunction with one of the sections listed.

These suggestions apply to a march-like number played at something faster than traditional march tempo. The band is assumed to be moving while playing. In cases where the band is motionless, performing no intricate movement, or marching at a slower cadence, the scoring may safely be written in a more complicated design and with many more divisions of parts.

There have been so many technical developments in recent years that one hestiates to recommend the best means of reproducing music, but one efficient and relatively economical means is by the Ozalid black and white process, in which the original part is written on a sturdy translucent paper and reproduced by chemical means.

# The Role of the Marching Band in the College Band Program

Paul R. Bryan/1962

The last few years have witnessed a crescendo of critical discussion concerning cultural awareness and training at all levels in our country. The band has come in for its share of scrutiny. The opening chapter of Richard Franko Goldman's book *The Wind Band* is an important and illuminating evaluation of the present situation. The critical view he implies, but does not state, is more clearly presented in the report of the Committee on College Bands to the College Music Society. In addition to these observations from outsiders, there can be no denying the questioning and unpleasant tenor of remarks among CBDNA members concerning marching band programs.

As marching techniques become more complicated and demanding, it is possible that we might lose sight of the proper lines of responsibility. Three points might be considered: (1) The role of the marching band in the college band program is secondary to the proper function of the band in the college music program. The latter, in turn, must implement the aims and needs of the institution of which it is a part. (2) The primary function of a band in an advanced educational institution ought to be its contribution to the musico-intellectual purpose. After all, there are no colleges training musicians to perform in professional bands. (3) The ultimate value is the contribution the band activity makes to the student, not what it (or the student) does to publicize or glamorize the institution. The truly fundamental issue is not the versatility, history, or perpetuation of the band medium, but its appropriate supporting role in higher education.

Divergent views are possible, or even probable, since each institution adopts its own set of principles and standards. However, I feel that leaders of college bands must aim for a position in the midstream of serious musical activity rather than on the periphery. A return to the philosophy that equated music with science or the humanities is not possible with the current dichotomy of music and athletics, which has arisen through overexploitation of the entertainment aspects of both. The versatility of the band medium, as well as its many nonmusical functions, makes change extremely difficult. But if the band is to approach the stature of other artistic media, it must be judged by artistic rather than entertainment standards. Our seriousness of purpose must be felt not only by the public but also by fellow musicians who neither participate in bands, understand their potentialities, or even are willing to listen sympathetically.

# The Future Marching Band

## Hubert Henderson/1962

It is difficult to be completely serious in discussing the marching band and I believe a majority of CBDNA members would agree that we are entirely serious about the subject only when rehearsing our own band. Our own band often inspires our most sedate mien, but we are each forced to smile a little when we think about the marching band in toto. When our band uses fire extinguishers it is no laughing matter, but when other bands use them we all agree they are somewhat ridiculous.

I understand that manufacturers of men's suspenders hold an annual convention. One of the solemn rituals at the closing session each year requires that all stand and drink a toast to the law of gravity. On the other hand, when space scientists get together their main topics of discussion involve means of circumventing the law of gravity. The college band director's ambivalent relationship to the marching band reflects both of these attitudes: we deplore its existence but we simply could not exist—in our present affluent state—without it.

The football show exists only because athletes get tired. The bandsmen blow so the players can catch their breath. What a curious situation in which to fashion a musical performance! No wonder we band directors are in a quandary—we are attempting to shine in a brief span of time that the star performers have relinquished, and for an audience that at best has only a secondary interest in our efforts.

There is a historical precedent for our predicament. The sixteenth century intermezzos, which were the forerunners of opera, originated to fill time between acts of stage plays. It is inconceivable that our halftime shows will develop into a separate, self-sustained form of entertainment, divorced from the sporting event that has given them birth, but it is entirely within the realm of speculation that either the band show or the game—or both—will undergo certain fundamental changes within the next decade.

Changes in the game that might affect us are obvious. The coaches may eventually breed players who can play sixty minutes without a break. Or the athletic powers may decide to utilize the halftime to give their freshman teams some experience before a live audience. These and other possibilities might occur and deprive us of our stage.

But more likely there will be changes in the shows themselves. Let us hope these will tend to minimize the more glaring inanities of current practices. I do not wish to belabor the present situation—we are all well aware of our shortcomings—and it is especially pointless to criticize college football when a former all-American sits on the Supreme Court and touch football games are played on the White House lawn. But some brief observations may be in order.

First, we enjoy captive audiences, but we are experiencing increasing difficulty captivating them because we are reaching the saturation point with almost all of our present techniques. Audiences have been exposed to countless numbers of bands, and the great majority of them are becoming alarmingly similar. We have become almost completely preoccupied with achieving uniformity and precision, and as we approach the archetype we become indistinguishable.

Second, we assume we are giving the public what it wants, but are we? To my knowledge no one has ever demanded that we feature baton beauties or platinum pompom'ers. No layman has ever asked for a fanfare, followed by a precision drill, leading to a working model of a perfume factory complete with the aroma of Chanel No. 5. I frankly believe the public does not know enough or care enough to realize what it expects from a band on the football field. Whatever notions the public entertains have been created by band directors who have slavishly followed the path of least resistance. Like successful politicians, we have become proficient in the art of the possible; perhaps, unlike politicians, we are beginning to have some doubts about the value of the possible.

If it is true that we need have no fear of audiences leaving the stadium, and if it is true that band directors are responsible for determining the public's level of acceptance, then we can safely venture into new and unexplored avenues for exploiting the best the band has to offer.

Band directors should consider the possibilities of writing original music for halftime shows, in the manner of Broadway musicals. Instead of borrowing published arrangements, or writing or buying original arrangements of familiar tunes—the choice of which more often than not is determined by the titles—directors or staff members will write original music related to a central idea. The music would incorporate all of the necessary variations of tempo, meter, rhythm, melody, harmony, and style in a well-placed presentation of theatrical elements, from a sparkling overture to a brilliant finale. Choreography, pageantry, and music could be welded into a show that would demand the best of not only the band but of allied organizations, including dramatic, dance, and choral groups.

With little more time than is now required to prepare and rehearse halftime shows, such a presentation is well within the capabilities of some schools today. We might well find acceptance of—even demand for—frequent repetition of a single show. Broadway musicals run six nights a week for years; why not a band show presented for five or six Saturdays throughout one season? Perhaps an original show, even one of modest dimensions, would thus save considerable time in overall preparation and rehearsal. It seems strange that with all of the time, energy, and money that has been spent on college halftime shows to date, not a single piece of original music has been written. Even burlesque shows have done better than that!

The recent furor over obtaining permission to arrange copyrighted materials for use on the football field is symptomatic of our predicament. Only in the radio and television fields is there a comparable fixation on the use of someone else's music, and both of these areas commonly are held in artistic disdain. Are we not equally liable for judgment as a wasteland by reason of our lack of ingenuity? How often do we hear a band director brag that he has never repeated a halftime show? Does he not mean actually that he has never placed in the same sequence ideas he has borrowed many times? And is it not likely true that such shows could not bear repetition?

We have often joked with athletic directors that the crowd really comes to the stadium to see and hear the band, not to see the game. If we repeated a single show throughout a season we might not prove this proposition, but we might prove the band's importance if people stayed away because they didn't want to see the same show. The athletic people might be completely convinced if crowds began to resent any interruption of the band and booed the return of the teams to the field for the second half. What poetic justice that would be! Imagine a coach's mortification if someday he had to request that the halftime production be reduced from thirty to twenty-nine and one-half minutes' duration because the fifteen seconds allotted to get his team from the dressing room to the kick-off position was simply not sufficient. *E pluribus tyrannus*, or may the worm squirm!

# The Marching Band in 1975: A Survey

Manley Whitcomb/1962

This CBDNA survey showed many inconsistencies in band directors' practices and beliefs. Ninety-eight percent of the CBDNA membership believes marching bands will survive to 1975. But 66 percent of the membership sees no need for the marching band's existence, although 64 percent of the young directors in the larger schools think there should be marching bands. "Young" directors were defined in the questionnaire as having less than five years of experience, and large schools were those with more than 4,000 enrollment.

Sixty-three percent of the membership believe there is a definite relationship between marching band activities and the purposes of the college in which they work. However, younger directors are doubtful of this relationship and directors who work in small schools are more doubtful than those who work in large schools. Thirty-eight percent believe there should be a definite relationship between marching band activities and the purposes of a college; only 10 percent believe there should not be any.

Seventy-nine percent are sure of their responsibilities to the administration and believe they should be sure of these responsibilities; however, only 50 percent are sure of their obligations and responsibilities to the academic aspects of the college and think they should be sure of such responsibilities. Seventy-six percent are sure of their responsibilities to the public; the older director in the larger college is the most certain of all.

Relationships with students are much more confused. Seventy percent are sure of the marching band director's responsibility to his students, although the director in the smaller college is inclined to be a little ambivalent. Directors do not seem to be worried about students continuing to play in marching bands; 71 percent believe student membership will increase. However, only 14 percent believe students should play in a marching band, which leads to the interesting inference that directors disapprove of students who choose to play in the marching band. Seventy-one percent do not believe students will be paid to play in the marching band, and 54 percent do not believe they should be. Only about 15 percent believe students should be paid to play in the marching band; the largest group to hold this belief is among older directors in larger schools and younger directors in smaller schools.

Forty percent of the respondents said they are able to control the extent, policies, and practices of the marching band activities. They are largely older directors; younger directors are more inclined to feel they cannot control these things.

Seventy-eight percent believe we are not doing the best we can with the marching band and that we should do better. Forty-two percent, mostly from larger schools, do not believe the marching band will be deemphasized, and only 34 percent of us believe that it should be. Fifty-eight percent believe the entire marching band program, including all possible aspects, cannot change appreciably, and 78 percent believe it should not.

The picture presented by the questionnaire is one of confusion and lack of direction, and shows a program almost entirely controlled by expediency.

# Marching Bands and Television Coverage: A Survey

George Cavender/1964

Our committee was supplied with a list of seventy-five college and university bands from all areas of the nation that had appeared on television during the past four years. The committee sent a comprehensive questionnaire to the conductors of these bands. A total of 82 percent of the conductors replied to our inquiry—a testimonial to their attitude and interest in the work of CBDNA.

The conductors first were asked if they felt a college band should appear in conjunction with professional football games, since these are usually televised. Seventy-five percent replied in the negative. A projection of this percentage over the entire CBDNA membership would indicate overwhelming objection, as a group, to our bands appearing on television in conjunction with professional football games. This finding might serve as a basis for future individual decisions and actions in this matter, and possibly as a guidepost should CBDNA feel some action should be taken as a group. As a committee it is not our prerogative to make any recommendations, but merely to present the feelings and thoughts of a large part of the membership about this controversial matter.

Members then were asked how they educationally defend the appearance of their bands on television at pro games. Ninety percent replied that they could not make such a defense. The remaining 10 percent defended the appearance largely on the terms that their particular appearance was in conjunction with a "charity" game. Some mentioned values of exposure and publicity for their college and university, particularly necessary and advantageous for small colleges.

The conductors then were asked if they felt the CBDNA should develop a credo relating to the appearance of college and university bands at professional games. Again, 75 percent felt there should be some action and a positive statement by the CBDNA. The remaining 25 percent also felt strongly on this point, arguing that the CBDNA was not a governing body and that television appearances were a matter for the individual school to decide.

The survey next asked whether the conductors felt it was ethical and proper for a band appearing on television to execute a formation with "commercial" implications. This question was directed at specific commercial formations such as the call letters of a network, and not the occasional show which is built around advertising jingles and ideas. Ninety percent replied that they felt such action was highly improper and had no place at the college level.

This question led to another portion of the questionnaire, which asked whether bands had received any financial remuneration for appearances at televised professional games. Amounts reported varied from nothing to transportation, meals and transportation, meals, housing, and transportation, and to sums as high as $8,000 for one performance. Several conductors reported they were offered as much as $600 if they would perform a particular work on a nationally televised game. Such an approach can be made by a composer with the idea that the credit units he would be awarded by ASCAP would more than repay the $600 expenditure. How widespread this bribery is, or might become, remains pure conjecture. But the practice does exist and the CBDNA should be alert and aware of its implications and our possible involvement.

The survey also asked whether television has had a detrimental or positive effect on the future of the college marching band. Eighty-five percent of the conductors indicated that they felt television has had a positive effect on the college marching band, largely because it provides national comparison for all bands in all areas of their performance—marching, playing, and show content and design. Such comparisons upgrade performances in general.

Conductors then were asked if any incidents had arisen either by playing or not playing for a televised game. Here an overwhelming 98 percent reported no unfavorable incidents. The few reported problems involved an occasional disgruntled alumnus writing in to inquire why the band hadn't played this or that song and so on. No major problems had occurred.

Directors were asked to estimate extra financial costs incurred because of televised appearances. Figures ran from very small amounts to $8,500. Seventy percent mentioned having to spend extra money for a televised appearance that they normally might not have spent. Conductors were asked if they felt the expenditures were worthwhile. Eighty percent replied that the extra expenditures were worthwhile from all standpoints. Conductors felt it benefited the college or university, the band, their students, and the entire program.

The survey asked if the CBDNA should ask for financial remuneration for bands appearing on NCAA games, if NCAA receives remuneration from the networks. Sixty-six percent of the conductors felt some remuneration should be requested under these conditions. The remaining 34 percent felt it was not a concern of the CBDNA, or felt such a request would curtail allotments made to their respective athletic departments by the NCAA, and in turn hurt their bands since they received help from the athletic department.

Conductors next were asked whether they were satisfied or dissatisfied with past television appearances in relation to coverage, response, problems, and extra pressure and time. Sixty percent felt coverage was poor and 40 percent felt it was good. Opinions were directly related to coverage an individual conductor's band received. Eighty-five percent felt that response to band television appearances had been very good by viewing audiences. Fifty-five percent were satisfied that television appearances presented no special problems and required little extra pressure and time; the other 45 percent were dissatisfied with the extra problems they entailed.

Since there has been dissatisfaction with the performances of certain announcers in covering band shows, we asked: "Do you feel the CBDNA should go on record asking the television networks to provide qualified commentators for halftime shows (as versus the collegiate "great" who is now an announcer and doesn't know a block band from a left oblique)?" The response was overwhelmingly in favor of this suggestion, with 92 percent of the conductors concurring. Names such as Glenn Cliff Bainum and Paul Yoder were suggested as possible announcers. The networks wouldn't think of broadcasting a baseball or football game without an authority to do the game and the color. Why should they present thirty to thirty-five minutes of television time devoted to band shows without a qualified commentator? The committee feels this is a possible oversight on the part of the networks and should at least be called to their attention.

The committee asked whether conductors would go on record in favor of "transparent" advertising (such as Gillette uses) over the band's performance. Sixty percent were emphatically against this suggestion, 30 percent were in favor of trying it, and 10 percent were undecided.

Conductors then were asked for their ideas on how to improve television coverage at college games. The following ideas were advanced:

(1) Television briefing and planning conferences between the conductor and producer should be held well in advance of a game. First meetings should be a month or two in advance.

(2) Commercials during halftime should be held to a bare minimum—possibly one per show.

(3) Qualified personnel should be employed to comment on and describe the band's activities on the field. The announcer could visit each band during the week's drill to get an idea of show outline, camera shots, color, and so on.

(4) Networks should pay greater attention to sound pick-up. They should have a microphone that is designed for maximum music pick-up, and not just for background or crowd noise.

(5) There must be an absolute minimum number of shots devoted to barelegged twirlers. Cheesecake footage is inevitable when

we place these young ladies right in front or in the center of the formations. Try using their talents in some other section of the field and formation.

(6) Adequate advance warning of television appearances must be given.

(7) Close-up shots of the band should be held to a minimum.

(8) No interviews or commercials should interrupt the performance of the band.

(9) Directors should provide the networks with complete information on their shows and what they are to present.

(10) The director of the program and cameraman might visit final rehearsals to obtain briefings on shots to be taken.

(11) All end-zone camera shots and all camera shots from blimps should be eliminated.

Directors were asked what type of show they found to be most effective for a television appearance. No one type of show proved to be the most popular. The major difference was that 90 percent of the conductors face their shows on camera when on national television, rather than playing directly to the stadium audience, as they do on a normal Saturday.

A television appearance with one's band is not the novelty it once was, and almost all conductors stated they held no extra rehearsals with their bands in special preparation for television appearances.

Conductors were asked what mechanics or techniques they had developed to obtain a better sound for their bands during television appearances. We list these for your consideration:

(1) Special instrument placement in formations.
(2) Smaller, more compact formations in the center of the field.
(3) Less extended formations, drills, and maneuvers.
(4) A tendency toward less motion.
(5) Playing directly on camera.

# Marching Bands in the View of Music School Deans, Department Heads, and Chairmen of Music Departments: A Survey

William Campbell/1964

Our subcommittee sent a letter to the administrators of 235 music departments or schools requesting a statement on their view of the marching band as it relates to their department, to music, and to music education in general. Eighty-two completed forms were returned to us. The return was slightly less than 35 percent.

Since this was not a questionnaire survey, but rather a written statement, evaluation was somewhat difficult. It did, perhaps, prove somewhat more revealing and varied than a standardized questionnaire.

Almost all the returns were congenial, worthwhile, and well-planned statements. There were two respondents, however, who could not understand why we had the audacity to inquire into their specific school situation and administration.

It would be impossible to cover all the thoughts that were expressed in the returns. We decided to present both positive and negative comments, in the order of importance to the administrators.

**Positive contributions**
(1) The marching band serves as a public relations agency in

influencing large groups of alumni and portions of the general public to support projects of the university and of the department.

(2) The marching band is considered a necessity in the training of music education students.

(3) Good performances by marching bands attract young musicians to institutions and thus serve as a recruiting means.

(4) The marching band is an important factor in creating school spirit and pride in an institution.

(5) The marching band appeals to university administrators and is the organization most closely identified with the music department in their minds. It therefore has beneficial effects on departmental budgets and goals that require administrative support. Good marching band performances can help every other activity of a music department.

(6) Marching bands provide a social outlet for students with some music training. It is an enjoyable use of leisure time and an important adjunct to the extracurricular life of the undergraduate.

(7) It provides light entertainment for occasions of the same nature.

(8) A good performance is a gratifying experience born of cooperative effort.

## Negative considerations

(1) The marching band lacks legitimacy as an academic activity.

(2) Playing outdoors while performing intricate maneuvers causes performances to be crude by musical standards. If improved musical performance and quality of music were stressed, it would be easier to accept the marching band as an educationally sound medium.

(3) The formation of the concert band is often delayed until one-third of the school year has passed. The large university is the exception to this fact, since it has more personnel and the better musicians may not be participating in the marching band.

(4) The amount of time spent by staff and students in marching band is disproportionate to the musical and educational results achieved.

(5) The money spent on marching bands could do much to promote an excellent academic music program. University administrators often look with favor upon marching bands (for public relations reasons) and therefore grant them large budgets, at the expense of the overall music program.

(6) Outdoor instrumental playing often damages individual performers' playing techniques.

(7) Lack of interest for marching band is shown by better student musicians.

# The Small College Marching Band

Glen Yarberry/1967

The most difficult problem facing the marching band has been the development of a sound educational rationale. I am not going to attempt to resolve the issue of entertainment versus education except to say that, like it or not, the small college is up against the standards and methods of schools twenty times its size. Television has brought the finest college band performances into nearly every home in the country. The longest professional football season has been lengthened and is followed, within just a few months, by an exhibition season. High school and college marching bands are pressed into service to entertain the millions who have gone pro-football-crazy. Television has managed to overexpose the western and the mystery program; could it be that an overexposure of professional football will spell its doom?

Many of my colleagues state proudly that the college band is the most unique of all music organizations. We have become part of one of the biggest businesses in this country today—intercollegiate and professional football. Our involvement cannot increase beyond what it is now.

Many of the students in small colleges involve themselves in a whirlwind of activity—marching, concert, pep, tour, and stage bands; orchestra; wind ensembles; opera workshops; and choir. Certainly performance is an integral part of one's musical development, but many students in the small school spread themselves too thin musically and academically.

Just how important is the marching band in the total education picture of today's college students? Achieving balance between students' academic program and their performance program is a much greater problem today than it was a decade ago. In my undergraduate days the marching band served the local institution and the members of the group; today we serve the nation.

Small-college marching bands have accepted the standards and procedures of large university organizations. Many small schools operate on minimal budgets with small staffs. Competition is keen for capable performers, and scholarship monies are scarce. One of my colleagues reports that in his school "the emphasis on academics seriously curtails 'extracurricular activities' such as the marching band, so that we struggle constantly for a share of the students' time; because of academic standards, we have problems in finding prospective student musicians who can meet minimum admission requirements. We have an enrollment fixed by arbitrary limit at 3,500. As a consequence, it is unlikely that our marching band will ever exceed 100 players. Finally, we are reaching an ever-increasing number of intelligent, sophisticated students to whom the marching band is anathema."

Nevertheless, many of the most artistic and precise performances on the college and professional gridirons today are being accomplished by these small colleges with lots of problems.

The small college has become involved either voluntarily or involuntarily in the greatest public spectacles of all time. We have organized chorus lines, pompom girls, twirling corps which twirl fire, flags, and fannies, a marching stage band, and concert bands with white stripes separating the sections. We have attempted to compete with the giants, fielding as large an organization as is humanly possible with small enrollments.

We have plundered our undergraduate students. We have given them little or no credit for an extremely time-consuming activity. We have alienated, in many instances, fine musicians with what some in our profession have called "a necessary evil." We have accepted the dictum that every school worth its salt must have a big marching band.

Some of my colleagues in the smaller schools believe we need to evaluate the past and carefully structure the future. We are looking to the leaders in the field of marching bands, those men whose groups set the national precedents by nationwide television appearances, for new directions. We are looking for that which is educationally defensible and sound. We are searching for musical acceptance by the knowledgeable music consumer. We are looking for mature, artistic, and entertaining fare for the football fan.

# Techniques

# PART 4

# Problems and Responsibilities of the Guest Conductor

William D. Revelli/1950

In high school, college, and professional music circles, the guest conductor serves as a kind of ambassador, reducing musical isolationism in all phases.

A guest conductor should be selected wisely. Some factors to consider:

(1) He should be an authority in his field, one who commands the respect and admiration of his colleagues. This means training, background, and experience.

(2) He should have an understanding of band problems. He should be an educator and builder as well as a superb musician.

(3) He should be a conductor who will complement and supplement the techniques and philosophy of the regular conductor, and thereby serve to balance the overall program.

(4) He must be personally sincere and natural. He will thus obtain the best results, rather than from any studied or affected techniques.

(5) He should know his music score thoroughly and establish ideals and standards for the final performance.

(6) He should evidence firmness and artistic integrity throughout his assignment.

(7) He should give credit for preparation and perfection. Some guest conductors claim all excellence for themselves, and assign blame publicly and without tact.

(8) He should leave behind a keen respect for performance both in rehearsal and concert by insisting upon an honest rendition of the printed page.

(9) He should make happy comparisons for purposes of encouragement and he should stimulate improvement.

(10) He should plan rehearsals, but be flexible enough to change as the pulse of the rehearsal necessitates. Essential and effective intermissions give an opportunity for rapid adaptation of the original plan. He should decide, after learning the state of preparation, alertness, and group personality, the appropriate mixture of drill, discussion, and inspiration.

(11) He should expect maximum results. He will not look for shortcomings found with other organizations, nor will he have a negative mind-set.

(12) He should remember that his words and actions will remain with his performers long after he has left.

Such is the guest conductor. Choose him wisely, prepare for him, assist him in action, and build upon the good effects of his visit.

We can expect many benefits from the visit of a guest conductor:

(1) A rejuvenated interest in performance by band members.

(2) An added respect for music and its performance because a performance was sufficiently worthy to warrant importing a guest for the concert.

(3) A sense of unity between neighboring localities, different sections of our states, or even different parts of the country.

(4) A general boost in performance quality, if the guest conductor demands such a standard of performance that expectations shift to a higher plateau.

In preparing an intercollegiate band for the guest conductor, many details should be worked out in advance by those in charge of arrangements:

(1) The choice of music should be agreeable to all concerned,

with a definite decision on the use of a specific edition. Music should hold interest, challenge, inspire, and demand the maximum musical ability of the band. The choice of a high type of music will help counteract the accusation that our organizations are fed a bad diet of musical junk.

(2) The balance of instrumentation should be decided upon in advance and proper distribution of parts agreed upon.

(3) The bandsmen should know their program thoroughly and be musically exact and accurate as to fundamental details. Too often, the guest conductor is handed an unprepared group. This is unfair and insulting. He should never be obligated to teach notes.

(4) The band should be trained to be sensitive and flexible so they will be able to follow the most subtle demands of interpretation.

(5) All matters of phrasing, breath marks, tempi, dynamics, intonation, fingerings, articulation, rhythm, cues, and so on, should be clarified in advance.

(6) Bands should be prepared in matters of courtesy, attentiveness, and general desirable etiquette. Have them feel friendly and comfortably acquainted with the conductor before they meet him.

(7) The routine physical setup should be arranged so no rehearsal time is lost and the conductor is able to concentrate his full attention on the artistic phases of the program.

(8) The physical comfort of the guest conductor should be attended to. His job is not an easy one, and his ease and relief should be guaranteed. Permit him the pleasure of some free time and protect him from too many demands and interruptions. See that his hotel reservations and transportation itinerary are the best, and don't overwork him or the band.

(9) The guest conductor should have data on the background and training of the band. Then his approach will be more sympathetic and constructive.

# Rehearsal Warmups and Intonation

Donald E. McGinnis/1969

Many band directors fight the forty-eight-minute-a-day rehearsal, trying to produce a musically superior product with no extra time. Using rehearsal time efficiently has become a craft in itself.

A beginning warmup should be helpful, instructive, and short. If you do not get to the music within a matter of a few minutes—a maximum of five—you have used too much rehearsal time and there is not enough left for the music. Often I bypass the opening scale—depending upon how warmed up the players, especially in the brass section, feel they should be. It should not be a problem for a reed player to wet his reed and start playing. It should not damage his lip endurance or control if he just suddenly puts on the reed, toots a note or two, and starts to play. He may, of course, not play as well as he would if he had a warmup. But college band directors have students with more mature embouchures, more mature players—players who can simply put the reed on (knowing where the position of that reed plays best on the mouthpiece by leaving it on from the previous day or the previous hour of practice) and be ready to go.

It is a different story with the brasses, and, to a certain degree, a different story with the flute. Flutists need the same kind of flexibility warmup as a brass player; on the other hand, the flute resembles the other woodwinds in that there is no impairment of the embouchure if one starts to play without a warmup—unless you are foolish enough to try to start with sustained, high-register tones at a pianissimo level, which makes flutists start pinching.

Double reed players have problems of endurance if they do not have their reed adjusted; they really find it helpful if you take time to let them get a little orientation at the beginning. The way you play the scale is tremendously important. I have been at many rehearsals where everybody simply plays a scale and starts to play. There should be a real intonation purpose in the scale. Every tone must be humored and in tune, with octaves and unisons perfectly in tune, as beat-less as possible, and adjusted for all other intervals.

Work constantly from this premise. Adjust the intervals so that you have a scale in which a second degree sounds like a second degree of a scale. In other words, your ear tells you if there is a chord underneath and somebody plays a melody above that scale, out of tune. If you have a discerning ear, you will realize that the player must play his notes in proper relationship to the chord that is already sounding in the accompaniment.

Many times I have heard bands play a slow Alberti bass figure in the clarinet section with a cornet singing a melody over this accompaniment. The clarinet in its middle chalumeau is usually sharp, and if the temperature is up it is abominably sharp. If the players have not been taught to listen and adjust those tones, it is unreasonably sharp. The cornetist starts on his open C, then plays his first valve, D, and then his open E, so he plays three notes that are going to be a little low in pitch when he starts out. If the clarinetists are playing sharp underneath, you say the cornetist plays flat, but the clarinets are the offenders!

Figure 2 shows a rough estimate of how the clarinet normally responds in its intonation pattern. Instrument manufacturers have a difficult time pleasing us because we ask for instruments that are everything to everyone, and this is impossible. If you send a clarinet down to Texas you are in one climate and temperature situation, and if you send it up to Minnesota you are in another—not only because of the temperature outside, but also because of the way in which the buildings are regulated for temperature, humidity, and so on. This causes an enormous difference in the response of the reed. For example, in a drier situation players probably should use a little more firmness in the tip of the reed, and in a situation that is humid, less firmness. Reed strength definitely affects intonation.

The low range of the clarinet, called the chalumeau register, normally sounds an arc such as you see in Figure 2. The E and F are a little flat at both ends of the chalumeau. The F-sharp to B-flat I label as throat tones because they are tones that are normally not overblown to produce another register. Throat tones often are referred to as bad in quality, but there is no reason why they should be. They have two real advantages: they are not expected to overblow to another tone, and thus can be tuned quite well on the clarinet, and they are what we call short-tube notes, more humorable by "lipping."

The farther away you get from the point at which you blow the reed, and the more fingers you have down, the less humorable becomes the note. If you tune to a note on the sharp side and then play a long-tube note that has a flat tendency, there is relatively nothing you can do about it—you are going to play flat.

So the best thing to do in the throat tones is to choose a mouthpiece that plays throat tones in tune with the entire register of the clarinet. If you have a clarinetist who is constantly sharp in his throat tones and must pull the instrument (as much as ¼ of an inch in some cases), then you are usually in serious trouble because he also has that gap inside when he pulls the instrument, and this causes notes in that immediate area to drop considerably in pitch. You then get a very irregular scale. When you ask the band to play a scale that crosses through the throat register, this player would spoil your intonation. You might have twelve clarinetists or eighteen, but just one bad apple in the barrel is going to ruin your intonation.

Your instruments should be checked out with proper reeds and with the mouthpiece that the players are going to use. Give a Stroboconn check at the beginning of the year and then continue to check from week to week. Keep your players aware of the level they have to maintain and how much their instrument can stand to be pulled, lest they have to insert tuning rings.

The gap caused inside the barrel by pulling an instrument is what causes the sag in pitch in the throat tones. Filling this gap by inserting rings that fit exactly allows the player to push the instrument in for a very cold situation, although the throat tones may be slightly sharp when the clarinet is not pulled at all.

A wood instrument such as the clarinet takes longer to warm up. Himie Voxman once told me he experimented with a number of clarinets and discovered that at normal room temperature of about seventy-two degrees it takes a clarinet twenty minutes to come completely up to temperature and remain stable. It takes the flute two seconds, probably, if you blow quite vigorously with a warm breath. So wood instrument warmups are important. Adjustments must be made throughout a rehearsal or concert.

You must constantly tune to your level. The B-natural and C-natural have a tendency to be sharp at the lower end of the clarion and then flat in the range of the E and F in the middle clarion. The upper clarion pitch (A, B, C) goes up again just as the chalumeau goes up on the A, B, and C. Those notes will tend to be quite sharp on some instruments, especially the alto clarinet (Figure 2).

The C-sharp is a special tone, for it is not played with the D-sharp key depressed to sustain it or to enliven the sound. This error is commonly made by some very good clarinetists. The next register after C uses venting, causing the harmonic structure to encourage the high register. The C-sharp is the tone you go to; it happens to be very close to the D-sharp key, causing the pitch to go abominably sharp if you use that key with it as a venting mechanism. However, by the time you get the distance away of the D-natural, venting enhances the quality of the tone and is often necessary with the tones in this particular range. The tones in that top register tend to be on the low side unless the player happens to be using a very brilliant sound and a mouthpiece that is conducive to playing sharp in the high register. Sharpness here often can be blamed on the mouthpiece but more often on the way the player has tightened his throat.

Hugh Henderson and I once discussed why the clarinetist goes flat when he plays loudly. I always have conjectured that in making the adjustment to the amount of sound wanted, the clarinetist must open up a great deal and take more reed with his lower lip. If he keeps the same amount of reed in his mouth when he crescendos, the tone is going to stop. He has to make an adjustment, so he takes more reed. Henderson conjectured that the excess flow of the air itself might tend to slow down the vibration of the reed with the intensity of the air. In this particular instance I am not sure that any positive research has been done. But you can hear that if you attack the tone softly and then loudly you can hear an enormous difference in the pitch of the two tones. If you observe the stroboscope you will see there is often as much as twenty to thirty one-hundredths of a semitone or "cents" difference. So the player must learn to make an adjustment in pitch levels.

Most high school and college players are hardly mature enough to blow the biggest sound they can possibly get in an instrument and still produce a fine tone and a good intonation pattern. For this reason I urge my players not to use a hard reed in band playing. An orchestra player often plays a heavier style in order to project through the heavy orchestral texture. But in a band it is difficult to get fifteen or sixteen clarinets to sound their best if they are blowing full force.

Many band directors insist that the clarinetists habitually play pianissimo. I have talked with some of my former students who play at the University of Michigan, and they have said that in order to accomplish what Dr. Revelli wants they adjust to a very soft reed and never play loudly. This is how he achieves that marvelous homogeneous sound in his section.

In all band instruments, the short-tube note/long-tube note situation exists. On many instruments in their second octave the long-tube notes, or the notes in which more fingers are down, result in a sharp tone. For example, in the saxophone the D-natural (middle D-natural) always will be sharp and the low D will be flat, producing what is called a stretched octave (Figure 3). In the oboe, it happens around the E-natural, sometimes E-flat, and sometimes F (Figure 4). In the bassoon, of course, when you overblow from the low G half-hole and get the G an octave above you are in the same situation—

too sharp (Figure 5). With the flute the worst tone is its open tone; the C-sharp is atrociously sharp (Figure 1). The D-natural is also a sharp tone. In order to keep the lowest tone from sounding too flat, you play the upper octave on the low side.

Short-tube notes can be considerably adjusted either up or down, for they use a very small amount of the tube. Another factor against you: not only are the notes of the shorter part of the tube generally on the sharp side, but they are also closest to your breath, and your breath temperature is 98.6 degrees. If the room temperature is at seventy degrees, one part of the instrument will be warmer than the other part; a saxophone, having a lot of tubing and being normally a little flat at the lower end of the instrument, has problems getting up to pitch. When it comes up to the higher tones there is no problem.

For every ten-degree rise in temperature, the instruments differ. If you are in a room that is around seventy degrees when the band starts playing or warming up, and it goes up to eighty degrees (do not be surprised if you check the temperature on your stage and find it goes even higher), the clarinetists go up four to five cents. They change less than some other instruments because they are made of wood and the density of the material is greater.

The cornets go up six cents, which means the cornets and the clarinetists would still be playing quite well together after a rise of ten degrees. But the sousaphones have gained three times that amount in the rise in pitch level. So it is often helpful to find a tuning level to your bass note. Jack Evans always tunes his band to the tuba. Of course this means you have to be well trained in listening to the octaves that would result in this method and get those octaves flattened off—not stretched.

If your group has been well trained, they will adjust all tones in playing a scale. For example, if the clarinetist plays a C-major scale, each time he plays the E-natural he sounds a note that is flatter than the notes that precede it. All clarinetists generally are sharp on A, B, and C, and flat on E and F. The good player will anticipate these problems.

A director should anticipate pitch problems before he begins the rehearsal. For example, in Nelhybel's *Symphonic Movement*, an

# REHEARSAL WARMUPS AND INTONATION

Figure 1 Flute

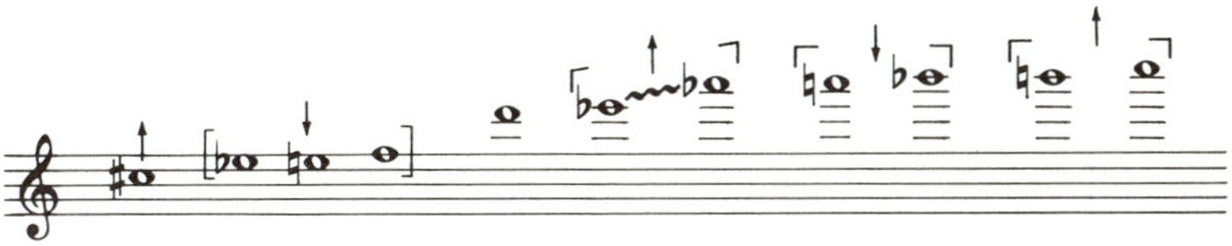

Figure 2 Clarinet

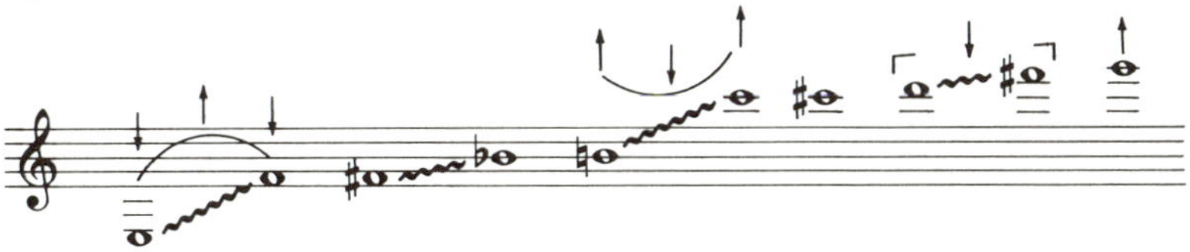

Figure 3 Saxophone

Figure 4 Oboe — FORKED

Figure 5 Bassoon

*ADD* AS NOTED TO *RAISE* PITCH

Figure 6 Flute

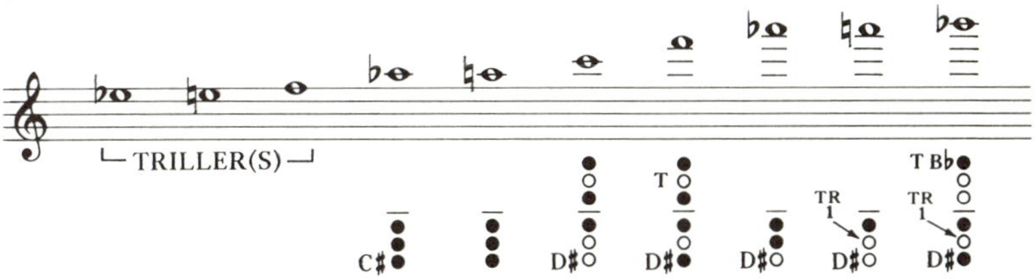

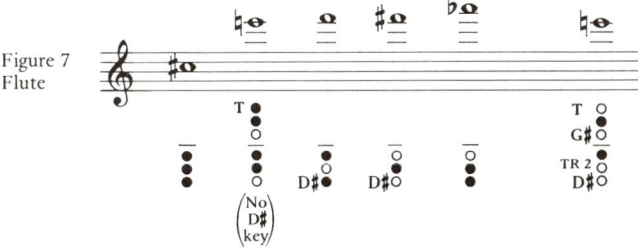

*ADD* AS NOTED TO *LOWER* PITCH

Figure 7 Flute

opening passage calls for an enormous sforzando chord out of which the second flutes hang onto a high C. The composer does not often take into consideration the fact that second flutes are not always the best players. It is difficult for the flutes to hold that pitch, and even at the magnificent performance given by Nelhybel and the Clarence High School band at the Midwest conference last year, my ear told me I wanted that C-natural to be a little higher. Probably the flutes were at pitch center, but when you strike a chord sforzando, the pitch is always going to fly a bit sharp, and an attack on the flute tends to be sharper than a sustained note of the same pitch. In rehearsing this piece, I ask my second flutists, instead of playing the sforzando, to start pianissimo at the level they were going to be at, or piano, for their sustained note. They are marked fortissimo decrescendo—just like all the instruments that play sforzando. Why ask them to start fortissimo and then struggle to maintain their pitch? If they start at pianissimo or piano they have the pitch under control before they have to sustain.

Even though the C-natural is a tone that would not normally be flat, listen to 90 percent of the bands that play the *Symphonic Movement* and you will hear the flutes sounding flat on that particular tone. By knowing the sharp fingering for that particular tone, and a very humorable fingering, you can help your flutes play that tone right on pitch. For example, if they play the high C as an overtone out of F and take off the thumb, it is immediately a sharp tone (see Figure 6).

How does one learn these things? James Pellerite has an excellent book on the basic flute fingerings and all of the alterations. If your flutes sound too flat on a certain note, you might consult this book and discover that the note can be played with a different fingering. Three other books which can help are Ralph Pottle's *Tuning the School Band and Orchestra*, Donald Stauffer's *Intonation Deficiencies in Wind Instrument Performance*, and Siennicki-McGinnis' *Etudes for the Advanced Clarinetist*.

By the way, I put another handicap on the players by insisting that the C be played without vibrato. Out of the brilliant sound and color of that opening chord I wanted a lifeless tone. I would guess that Nelhybel did, too. If you listen to the orchestras of his native country you will discover they play with less vibrato than our American orchestras. His ear has undoubtedly been tuned to hear the straighter tone. On the other hand, I heard the Czech Philharmonic this fall and I have never heard so much clarinet vibrato in all my life. It was a thin, facile tone, matched by the flutes. Things are changing over there just as they change here.

If a flutist wants to sustain that high tone, he can take a fingering that is sharp so that he can lip down. Every note you struggle up on is murder, so I often indicate on the flute parts to push in for a certain situation, pull out for another. Within the course of a composition they tune at the beginning, pull out for a certain situation and push in for another. When they play a march that is usually loud and high, they would pull out. Figure 7 shows flute fingering adjustments.

Another pitch problem occurs at the end of the slow section in John Barnes Chance's *Variations on a Korean Folk Song*. The sustained A-flat keeps going down in pitch, with the clarinets going up. Soon we have such a short octave that it sounds miserable. I have the flutists in this particular case add the fingering for the right hand low register C-sharp to the already existing A-flat fingering, which raises the pitch and makes control of the tone easier.

There are many situations where the flutist has to end on an E-flat or an E-natural of the right hand at the top of the staff. This is a difficult thing to do. Add a trill fingering, either the second or the first triller (it does not hurt if you experiment a bit). It should stabilize pitch, tone quality, and control. The E-natural, were you to attack it with the second triller on, is far too sharp. But sustained, that E can go hopelessly flat. The best way to stabilize it is to add the first triller. If you checked it on the stroboscope it would not raise the pitch. However, the second triller brings it into focus.

The problem of sharping is always existent when we get to the high register of the flute, oboe, clarinet, bassoon, or saxophone. For example, the saxophone has a poor middle register. The open C-sharp on the saxophone is almost always flat. Then right next to it you have an extremely sharp D and D-sharp, and sometimes E, depending on the structure of the instrument. The high register of the saxophone normally goes up in sharpness.

The high register of the clarinet does not go sharp from the D up through the F-sharp, except in the hands of people who pinch a lot (Figure 2). If you get above that you are playing very sharp tones. For instance, the high G always becomes sharp and if you ever have to play G#, A, B♭, B, and C, those notes become quite sharp.

Oboes are always sharp on their A, B, and C (Figure 4). Other troublesome notes on the oboe are especially the E-flat and E-natural in the upper-middle range. The flatness in the low register is a problem. For example, at the end of the first section of the Persichetti *Psalm*, the clarinets come in on a unison with a low register oboe tone. After ruining about three tapes trying to record this particular measure, I asked the oboist to leave out his note. It was marvelous—we no longer had the flat oboe and the sharp clarinet, and we were in business. I asked Persichetti what he thought, and he said, "I probably should not have written the note for the oboe. I was thinking musically instead of thinking in a certain instance where that particular instrument could no longer make the adjustment to the tone."

In the beginning of the *Variations on a Korean Folksong* the oboist enters on an E-flat. The flutes have just finished this particular passage and they end on E-flat. The oboist has to attack pianissimo when he enters on the unison with them. Every time you come to it the flutes are shading off, which means they are going flatter and flatter, while the oboe is sharp.

Bassoonists have a sharpness problem in the low register, especially with the low D and F. The C-sharp, D, E, and sometimes the F, are flat tones.

It is a very important aspect of flute legato to keep the breath flowing through a smaller aperture of the mouth, and keep a line of sound between notes so as not to hear a lot of finger popping and emphasizing of certain notes. This lets the subordinate notes remain completely unemphasized and insignificant. If the flute is asked to play softly with the clarinet, he has a problem. The clarinet starts out on F. The flutist must warm the instrument before playing the unison with the clarinet and must be conscious of holding up during every one of those passages. It is difficult for the flutist to keep the line flowing, although the clarinetist does it so easily.

I had the pleasure of playing in an orchestra when Stravinsky conducted the *Symphony of Psalms*, and his colleague Robert Kraft did the *Symphony in Three Movements*. Listen to Stravinsky's recordings and note the style. It is an extremely short style—some of it seems much too short, much too pungent, and it dries out the sound to a degree where you do not get the quality you would like to have. In the rehearsals of the *Symphony in Three Movements* Kraft would say, "Orchestra! Staccatissimo!" "Beep!" "Bup!" and so on. If you work with that sound in mind, you will begin to get some of the pungent clarity characteristic of modern music. It gets away from legato slush.

For a number of years I had difficulty teaching, playing, and working on dotted rhythms, until I studied the flute and practiced the *Taffanel-Gaubert Method for Flute* (published by Leduc). Phillipe Gaubert says the dotted rhythm, if played in a clear manner in music other than of a legato nature, should be played from the sixteenth note rather than from the dotted note. It should be played with pungency, almost a roughness of sound in the dotted note. Use one syllable in the little note and then a different syllable in the dotted eighth. He uses the term te re—in French pronounced "tuh-ruh." I have had any number of students try to say ta-Ta, ta-Ta in dotted rhythm as fast as they can. Instead, dull it and say, tuh-Tuh, tuh-Tuh. Now make the second note a "D" sound: tuh-Duh, tuh-Duh. Flip the end of the tongue. Now you can get some speed with it. It applies just as well to brasses if they are not trying to play too heavily.

In rehearsing a syncopated $\frac{12}{8}$ passage, the problem is to keep the first of the two slurred notes from being shortened. Restructure it into two bars of $\frac{3}{4}$ instead of one bar of $\frac{12}{8}$ and practice it that way. This takes a lot of flexibility and you have to be playing a lot to do it. But that type of routine, rehearsed in detail before you put the section into the written pulse context, is extremely helpful.

Finally, I have listed the rehearsal phrases I use with my band. I'm not sure why someone else should want to use them but you are welcome to them.

## Rehearsal phrases
(1) Prepare the attack—attack clearly.
(2) Listen for the releases—ensemble.
(3) Tune to the bass note of the chord.
(4) Clarinets keep pitch down, so flutes will not sound flat.
(5) Clarity, pungency, accent.
(6) Follow the beat; do exactly what the baton says.
(7) Dynamic inflection
(8) You must believe that you can play still softer.
(9) Melodic flow—fluidity in technic
(10) "Hit" the note versus "lift" the note.
(11) Press-release: almost a tenuto style
(12) Space
(13) Play the little notes:  "Hook" the sixteenth note:
    *Allegro*
(14) Group the notes in rhythmic motion (group the sixteenth note with the next notes).
(15) Always have a lead pencil at rehearsals for dynamics, wrong notes, slurring and grouping.
(16) Sing!
(17) Find the melody in every measure: find the peak of the phrase.
(18) Subordinate your part to the melody. If you cannot hear it, you are too loud.
(19) The composer cannot possibly indicate all nuances and subtleties; they must be added.
(20) How short is short? How long is long? How loud is loud? How fast is fast?
(21) Play lighter in virtuoso passages. Keep the air stream working for you.
(22) You must begin and end absolutely together—and ideally play everything between.
(23) Longer notes for forte volume, shorter notes for piano (and vice versa)
(24) For control in pianissimo, close the oral cavity and support firmly (mild hiss).
(25) When music is rapid, don't try to tongue too short.
(26) Don't stop the tones with the tongue when you want legato or melodic shaping.
(27) In fact, when should the tones be stopped that abruptly?

(28) Wait for rapid notes (or grace notes); then play them quickly and succinctly.
(29) Use the same sound on every note:
(30) Use different sounds on each note:
(31) Use the same volume on each note.
(32) Tempo rubato—bend the phrase.
(33) Play on top of the sound (or tempo).
(34) Do not change either pitch or tone quality for forte-piano, crescendo, or dimuendo.
(35) Center the tone and the intonation.
(36) Intonation is often a matter of sheer pride and determination.
(37) Play exactly (not approximately!) what the composer wrote: notes, slurs, dynamics, rhythm.
(38) Don't run away from the first note. Set it with accent and/or tenuto. Your tempo deviations are usually in consecutive notes of the same value.

**Ways to practice a difficult passage:**
(1) Slow-fast
(2) Diverse articulations
(3) Diverse rhythms
(4) Group threes in four, group fours in three, and so on
(5) Diverse groupings; especially uneven ones such as five or seven
(6) Diverse accents or tenuti
(7) Combinations of any of the above
(8) Re-bar the passage:

(9) Delete the rest(s) and practice from the note
(10) Divide the difficulty:

# Intonation for the Band Conductor

Mark Hindsley/1971

The title of this article has certain implications. First, I shall be writing not only for but also as a band conductor, not as a performer, studio teacher, retailer, manufacturer, or scientist; I may not agree at all times with other groups; I may not even be in agreement with other band conductors. Second, I shall be writing on band intonation, whose elements may or may not all be in common with those of other instrumental, or choral, ensembles.

It is my intention to develop my subject from three primary standpoints:

Part I—What is good (or desirable) intonation, and what we may aspire to in securing that intonation for the band.

Part II—Selecting instruments, and modifying them when necessary and advisable, to make good intonation not only possible to achieve, but to insure that its achievement is as natural and easy as possible.

Part III—Tuning procedures and "intonation education."

The pitches of the tones in our modern scale of twelve tones in

Editor's note: Reprinted from *The Instrumentalist* (September 1971, pp. 66-69; October 1971, pp. 66, 68-69; November 1971, pp. 61-64; January 1972, pp. 59-62); © The Instrumentalist Co. (1971, 1972). Used by permission of The Instrumentalist Co.

one octave, or the way the scales are "tempered," furnish the main if not the full criteria for what we call intonation. The pitch of a tone is determined usually by the number of vibrations in a period of time—like the second. I say "usually" because under certain conditions there may be a change of pitch and vibration frequency between the source of the sound and the person who hears it.

There are scales of three different and well-established temperaments with which we should be concerned:

The just scale is based on nature's harmonic pattern of the open tube or the stretched string. With the fundamental as the first tone of the pattern or series, the second tone is an octave higher, produced by vibrations twice as fast, or with a ratio of 2 : 1, the simplest ratio. The third tone adds a perfect fifth, with a ratio of 3 : 2. As we proceed upward the intervals and ratios become consecutively smaller until the half step in the diatonic scale has a ratio of 16 : 15.

From the just scale and its primary ratios are derived the so-called consonant intervals of the perfect fifth and fourth, and the major and minor third and sixth. However, within this scale some of these intervals do not have the primary ratios cited, therefore the scale cannot be completely depended upon for consistent consonance. To be more specific, within the diatonic form of the just major scale (two whole steps and a half step, three whole steps and a half step), the perfect and consonant fifths are C-G, E-B, F-C, G-D, and A-E, but D-A is an imperfect, contracted, and non-consonant fifth. It so happens that all the major thirds in this scale (C-E, F-A, and G-B) are equal and consonant. The minor thirds E-G, A-C, and B-D are equal and consonant, but D-F is contracted and non-consonant. (The inverted fifths and thirds become fourths and sixths and have the same consonant or non-consonant properties.)

Although the two minor seconds, E-F and B-C, and their inverted major sevenths are equal, the major seconds and minor sevenths come in two sizes: C-D, F-G, and A-B are larger than D-E and G-A, with the reverse situation in the inverted sevenths. A study of the chromatic and enharmonic tones would show more inequalities and inconsistencies. The just tempered scale, then, may be considered as most valuable though somewhat unreliable harmonically, and as quite erratic melodically.

The Pythagorean scale is a "synthetic" scale, featuring perfect and consonant fifths and fourths throughout, diatonically and chromatically. None of the major or minor thirds or sixths are consonant from the ideal, simple ratio standpoint, but they, along with the major and minor seconds and sevenths, are all equal to each other. The equalities of the diatonic intervals, in contrast to those of the just scale, foretell the evenness of the Pythagorean temperament melodically. All the tones may move adjacently either way up or down, with equal "gravitation."

Another feature of the Pythagorean scale is its placement of the chromatic tones; the sharper tones are placed "off-center" toward the next higher tones on the way up, and the flatted tones are placed equally off-center toward the next lower tones on the way down. (This contrasts greatly with the just scale, where the "sharps" are all flatter than the "flats" and the "flats" are all sharper than the "sharps"). The Pythagorean chromatics are thus all "gravitational" in their natural directions. And even the natural half-step diatonic intervals E-F and B-C are closer than in the other scales, making the E and B quite proper "leading tones" to F and C.

The Pythagorean scale, then, may be considered as valuable, consistent, and reliable melodically, but not one on which we can rely or can approve harmonically.

The equal-tempered scale is also a "synthetic" scale, dividing an octave into twelve equal half-step intervals and eliminating unequal enharmonic (C♯ has the same pitch as D♭, D♯ the same as E♭, etc.). This scale long ago became a technical necessity for keyboard and mallet instruments, to make multi-key, modulatory, and innovative harmonic performance possible and practical. This scale makes it possible to play equally in tune or out of tune in all keys. In other words, it is very frankly a compromise temperament, both melodically and harmonically.

From the description I have given of these three differently tempered scales, a broad statement may be made that the Pythagorean scale should be used melodically, and the consonant, simple ratio portion of the just scale should be used harmonically. Actually it is theoretically possible for singers and for string and trombone players to do just that. As we have noted, however, this combination is impossible for keyboard and mallet players; it is also a practical impossibility for players of wind instruments other than the trombone, for it would involve humoring the pitch of each tone in the diatonic major and minor scales over a range of 33 1/3 "cents" (one-third of a half step or semitone), and in the chromatic scales over a range of 74.3 cents (almost three-fourths of a half step). These extreme variations ordinarily cannot be made in many wind instruments without considerable loss of tone quality and/or control.

It is my conclusion that we should try to have our bands play in the combination of the just and Pythagorean temperaments. Theoretically and for practicality, wind instruments should be tuned to equal temperament in manufacture and adjustment; in their playing we should go as far as possible toward the tone pitches of the other temperaments. We should prefer the Pythagorean scale for melodic lines, but at the very worst may have to accept the equal scale. We should prefer the consonant, simple ratio relationships of the just scale harmonically, but at the very worst we may have to accept the harmonic relationships again of the equal scale.

I say we should prefer the combination of the just and Pythagorean, but I have found that a majority of band conductors and graduate college band students actually prefer the equal temperament, more so melodically than harmonically. This reveals our dominant "ear-conditioning" by the piano and mallet and wind instruments. Not only have these instruments affected our hearing within the short range of an octave scale and a few close chords, but they have affected our hearing in the long range from octave to octave within the normal six or seven octaves in which we "operate." And for many players it may be apparent that the scales they play (and evidently prefer) do not fall within any of the three temperaments or combinations of temperaments which I have described.

I had been aware for some time that pianos are not tuned "straight up and down" in octaves, that the top tones on the piano are relatively much sharper than the middle tones, and the lower tones much flatter. I accepted as fact what I had heard along our musical grapevines, that the human ear expects sharpness in the high register and flatness in the low register. I learned, however, or was or became aware, that the organ was not tuned in any such manner, rather that it was indeed tuned straight up and down. When we purchased a transistorized electric organ in which every tone could be tuned separately—rather than in perfect octaves—I decided to try an experiment. After having our piano freshly tuned, I tuned the organ precisely to the piano. Although the piano sounded fine to me, take my word for it that the intonation of the organ was about as atrocious as you can ever expect to hear.

It was then that I telephoned our university piano tuner and technician and asked him the perfectly simple(!) question, "How do you tune a piano?" He replied, "Which piano?" He continued that no two pianos were necessarily alike, although certain makes and models had tendencies which could be anticipated. (How like our wind instruments after all, I thought.) He went on to say that it was his practice to "set the temperament in an octave near the middle of the piano. Using a stroboscope (the portable "Strobotuner"), he then worked upward and downward in octaves, not necessarily to an exact octave, but to the first overtone of the lower octave, which more often than not is not the same. (The "bands" of the stroboscope make it possible to identify at least part of the overtone series.) Tuning to the first overtone makes for reinforcement of sonority and resonance, reducing conflicts among frequencies of the fundamental and the harmonics above. It also points out the curious and perhaps lamentable fact that (intentionally or unintentionally) the piano as now built (and very likely as it always has been built) produces imperfect harmonics, by nature's standard, in the upper and lower registers. Whether pianos could be built to produce perfect harmonic series I do not know, but I suspect that if such pianos were to be built, few of today's pianists would accept them. I am trying to make the point that to a great extent, in wind instruments as in pianos, we may become "slaves" to the instruments we play, both in what we accept as being in tune, and in how much we can do, or are willing to do to change their intonation for the better.

I had been aware also that of the string instruments, the violins, violas, and cellos tuned in perfect fifths, and that perfect fifths were two cents sharper than fifths in equal temperament, thus causing a "stretch" of six cents from the lowest string to the highest, or vice versa, or almost four cents an octave. For some time I considered this a valid reason for wind instruments becoming sharper as they play higher, and flatter as they play lower. I did not take into account that the string bass tunes in fourths rather than fifths, with exactly the opposite results from the other strings, a contraction of six cents from high to low string. How all the strings got along in their overlapping registers did not bother me. Nor did I take into account that in the overlapping registers of wind instruments what was the low register in one could also be the upper register of another, thus making unisons quite impossible, if a policy of "stretching" were followed along with customary tuning procedures. Customary tuning procedures indeed! It finally occurred to me, or dawned on me, that the cellos and string basses did not stretch the octaves when tuning their A's one and three octaves below the common A of the violins and violas. And when the strings use harmonic tones in their performances I do not think their instruments are so imperfect that those harmonics are stretched as they are in the piano. So I concluded that if strings play sharper as they go higher, it is because they want to, rather than because of any characteristic or deficiency of their instruments and voices—and they are out of tune whether they know it or not.

By recording the pure tones of oscillators I have found that most band conductors and graduate band students can tolerate out-of-tuneness in open octaves to the extent of two cents, but beginning at three cents the sound is objectionable. (Incidentally, in unisons, the tolerance was found to be one cent with two cents objectionable.) These tolerances are considerably lower than the four and six cents I have read elsewhere as being tolerable, even acceptable. If only band conductors were able to demand and secure these close one and two cent tolerances with the instruments of the band!

I have heard about great orchestra conductors who reportedly have had to ask their groups not to play so well in tune, because it made the music so gray, so lifeless. I believe I have heard much music played perfectly in tune, but never have I had the experience of hearing music so well in tune that I could complain about it. There are other ways of making music colorful and alive than playing it out of tune.

Some of our colleagues belittle the use of electronic devices to measure and teach intonation, who would possibly decry all this folderol about temperaments and scales and cents, and who would say so smugly, "all that matters is the ear." To be sure, the ear is the final authority, but I have learned not to fully trust anyone's ear, least of all my own. To be sure, the ear can and must be trained, and one of the good (maybe one of the best) ways is through the eyes looking at a stroboscope while the ear is listening—with proper interpretation and in the light of an understanding of what intonation is all about.

The stroboscope has been invaluable to us in the work we have done in connection with the second of the three objectives stated earlier: selecting and modifying instruments to make good intonation possible and relatively easy to achieve. We have taken for granted that wind instruments should respond naturally and accurately to the readings of the equal-tempered stroboscope, and that there is a certain point of focus of each tone which is the proper point of departure from which to go up or down to meet the requirements of the other temperaments and other performance exigencies. (I have also taken for granted that everyone is acquainted with the stroboscope, and no doubt its universal and exclusive trade name in our field, the "Stroboconn.")

Now it is time for me to start an "inventory" of what we have done at the University of Illinois in the matter of selection and modification of instruments.

**Flutes, piccolos, oboes, and English horns**

We did not have to select or purchase any flutes or oboes, for the students' own first-line instruments proved entirely capable of being played in tune when kept in proper adjustment. I will have more to say about tuning procedures and tone production later. We have had one beautiful and beautifully in-tune C piccolo for concert band use for close to fifty years. We did purchase a group of C piccolos for marching band and supplementary concert use when the changeover from D to C instruments was being completed in published music. We could not afford, or did not wish to invest in a large group of first-line instruments, so all we could do was choose the least sharp and the most even scale of the second-line piccolos. We had occasion to purchase English horns, and were successful in securing very fine and very satisfactory instruments.

**Bassoons**

We objected to three main faults of the bassoon: the frequent unevenness of the scale, the sharpness in the register below the bass staff, and the sharpness at the change of register with the "whisper" key, particularly the G fourth space. We had the good fortune of being able to work with Hugo Fox at South Whitley, Indiana, when he was in the early stages of making the instruments that bear his name. With a few trips to his then small factory, at first taking along our own Stroboconn at his request, Mr. Fox tuned an instrument which became a model for the set we purchased and for his entire production, and which removed quite successfully the first two objections: the unevenness of scale and the sharp low register. The sharpness of the middle G could not easily be corrected because with the same fingering, except for the whisper key, the lower G was in tune, and the instrument simply overblew sharp in the octave above. My amateur solution to this problem was to add a key mechanism which would reduce the clearance of the pad over the low F hole sufficiently to bring the middle G in tune, merely by straightening the normally curved third finger of the right hand. I installed this key on the set of instruments we purchased, and had every reason to believe it was a practical and successful improvement and solution. However, my amateur mechanical work was not impeccable, some of it fell apart, and I was guilty of neglecting to follow through on this modification in a professional manner. Then, in our affluent society more and more of our players were bringing in their own Foxes and Heckels which they wished to play, so we have lived with the sharp G, always exhorting the players to use another key already on the instrument, and another finger, to maybe bring the pitch down.

## Contrabassoons

We had no occasion to replace the one instrument in our inventory, and with proper attention to adjustment it has been adequate.

## Saxophones

We found that most saxophones were quite sharp above the treble staff when played with the rather firm embouchure needed for a suitable concert-type, ensemble tone. We were successful in being able to find and purchase a set of instruments without that fault. Then, by adding strips or layers of cork to the upper curves of the tone holes that produced sharpness in both the first and second octaves, we minimized our problems still further. The octaves D-D and A-A were still often quite troublesome, with the lower tones flat and the upper sharp, and we tried to compensate with auxiliary fingers. More recently we found alto saxophones that are quite satisfactory without much adjustment or use of auxiliary fingerings, but the tenors and baritones are still somewhat inconsistent and unreliable.

I am greatly disappointed that we have not been able to completely solve at least the major intonation problems of the saxophone, and that I have had few ideas to help. My impression is that this instrument has been victimized by jazz players, whose loose embouchures and wide vibratos paradoxically make good intonation more nearly possible and cover up many imperfections.

## B♭ soprano clarinets

I have saved the clarinets until the last of the woodwind family because of their particularly unique and complicated problems. Soon after acquiring a Stroboconn, I began testing the instruments and players of the concert band. Incidentally, we had been using A=442 as our tuning pitch prior to this time. When I found that several fine clarinet players had difficulty reaching even A=440, we changed to A=440 as a tuning standard and held it there from then on. But the tests I made revealed other unexpected inconsistencies among instruments and players, inconsistencies so great we felt something drastic had to be done. We were fortunate to be granted a series of appropriations that made it possible to purchase instruments to equip most of the sections of the concert band, including the clarinets (and excluding the flutes and oboes, which we felt it unnecessary to purchase because of reasons previously given). The great adventure of selecting and modifying and using these instruments (the clarinets) was on.

What we looked for in clarinets basically was an instrument which was in tune, or could be made to be in tune, in the low or chalumeau register (low E to first space F), and which overblew exactly an equal-tempered twelfth in the upper or clarion register (B third line to C above the staff). Neither of these characteristics was easy to find; most clarinets were either sharp in the middle of the clarion register; most were also sharp, quite sharp, at the top of the clarion register for almost all our players. We were glad to settle for an instrument that was still somewhat sharp in the middle of the chalumeau register, but really well in tune from approximately D fourth line to A above the staff, a part of the clarion register which is not affected by the size of the register hole or the clearance of its pad. We could take care of the fifteen cents average sharpness at the top of the clarion register by reducing the size of the register hole with thin aluminum tube inserts of different lengths, although this would ruin (flatten) the thumb B♭ in the throat register (third line); when these inserts caused flatness in the lower tones of the clarion register, we could make a correction by boring a small hole in the bell (usually less than a quarter-inch in diameter), at the approximate point of the next imaginary tone hole (about 1⅜ inches from the top of the bell), although this would also sharpen the bottom of the chalumeau register, except B♭, by taping up the individual holes and/or adjusting the pad clearances. To restore the thumb B♭, we installed the S-K (Stubbins-Kasper) mechanism with its supplementary B♭ tone hole. The middle of the chalumeau register had to be lipped down or brought down by the low F key or by pulling the middle joint in isolated passages using the errant tones. For the high or altissimo register (above high C), created by the troublesome fifth harmonic which we shall discuss more fully in the brass instruments, we could only pray and try out some new fingerings.

Twenty or more years ago it was difficult to find a clarinet that met the two basic requirements: a good chalumeau register and a good middle clarion register. We found it not quite as difficult when we changed some of our instruments about five years later, and others just a few years ago. I would hope it is not difficult at all today, but I still have doubts.

Without question the clarinet is our most inflexible instrument from the standpoint of intonation, without undue sacrifice of tone quality. One of the reasons is that the best tone quality is found near the top of the possible pitch variation; it is difficult to play much sharper than this optimum point, and playing much lower soon destroys quality. It might be that the fact the clarinet is the only one of our wind instruments that acts as a closed tube (overblowing only to the odd-numbered harmonics) is a factor in this inflexibility. Since players differ from each other in intonation even when using the same equipment throughout and producing equally good tone quality, we must find some mechanical flexibility to compensate for these differences. Even individual players change from time to time and need to make adjustments in their instruments. The mouthpiece, the reed, and the barrel are all interchangeable and may be experimented with. The primary need in flexibility, however, is in the ability to control the overblowing of the twelfth. To do this we must disconnect, or divorce as much as possible, the register hole from the thumb B♭ hole, so that the register hole can be changed in size as desired. (We have done this recently with interchangeable tubes threaded on the outside to insert into the bore of the instrument with the aid of a socket wrench.)

After all, what is so sacred about using the same tone hole to make a thumb B♭ and as a vent to facilitate overblowing to the twelfth? This hole is not located far enough down on the instrument for a properly placed B♭ and is too small for good tone quality on this tone and for stable intonation. Isn't the correct overblowing pattern more important than this single, chromatically fingered throat tone? It really isn't necessary to choose, and we can have both good overblowing and a good thumb B♭ by installing a mechanism such as the S-K, which as previously noted adds a completely new, properly placed and sized hole for a completely independent B♭. Perhaps still other mechanisms and/or fingerings could be invented which would be better than what we now have.

It should be repeated here that when we reduce the size of the register hole to bring down the pitch of the top of the clarion register, we must be prepared to make a compensating adjustment at the bell to raise the pitch of the clarion tones affected there, and then to lip the very lowest tones in the chalumeau register downward, if necessary, while playing.

For these past many years it has been our practice to "fit" our clarinets to the individual players, or vice versa, much the same idea as fitting a person with eye glasses. As a player changed, his instrument could be adjusted or he might benefit from still another instrument. It has required a lot of work and patience, but the results have been most rewarding. Here is a good example of making all the mechanical adjustments possible before expecting human adjustment; of trying to let the player be the master of his instrument rather than its slave.

### E♭ soprano and alto clarinets

We used these instruments only when absolutely necessary. The soprano E♭ was treated as a solo instrument, and we were able to find satisfactory combinations of instrument and player. We used the alto clarinets both as solo and section instruments on occasion, and actually were able to find and purchase instruments more nearly perfect in intonation than any others in the clarinet family. Our only problems came when we tried to mix these beautiful instruments with other makes and models of lesser stature.

### Bass clarinets

The bass clarinets we chose were in tune in the valuable chalumeau register only when we pulled them rather extremely in the middle and at the bell and doctored up a few tone holes. The manufacturer made permanent extensions at these two joints in our complete set and they have worked out well. The clarion register has been difficult to control, and is not too reliable in intonation, so we have avoided the use of these instruments in sensitive spots above the throat register as much as possible.

**Contrabass clarinets (E♭ and B♭)**

Selection has not been a problem here, and the instruments have required only routine maintenance and adjustment. Again, we have considered these instruments of primary value only in their lower registers.

**Cornets and trumpets**

When discussing the just-tempered scale, I may have written rather glibly about nature's harmonic series and the consonant nature of the tones derived from its simplest ratios. I have also discussed the nonconformist piano, and various departures from the "straight and narrow" by some of the woodwinds, which normally employ only from three to five of the long series of harmonics. It would seem that Mother Nature herself may not always be perfect, and when combined with human nature there is never an end to imperfection. Pity then the poor brass instruments, which have to contend with up to twelve or more tones of the harmonic series. Think what human nature can do with all those tones to play with! On a three-valve instrument this counts up to some eighty-four tones to work with; twice as many as are needed in a 3½ octave range. There are even more in a four- or five-valve instrument or a double horn with its two sets of valve slides. How can all these tones possibly be sorted out?

Really, it doesn't have to be as bad as I have made it appear, and seldom is, but the combination of harmonics and valves makes a formidable team which can be wonderful . . . or terrible. Let's review the harmonic series of the open tones of the cornet and trumpet: fundamental, octave, perfect fifth, perfect fourth, major third, minor third, an unusable out-of-key seventh harmonic, a third octave, a large major second, a small major second, an unusable eleventh harmonic, and a twelfth harmonic an octave above the sixth. It is possible for master craftsmen to reproduce this series exactly, and they are sometimes allowed to do it. They may also reproduce the series quite faithfully when the valves and valve slides are added, even with the handicap of only one bell. The two "flies in the ointment" are the fifth and tenth tones in the series. Although in tune harmonically when they appear as major or minor thirds or sixths in a chord in the key of the particular harmonic series, they are quite flat in the Pythagorean and equal-tempered scales. For this reason, neither the fifth nor the tenth tones are satisfactory, melodically, in any key. Neither are they acceptable, harmonically, in most of the keys. In the simplest example, the written E, fourth space, played "open," is in tune when it is combined with a just C and a just G in a major chord, but it is badly flat as a fifth in a chord based on an equal-tempered or Pythagorean A (15.6 and 21.5 cents).

It is the rare instrument maker who is content not to tinker with this fifth harmonic. And by means which are largely beyond my understanding he is able to bring one of these tones, the open tone for example, in tune as an equal-tempered tone, without affecting the other tones in the series. However—and here is the "rub"—I never have found any instrument in which the fifth harmonic of the open tone had been "corrected" and in which the fifth harmonic of the first or second or third valve tone could also be corrected without displacing at least one other tone in the series. Usually when the fifth harmonic is raised, it also raises the sixth harmonic and perhaps lowers the third, both of which originally should have been in tune in all the temperaments (a bare two cents sharp as an interval of a slightly imperfect fifth in equal temperament). And usually those who attempt these "corrections" do so with the philosophy that they are making certain tones "a little sharp" in order that others will be only "a little flat." In other words, instead of one tone out of tune for each such correction, there are apt to be two or three or more. Such is the price of compromise.

Now come the problems of the valves and valve slides. The second valve may lower each open tone one half step and the first valve may lower each open tone one whole step, but the second valve slide in that case is not long enough to lower the first valve tone a half step, nor is the first valve slide long enough to lower the second valve tone a whole step. Again the urge to compromise asserts itself. Again a simple example: Let us suppose that both the first and second valve slides are lengthened just a bit so that their separate tones will be only "a little flat" and their combination tone only "a little sharp." And let us suppose that the third valve slide, which is said to lower the open tone 1½ steps, is made long enough so that its combination with the second valve is only "a little flat" and its combination with the first valve is "not as bad as you otherwise might think" and the combination of all three valves is a "lost cause anyway."

In the instruments available to us there are many variations of harmonic patterns and valve slide lengths with all sorts of intonation results, almost all committed to compromise in a great majority of the tones. It was my feeling that it would be better to select and modify an instrument which would have the greatest possible number of tones in tune in equal temperament, and then by other mechanical means make it possible to play the remaining tones in tune by providing the right lengths of tubing.

We found an instrument, both a cornet and a trumpet, in which the harmonic series was nearly perfect in both open and valve tones, with a flat fifth harmonic throughout. The second valve slide was of exact length to lower the open tone one half step. The first valve slide was short enough to play the fourth line D in tune, but all the other first valve tones were sharp, so we pulled this slide some 3/16 inch. The third valve slide was of the length required to play the two-three valve combination in tune; we shortened it to make it play exactly 1½ steps below the open tone, and took a 3/16 length of what we had removed to add to the first valve slide so the latter could not be made sharp in its basic series. We now had an instrument on which sixteen of the twenty-five tones in the two octaves C-C could be played in tune with open or single valve tones (C, E, F, F♯, G, A, B♭, B, C, F, F♯, G, A, B♭, B, C). By using the ring on the third valve slide we had the means of achieving the right tube length and good intonation for five more tones (low C♯, D, D♯, and the two G♯'s). To raise the pitch of the four remaining fifth harmonic tones C♯, D, D♯, and E near the top of the staff with normal fingerings, we put a ring on, or connected to, the main tuning slide which permitted closing this slide sufficiently with the thumb to bring these tones into proper pitch. And all this without compromise!

In addition, the main tuning slide was equipped with double-acting springs which permitted the player to push or pull the slide either way while playing, to augment what he might or might not do in humoring the tone, without loss of control or quality. With these arrangements it put all the responsibility for playing in tune on the player, for the instrument was fully capable of it. This was another step in our crusade to let the player become the master of his instrument instead of its slave.

Most cornets and trumpets are now normally equipped with a ring on the third valve slide to permit the slide's extension when it is used with the first or second valve or both. The moving of this slide should become a part of the regular fingering of the instrument from the beginning of instruction, when the duration of the tones in question is sufficient to make such slide adjustment possible and practical. I am familiar with the trigger which also extends the first valve slide, and which is often used instead of or in addition to the third valve slide ring. I am also aware of the ring or "saddle" on the first valve slide, which permits sensitive manipulation either way from a slightly extended position. However, the double-acting main tuning slide does all the first valve trigger or ring or saddle can do and far, far more. This main tuning slide, though, cannot be operated over a sufficient length to permit its substitution for the third valve slide extension.

After some twenty years experience with it, the instrument I have described, with normal harmonic series, precisely and individually tuned valves, and movable third and main tuning slides, is still the "one for me." Many experts can and do play quite satisfactorily in tune with other instruments, but with "my" instrument even these highly talented performers could do it more easily . . . and the rest of us mortals need all the help we can get to play in tune.

**Euphoniums**

At first we could find no euphonium without a decidedly sharp sixth harmonic, but we took the best we could find and modified it along the same lines as described for the cornet and trumpet. Later we found an instrument somewhat better in tune, and which was equipped with "compensating valves." We chose the three-valve model (extra tube length is added to all tones using the third valve when that third valve is used in combination with either or both the other valves). The manufacturer was most cooperative in altering the lengths of some of the slides to our specifications; he adopted these measurements as standard for regular production; we found our intonation improved, with less effort on the part of the player.

Our players today prefer the four-valve euphonium with compensating valves (and with bell-up rather than bell-front). The fourth valve does indeed help correct a few tones, but does not compensate in valve combinations without the fourth valve. The value of the extra range provided by the fourth valve is questionable. I have an idea that the fourth valve is as much a status symbol as anything else (on the tuba as well). This is one of our difficult problems in intonation: the make of the instrument, and its accoutrements or lack of them, often become more important to the player than intonation. Only a thin line separates an American-made from a foreign-made instrument in either direction, a status symbol from a gadget. And when a player thinks one instrument is better than another, it usually is—for him, and for his purposes and standards. It is our job to try to educate him, to convince him that playing out of tune as an individual or virtuoso soloist is really as bad as playing out of tune in an ensemble.

There are now euphoniums with good basic harmonic series, four valves, and movable tuning slides. We purchased some of them, and considered them near-perfect instruments. Now if we could add the third valve compensating feature they indeed would become super-perfect instruments.

**Tubas (Double B♭ only)**

Our solution to good intonation in the tubas was quite similar to, and actually preceded, that of the euphoniums. We selected a three-valve compensating instrument with a remarkably good harmonic pattern. The manufacturer changed the length of the main tuning slide, the valve slides, and one of the compensating loops according to our findings, and adopted these specifications for future production. With a minimum use of alternate fingerings we found the instrument remarkably in tune, and our section one of the most dependable for intonation in the band. However, the tuba majors came to prefer a larger bore four-valve instrument which became available. It was our decision to change to this latter instrument, for it was indeed a fine one—in tone quality, response, and potentially in intonation. The students liked to play it better, and undoubtedly they felt a rise in their status (besides having four valves it was also bell-up rather than bell-front), but we had more intonation problems within the section, as well as between the tubas and other instruments, than we had with the former set of instruments.

## Horns

We did little with the horns except to select two makes and models which were entirely satisfactory from an intonation standpoint. Some of them required shortening of one of the main tuning slides, and all of them needed critical internal tuning by pulling all the valve slides and keeping them so pulled. Still, the apex of status swung back and forth between the two makes, and both suffered from competition with other makes and models not as well in tune but endorsed by and bearing the names of horn heroes. The heroes no doubt play or have played their horns perfectly, but the students do not do as well.

## Trombones

Again we did nothing here except to select instruments for size of bore and desirable tone quality and response. We did not consider the harmonic pattern of particular importance in the trombone because the players could always find the slide position for the right tube length for any tone. We were disappointed, however, in two ways: (1) all the trombones, the tenors, at least, were sharp in some of the sixth harmonics of the series, a result of making the instruments with essentially corrected fifth harmonics; and (2) the players were reluctant to bring down these sharp tones (high E♭, E, and F) to proper pitch by extending the slide an inch or so from the positions of the octaves below. I believe I would prefer an instrument with an in-tune sixth harmonic and a flat fifth; it might be easier to teach the players to shorten the positions for B, C, and C♯ above the staff and use fourth position for D. The player would always prefer to sharpen rather than flatten the tone. He has the means to do both on every tone on his instrument except the low B♭, which, without the now common F attachment, he can only flatten. If he does not play in tune, it is solely because he does not recognize in-tuneness.

**Mallets**

We soon had our celeste and chimes retuned from A=442 to A=440. Later I personally retuned the celeste to achieve a straight up and down pattern, rather than the maker-tuner's pattern of "stretching" (somewhat matching the piano). We found in our inventory a set of wonderful, thick steel bells which had not been used at least for a long time, apparently because they were tuned to A=440 in a straight up and down pattern—just what we wanted! Within the past few years we purchased a new celeste, xylophone, and marimba, after with great pleasure and satisfaction finding them in tune with themselves and with each other at A=440. We now had no difficulty in matching pitches between and among winds and mallets and harp.

In 1954 I prepared a series of "tuning guides" for wind instruments, and had them affixed inside the concert folios for ready reference and study by all band members. In the early 1960s they were incorporated in a book by Ralph Pottle, who also published the tuning guides separately in card form.[1] The gratifying sale of the book and of the guides, through several printings, has indicated the general desire of conductors and teachers to really get hold of the intonation problem and to do something about it. And I

---

[1] Both *Tuning the School Band and Orchestra* and the guides are available from Ralph Pottle, 407 N. Magnolia St., Hammond, LA 70401.

honestly believe that more bands play better in tune now than ten or fifteen years ago.

The tuning guides deal primarily with "mechanical" tuning, i.e., with adjustment of joints and slides. They assume and/or encourage the careful selection and any necessary modification of the instrument. Also, it is explained that in many of the instruments most of the joints and slides can be rather permanently set on an individual basis, their setting tested by experience, and only then adjusted further. Tuning by and for the band ensemble can thus be limited almost entirely to a single tone for each instrument. For the woodwinds this tone should be one at or near the "top" of the instrument (near the mouthpiece), where changing the length of tubing causes the greatest change in pitch. (Tuning the clarinet to third space C at the barrel or mouthpiece is an extreme example of unintelligent tuning, but one which unfortunately has not yet been stamped out.) For the brasses the tone should be the key tone of the instrument near the middle of its register. Concert B♭ is used for the flutes, all the E♭ clarinets, tenor saxophone, and all the B♭ brasses; concert F is used for bassoons and horns, and concert E♭ is used for all the B♭ clarinets and E♭ saxophones.

At Illinois we encouraged tuning to these tones by attaching a tuning bar of the right pitch to a chair at each desk of players. We frequently sounded the tuning tones and various other tones of oscillators provided by the Petersen Chromatic Tuner over a range of five octaves. We also made available a Stroboconn and a Petersen Tuner for individual reference between rehearsals. And we used to a limited extent a remarkable and rather new electronic instrument called the Johnson Intonation Trainer. This is a keyboard instrument having two scales: one tuned permanently to equal temperament, and the other susceptible to tuning each tone and its octaves through a wide pitch range by turning a set of knobs. The Johnson Intonation Trainer provides a ready and accurate way of studying and demonstrating temperaments, melodically and harmonically. Ideally its use should be extended to the individual and to small groups of players and classes. The instrument can make an effective contribution to proper ear training.

We have had still another device to test instruments and their players and to develop sensitivity to pitch in unisons, octaves, and primary chord intervals. We recorded our electric organ in octaves, in equal temperament, in the first phrase of the melody of the Doxology in all twelve keys. We wrote out this phrase for each instrument in such a way that every tone in the normal register is represented. In one third of the keys the instrument plays in unison or in octaves with the recording, in another third it plays in one harmonization of the melody, and in the final third in a different harmonization. We called this set-up our "Intonation Doctorology," and let me assure you that it really "separates the men from the boys" in the instrument-player combination, and does indeed "doctor up" intonation.

It is typical for many flutists, especially the younger ones, to keep the headjoint all or nearly all the way in, and then possibly to blow down to tune. I say "possibly" because many of them have been conditioned to hear and to tune sharp to the tuning tone. But if they have blown down in tuning, when they start to play in ensemble they will revert to their sharpness. Some of this is no doubt in self defense, because of the usual sharpness of so many clarinet players in the upper register.

Because of the unusual perfection of the flute as an instrument, I have found a device which has produced quite good results. It is to use the fingering of the low E♭ to produce the harmonic B♭ above the staff. This harmonic tone is not so susceptible to humoring as is the tone with the regular fingering (again especially with the younger student), so I ask the player to adjust the headjoint until the harmonic tone is in tune, and see that the headjoint is pulled far enough to make this possible. Then I ask the player to produce the same pitch with the regular fingering. This procedure achieves, to a remarkable degree, two results: (1) tuning the instrument mechanically, and (2) stabilizing the direction of air through the embouchure and into the blowhole for optimum tone production. It is possible to play the flute well in tune through three octaves.

Oboe players have a tendency to take too much reed in the mouth, which results in (1) uneven intonation at the change of octave around third space C, (2) flatness in the low octave, and (3) sharpness in the second octave.

Bassoons and E♭ saxophones can be very far out of tune when the conventional B♭ concert pitch is used as a tuning tone.

The best tuning on the B♭ soprano clarinet is achieved when we tune to the thumb F (concert E♭), change register tubes so that this F will overblow a perfect twelfth to an in-tune high C, then tune the middle joint just above the staff, and tune the bell to B third line, if necessary boring a hole in the bell to correct flatness caused by reducing the size of the register hole. It is then possible for the performer to play this instrument well in tune throughout its normal register.

Every one of the above examples can be convincingly demonstrated by tape recordings we have made.

I once asked the whole soprano clarinet section to keep their instruments closed at the middle and at the bell and to tune with the barrel to third space C (concert B♭), which, as I have said, is what is still being done in so many bands. I then had my section play a harmonized chorale. I may say that I was surprised at how well they played with this tuning, and for a few moments wondered if the more complicated tuning I had been prescribing was all that worthwhile. However, I then asked the players to tune to the thumb F (almost all of them had to change the prior adjustment of the barrel to do this), then to G above the staff (more than two-thirds of them found it necessary to pull at the bell). When we repeated the chorale with the new tuning, the difference was amazing. The experience was dramatic proof and reaffirmation to both players and conductor of the worthwhileness of detailed and exacting mechanical tuning. It also served to remind us that we could be lulled into accepting a standard of intonation considerably less than perfect, considerably less than the best.

I can tell you of a still more contrasting "before and after" experience. One September we accepted eight new soprano clarinet players into the concert band. Six of them were freshmen, one a sophomore, and the other a graduate student. All of them had been first chair players in their high school bands, and all but one brought in their own first-line instruments. I called them together to test them and their instruments on intonation. I asked them to tune to B♭ concert without further instruction or comment, then we played and recorded a scale and two four-part chorales. In this case, the intonation was surprisingly atrocious, even worse than I could have anticipated. Then began the process of choosing and adapting for each of the players an appropriate instrument from our set, on a tentative basis at this meeting, with a somewhat more detailed—yet still incomplete—checkup in the following few days. At the beginning of the next band rehearsal, without time for warm-up, I asked the eight players with their new instruments to sit in the front row. We tuned to the thumb F only, then repeated and recorded the scale and the two chorales. The improvement was almost unbelievable. Though the intonation was not perfect, the potential for perfection was already there.

Arthur Williams, former band conductor at Oberlin and a brass specialist and expert, has written, "In the hands of a brass player who has learned how to listen skillfully and appreciate varying degrees of sharpness and flatness, the mechanisms which permit this player to sharp or flat any tone that he can sound so as to play it in tune with any other instrument and still play a tone which is resonantly centered as to quality (this) is the mechanism we must eventually all learn how to use and accept."

I also quote the tuba virtuoso and professor at Indiana University, the late William Bell. "Having found an instrument with good open tones and one on which the first, third, and fourth valves can be manipulated with the left hand, there should be no excuse for playing any note out of tune."

This concept of "tuning while you play," which string players and singers and trombone players already can do, is one which is readily adaptable to valve brass instruments and its practicability proven. So many players say they can play their instruments in tune by lipping only. There may be some merit in conquering the intonation of an imperfect valve brass instrument without slide manipulation, like the merit in climbing a mountain because it is there. However, the ultimate goals are to achieve perfect intonation and to get to the top of the mountain, and there is no more sense in depriving the brass or other wind player of valuable tools on his instrument than there is in depriving the mountain climber of rope, axe, and piton.

By way of approaching a conclusion, I wish to quote a few pertinent sentences from the book *The Art of Oboe Playing* by Robert Sprenkle and David Ledet.[2] This chapter is so fine a presentation of general intonation fact and philosophy that, with the publisher's permission, I had it duplicated and distributed to the concert folios of our bands for study and reference. I quote: "Powerful disruptive forces result from the divergent tendencies of various musical instruments. . . . The use of an accurate, impartial device like the Stroboconn is perfect for measuring the extent of these divergences. This information, to be useful, must be properly interpreted in an unemotional and objective way which is only possible in an atmosphere of mutual respect and cooperation. . . . Ensemble playing is a democratic process, and the pitch problem can only be solved by sharing it. . . . The mistaken idea that being sharp will provide brilliance to the tone is a cheap way of taking advantage of other players, because sharpness is a comparative condition and can exist only when someone else is flat. . . . Some musicians prefer the Pythagorean tuning, some the 'just' intonation, and others the 'tempered' scale. We probably use them all at different times and in different passages, but only the 'just' intonation will tune vertically through chords. In any case, the differences in these systems of tuning are less than the errors that usually offend our ears because of carelessness. Learning to play in tune is a complicated process, requiring sensitivity, control, and understanding."

The wind and percussion instruments that are available for our use in bands surely have benefited from the technological period in which we are living. The finest tone quality and the greatest facility are readily available to our bandsmen. However, many problems of intonation remain. These are handicaps to the player who is challenged to overcome them by a combination of physical, mental, and musical effort. There would seem to be an alliance of inability and resistance in the matter of building into some of the instruments good basic intonation properties. There is a tendency on the part of

---

[2]Copyright © 1961 by Summy-Birchard Company, Evanston, Illinois. All rights reserved. Used by permission.

nearly all concerned to accept undesirable tendencies as "handicaps to be lived with forever" instead of "problems to be solved." In so many cases, response and facility are considered before and above intonation; and much of the time "response" is apt to be measured in terms of "brilliance," which often is only "sharpness." When one instrument is not as sharp on some tones as another, the first instrument is often pronounced "stuffy." Until we are able to convince ourselves, our own players, and the manufacturers that we do not want sharpness, or flatness either for that matter, we will continue to have instruments that are unnecessarily difficult, if not impossible, to play in tune. Knowing the characteristics of so many deficient instruments, I marvel at how well in tune some bands play, and deplore and sympathize with others that play badly out of tune. Instruments built with more intonation accuracy and standardization would make it easier for the good bands to play in tune, and more nearly possible for the others. Certainly technology will provide this for us, if we will recognize the problems and agree on what we want. I do not wish to put too much blame on the instrument makers, for no doubt they are responding in large measure to what we will accept. I believe we ourselves are the key to better intonation in instruments, individual players, and organizations. What we hear, what we learn, what we know, what we teach can make the big difference in band intonation. I hope this article has made some contribution to that end.

# The Profession at Large

# PART 5

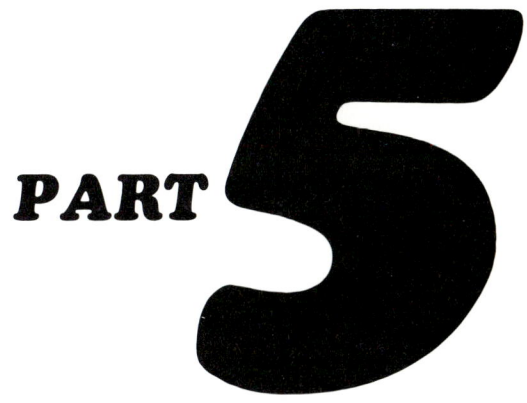

College band directors, generally, have always taken a keen interest in secondary school music education. Ray Tross's 1963–64 survey found that 93 percent of his sample's college conductors made regular visits to public schools and 51 percent were involved in private teaching of younger students. Sixty-one percent conducted clinics with high school bands prior to festival time, and virtually all were involved with festivals as adjudicators, some working in as many as twenty each year!

The time devoted to these activities represents the genuine interest of most college conductors in music education. This dedication is captured in an anecdote once told by past CBDNA president Richard Bowles of the University of Florida:

> A few years ago, Charlie Spohn, John Butler, and I judged the North Carolina state band contest. We started out on Tuesday evening, judged all day Wednesday, Wednesday night, Thursday, Thursday night, Friday, and finally finished up Friday night about seven o'clock. We got in John's VW and drove

through a miserable cold rain on a very dark night about ninety miles to the next contest site where we started in judging Saturday morning, went straight through Saturday night, ending up by giving the local host a IV. Eighty-one bands later, we staggered out of that high school gym and got back into John's VW to go to the hotel, and John turned to me and he said brightly, "Isn't it astonishing how rapidly the time passes when you're doing something you really enjoy?"

# The Influence of Contests on University and College Bands

L. Bruce Jones/1950

The history of competition in music dates back almost as far as the history of music itself. From the earliest times, performers have vied with each other in various ways. It was a favorite pastime in the eighteenth century for organists to "play down" one another in improvising on given themes. Organized festivals with prizes and awards appeared in England in the seventeenth century, and some are still in existence today.

Competition in school groups has been widespread since music became a part of the schools of this country. Halftime shows are not contests, but the element of competition is a definite one. Even though the directors and bandsmen refrain from competitive spirit, the public invariably makes a comparison. Sometimes such rivalry is more intense than that of athletic teams. So if we have music, we will have competition between groups representing different schools.

Another type of competition is present in all music groups, both professional and amateur: the ranking of players within the organization. Every musical aggregation, be it high school band or symphony orchestra, assigns its players to chairs in the sections; this placement, based on performance ability, is naturally competitive and could not be otherwise. No matter what the status of the group, the aim is to perform as well as possible, and this can be done only by having the players properly assigned throughout the sections. Placement is determined by some form of audition, and rivalry for the higher positions is keen, whether for increased pay or the satisfaction of higher attainment. Players, whether professional or in school, are willing to work long and hard to attain a high standing within their group. Such informal contests are inevitable.

Secondary school band competition has a direct influence upon the university band. The achievement of the high school band is the sum of the attainments of its individual players, who, in turn, will be the components of the university band. What, then, is the effect of contests on the work of the individual bandsman and upon the band itself?

In order to build a fine high school band, you need interested, hard-working bandsmen, backed by the financial and administrative aid of parents and school authorities. There is no sounder or more effective appeal to these groups than the appeal of competition. To students, gaining high rank in an instrumental music contest gives as much satisfaction as winning an athletic event. The need for approval from one's peers is an intense motivation for long hours of practice and rehearsal. Competitive events emphasize more vividly than any other way the need for rehearsal space and equipment, instruments, a library, and uniforms. Parents, communities, and schools will cooperate to provide these necessities in order that their bands may have equal opportunity to do outstanding work.

School music competition has had an important influence on the quality of music published. Contests have progressed steadily toward the selection of the best in music materials. It is difficult to imagine anything else that could have so stimulated the publication of fine music for school bands and orchestras.

The same is true of performance level. A performance that rated at the top in a given year would receive a rating two or three places lower a few years later. The capabilities of high school bands have grown because competition spurs on even good bands. If there are no losers in a festival, there will be no progress, and music in our schools will be condemned to fall to the standard of the least proficient. It is a regrettable sign of the times that many are content to do anything only well enough to get by.

Some stimulus is needed to improve quality in anything. Countless products have been improved because competition for sales has stimulated the imagination to make a good thing better. Because our business world is and always will be competitive, every manufacturer knows the only way his sales will increase is to make his product better or to advertise it better than his competitor. How does he know his product is better? Because it is compared constantly with similar products in the open market, and the verdict is in the sales reports. If he had no knowledge of sales, he would have no way of checking its appeal to the public.

So the director and his group may build a good organization, may feel they put on a creditable performance, but until the group faces impartial comparison with other similar organizations, no one will know how it actually rates. The contest is the sales report, which guides the future progress of the band.

The manufacturer is not "hurt" when he finds his sales not increasing as they should; he accepts the facts and seeks ways to improve. Similarly, the director learns how to correct the weaknesses and emphasize the strengths of his group; the student who wins less than top honors in a contest can view the experience objectively as a gauge of present achievement and a guide to future study and practice. There will be no damage to personality; on the contrary, the realization that competition is a law of life will be invaluable throughout the life of the individual.

It is strange that contests have been looked upon disapprovingly by educators who approve, tacitly at least, other activities of the band that cannot be so clearly defended on the basis of educational value. The usual obligations of a school band—parades, athletic events, and so on—demand music largely of the popular, entertainment type that asks less of the student and contributes less to his musical development. Can it be that these objectors look only at the money-raising phase of the athletic event and automatically approve anything that contributes to its appeal?

The basis for judging should be the effect on the student, rather than on the budget. The competition festival offers the band a sound educational objective. The music is of high caliber; the intensity of effort, and the accuracy of preparation necessary to a creditable performance demands the best use of practice time and the best teaching methods.

Comparisons have shown that instrumental music groups that have participated in competition are better performers of an entire year's repertoire. The experience of preparing for and playing in a contest makes the student better able to play all other music well. Having once experienced the thrill of a fine performance, the participant is dissatisfied with a lower standard.

The widespread practice of requiring all competing bands to participate in a sight-reading contest is one of the most effective means of insuring a large repertoire. I know of no better way to develop a good sight-reading band than competition. This practice insures acquaintance with a large amount of music and encourages the student to evaluate the music he plays. He becomes musically literate, able to read his part without the aid of other members of his section.

The student who has been trained to recognize the aims and values of instrumental activity will look forward to the opportunity to play for competent critics. He will recognize his responsibility for honestly presenting the mood and message of the composer. Knowing his efforts will be evaluated is a powerful incentive for careful preparation. An intelligent student will scarcely expect to attain perfection; he will realize the comments of the adjudicator are signposts of his progress and use them as a guide to further attainment. In order to assure these benefits, the qualifications of the adjudicator must be closely scrutinized. He must be widely acquainted with band literature and understand the purposes and values of the competition or festival. He must command the respect of the contestants if his comments are to be of value.

The benefits of any educational activity should be realized by all participants. In band contests everyone competes, not just a select few. Each bandsman takes part as a member of the concert and marching band and may elect to compete as a soloist on one or more instruments; he may participate in one or more chamber groups. He may be eliminated in his own school but the values inherent in the study and practice of the music will still be his.

The purpose of education is to prepare the student to adjust himself more efficiently to the demands of living. We must place high priority on those activities that present problems and challenges inherent in the life of every adult, whether he be a day laborer or scholar. Life in the United States is characterized by competition more than by anything else. Competition is the basis for the growth and development of our country. We find it in every area of human endeavor; there is no way to escape it. We as a people like to see how we measure up against the other fellow. We like to check our job, our school, our church, our town, against all others and feel a glow of pride or a determination to improve.

The instrumental music contest provides a realistic medium for teaching the student to accept and meet competition in a wholesome, effective manner. Contests develop valuable and permanent personal traits, habits, and attitudes. If we adopt a protective attitude toward the student, shielding him from the fact that he must earn his place by playing better than others who play well, then we have failed to give him a tool indispensable to his future career.

The student who participates in competition develops an appreciation for the work of other students, respect and approval if such work is excellent, and tolerance and understanding if it is marred by mistakes or insufficient preparation. He learns courtesy and good sportsmanship toward his competitors and often forms friendships with them that are in no way marred by the fact that each seeks to outdo the other in the contest.

None of these byproducts is automatic. It rests with the director to see to it that they are fully realized. But many directors do not have or do not succeed in transmitting an understanding of the values of competition in instrumental music education. A large proportion of directors and students believe that if they do not win a high rating, they have lost everything. On the contrary, a contest in which a band ranks low can be of far greater value than one in which it wins the coveted first place. A good rating is not in itself the ultimate goal.

Frank Beach has said, "We come together in clinics and competition-festivals, not to win a prize but to pace one another on the road to excellence." The rating is only the road sign; excellence is the destination. The director must keep clear in his own mind, and make clear to his students, that personal development and the building of a better group is the real reason for their efforts. Students who have been taught to evaluate their progress intelligently in daily work will suffer no damage to personality when they come up against another student or band that is farther along the road to excellence than they.

In the last analysis, the worth of any instrumental music program depends almost wholly upon the director. How can the director measure his work or realize his strengths and weaknesses unless he compares his work with that of his colleagues? And what better laboratory for testing can be found than a contest? Adequate training is a prerequisite for any teacher. Refresher courses, summer camps, and clinics are valuable. But as an urge toward honest, hard labor, there is no greater compulsion than seeing your work in impartial comparison with the work of others in your field.

On the other hand, there is no greater satisfaction than knowing, because you have seen it demonstrated, that you have given your students high ideals of musical performance and inspiration for sustained, intelligent endeavor. If a director chooses the anonymity of the classroom and denies himself and his students an opportunity to measure their progress, he condemns himself to mediocrity.

There must be vision and a goal if there is to be progress. The vision brightens and the goal rises higher as we see what it is we lack, and what it is we have that is good and worthy of pride. When we no longer want competition, when we no longer desire to measure our worth against others, when we no longer wish to check our standards, our methods, and our results against others, we shall have lost a great part of the American spirit that has made this country one of the great nations of the world.

We have an unparalleled opportunity to train students in accepting and meeting intelligently the competitive principle that is the foundation of our American way of life, and of democracy itself.

We cannot afford to neglect this opportunity; we must not allow short-sighted, protective thinking to obscure our responsibility to preserve this heritage for our students.

Those criticisms of the contest that can fairly be made are actually criticisms of its organization and management and not of the principle of competition. Let us keep the true purposes and values of competition clear in our minds, and we shall be able to perfect the details of management. The competent, intelligent competitor and the able, honest judge are prerequisites to a truly effective contest.

The future of instrumental music as a worthy cultural activity in itself and as an effective, realistic preparation for life, depends upon its leaders. We must strive for better opportunities for effective training and a continued chance to measure the results of our work with that of our neighbors through well-run competitive events.

Thus we shall rise above the plateau we have attained and reach for constantly improving standards of excellence. Our high school bands will continue to produce better musicians, more industrious workers, and more intelligent citizens. College bands inevitably will become finer, more proficient musical organizations.

# The American Music Heritage

Frederick Fennell/1956

Our music heritage in the United States embraces what we feel to be the best of all that has gone before. Like the other arts and sciences, music in our country has evolved its own particular profile that reveals not only past achievements from great cultures in the world, but also possesses a healthy individuality that belies the now weary criticism that it is derivative. Institutions are constantly open to challenge, including those by which men seek to govern for the common good. The pathways of history are strewn with the casualties of evolution; that which man has ruthlessly discarded seldom rises again to challenge what we accept as his progress.

Our republic, which was founded upon the simple premise of the dignity of man and his inalienable rights to those pursuits considered to be God-given, began its existence with a blazing manifesto that is still the hope of the free world. This priceless document was the beginning of the American heritage. Its clarity of concept and its unequivocal granting of freedom's franchise to all citizens are the distillation of previous efforts and achievements in self-government. When these ingredients were filtered through the fertile minds of Thomas Jefferson and his colleagues, man had a new testament to his freedom.

From the Olympian heights of his mind and spirit, Jefferson was able to review the broad panorama of intellectual and political history. He could see sixty centuries of magnificent architecture by the Egyptians, the Greeks, the Romans, and the Chinese. He could survey twenty-two centuries of drama from Euripides to Shakespeare; the manifestos for freedom and dignity which culminated in the Magna Carta; the covenants of justice by way of Greek and Roman law; and the dark centuries of feudalism and wanton usurpation of the rights of many by a supposedly divine few. All these and more of men's acts, deeds, and records lay open for acceptance or rejection by those who forged the American heritage. There was Christ, there was the Bible; there were Confucius and his people's twenty-one centuries of thought and action; there were the explorations of the Phoenicians, the Italians, the Dutch, the Portuguese, the French, the Scandinavians, and the English; there was the medicine of Hippocrates; the arts of glass, bronze, iron, steel, copper, wood, canvas, and oil; the skill of the tiller and the sailor; the force of gunpowder; and the incomparable sound of the violin. Thus the American heritage began with an inheritance from the world.

This inheritance at the republic's founding also included the glorious art of music—a millennium of it from Ambrosian chant to the pages of the *Haffner Serenade*, still heavy with Mozart's undried ink on the same afternoon that John Hancock penned his bold and equally wet inscription.

Granting the rich inheritance with which the American music heritage began, it is not surprising that we finally have emerged as a people worthy of that legacy. For years we have been ignored or branded as totally without aesthetic sensibility in our worship of mechanical and scientific ingenuity. But our arrival in the arena of the arts, however late, is complete and our standing in the creative and recreative olympiad is one for which we need feel neither shame nor false pride.

What were some of the great music forces at work in Europe when Washington was inaugurated as our first president? What music institutions did we have?

At the Esterházy palace in Austria, Haydn was rounding out

thirty years as history's most productive composer in residence. In the field of education, the members of the National Guard Band in Paris had become the nucleus that founded the Paris Conservatory. Christian Cannabich and the court orchestra in Munich were continuing their perfection of the art of orchestral playing and inspiring Mozart to complete his last four great symphonies. Charles Burney, concluding his first wanderings over the continent, was publishing the first history of music in the English language, while Beethoven, at age seventeen, was arriving in Vienna to begin his musical conquest of that city. The year of Washington's first inaugural, marking the climax of our own revolution, saw the vicious outbreak of France's ten-year civil war, which consumed ancient institutions like a wind of flame. As it burned it also refined new institutions, among which was the establishment of the truly public concert with emphasis upon outdoor gatherings. The French Revolution thereby became the greatest single influence upon the development of the band.

In Philadelphia, the ten-player United States Marine Band, modeled after the Prussian bands of Frederick the Great, began its uninterrupted service to the nation. The Moravian settlers in Bethlehem, Pennsylvania, had firmly established their importation of German musical life, complete with organ, orchestra, trombone choir, and collegium musicum.

These promising beginnings produced only stunted growth for the next 130 years, during which expansion, internal and external conflict, and political, social, and industrial upheavals all but consumed "our lives, our Fortunes, and our sacred Honor." Musically we were content to import whatever came, caring little even then for the home grown article. But we had homegrown composers, however imitative and lacking in worldly fame. We had marching tunes for fifes and drums borrowed from everywhere and adapted to our own purposes. Deep in the Appalachian country our songs and those of other lands were being recast in the furnaces of time, awaiting use in the twentieth century. The fields of the South and the decks and wharfs of our waterways heard old and new rhythms and chants. People danced jigs, reels, minuets, and hoe-downs. People sang to the glory of God and for the salvation of their souls.

It was not Schubert lieder or *Götterdämmerung* or even *Rigoletto* that was sung, but it *was* singing, it *was* dancing, and it *was* ours. We even had composers of genius who died penniless and unrecognized. At the same time that Wagner was producing his great opera on the subject of the high German art of minstrelsy, we were in the thick of a minstrel show of our own concoction—one which mirrored our musical and theatrical needs at the time as perfectly as *Die Meistersinger* represented the culmination of ten centuries of Germanic contrapuntal, vocal, and instrumental art.

While Wagner was pamphleteering up a storm in protest against the pitiful artistic conditions of the German state opera theatres, our kind of opera houses sprang up by the hundreds overnight along the trails to the California gold fields. By the time Puccini had crowned the golden age of Italian opera with *Madama Butterfly*, we had given the world such useful inventions as bifocal reading glasses, the cotton gin, the steamboat, the reaper, motion pictures, the air brake, vulcanized rubber, the telegraph, the telephone, the camera, and the airplane. True, we were short on Schuberts, but with our technological achievements we were able to crisscross the nation with a network of railroads to bring us the music and performers of every country of the world.

As our westward expansion siphoned off the vast populations on the eastern shore, those who fled religious and political oppression abroad took their places in the cities or joined the westward migrations, bringing the music of their native countries. Among them were the Irish bandmaster Patrick Gilmore and the German orchestral conductor Theodore Thomas. These two men did more to shape the development of the American instrumental heritage than any men before or since. Lowell Mason, a Boston school teacher and pioneer in the building of the American music heritage, had begun his work to introduce the teaching of music in our public schools. Thomas Edison had invented an arresting little gadget from which the approximate sounds of Sousa's band were reproduced with the possibility of almost unlimited repetition. Orchestras had sprung up in Minneapolis, Cincinnati, St. Louis, and Chicago. Singing societies, opera houses, vaudeville theatres, musical gardens, and amusement piers had grown by the hundreds.

All this activity was principally imitative. But New Orleans witnessed the evolution of a musical genre that was its own: jazz. It belongs to us and we are proud of it. Jazz spread to the most remote corners of the land with unprecedented speed in acceptance, launching a great instrumental renaissance. That renaissance was accompanied by the development of music schools and departments in colleges and universities, which continue to pour forth an unending flow of young people who preserve and enrich the American music heritage.

The college band is certainly among those institutions that can shape the music heritage of our young people and generations yet unborn. To them, as to us, goes the inheritance of the now taken-for-granted genius of Stradivarius, Blummel, Wieprecht, Boehm, and Sax, who gave us instruments upon which to play; the incomparable music of Mozart and all his colleagues who fashioned our music literature; and the combined efforts of thousands of bandmasters, educators, publishers, physicists, and instrument manufacturers who overcame apathy and ignorance in the furtherance of a native music culture.

Never before in history has there been so magnificent an opportunity for the common musical good as exists in the thousands of music rooms across our land. But if we are not careful, that fabulous opportunity is going to pass us by. It will elude us if we are not aware in the first place that it *is* an opportunity. It will be lost if we are not equal to the opportunity, once we grant that it exists. We must lead from strength and not from fear. I am not concerned about any lack of technical skill or the respective abilities of directors to promote our organizations. I am not disturbed by those whose strange philosophy consists mainly in making the world safe from the symphony orchestra. I am not convinced that because the college band is at once a musical experience, a social resource, an educational institution, and an indoor and outdoor minstrel show, that it is too many things to too many people to be anything to anybody. But I am very concerned that we maintain a true music leadership passionately devoted to the art of music in all its manifestations. Many are the diversions that distract us from the simple pursuit of the pure art of music, but if we do not make the revelation of the art of music our whole reason to exist, if we do not worship at its shrine with devotion, curiosity, and courage, the band will be strangled with our own citation cords or impaled on our own batons.

It is our duty to know the strength of our position and to use that strength for the good of all music. To be a music leader one must first of all be a music citizen, and citizenship is what a heritage is all about. That ten-inch platform which raises a conductor above the floor of his musicians does not make the man who stands upon it a conductor. He must be willing and able to assume the full office of that leadership. He is in a position to contribute immeasurably to the further enrichment of American musical life.

I do not advocate more hastily prepared or ill-conceived concerts, or the increasingly casual awarding of academic degrees. These will not enrich the lives of anybody. We all have had our gripes about what happens or what does not happen on the radio or television, but how many of us do anything about it, individually or collectively, with the hundreds of students who might share our views? Our hard-won heritage is an eloquent testimony to battles won against formidable forces. The victories of the past are also a clear indictment of our apathy and our lack of curiosity, devotion, and courage. If we and our students did more than gripe during intermissions about unimaginative programing, we might soon hear something more ambitious.

Let us not look with remorse upon the fact that Italian opera at the Metropolitan may not be performed as idiomatically as it is at La Scala. Rather let us rejoice in the beauties of *South Pacific*, *My Fair Lady*, and television's gift to the world, *Amahl and the Night Visitors*. Let us applaud the growth of opera in any form. Let us be encouraged by the bright prospects of musical theatre as we see it and as we fashion it.

Let us not feel inadequate because the splendid Carabineri Band of Rome has that "Noah's Ark" instrumentation that suits them and their social and musical structure so well and suits us not at all. Rather let us seek to solidify what has been forged in the past forty years as our own kind of wind band—to serve it and its fast-growing literature with a full measure of our minds and hearts.

I would rather read our history at sunrise with Benjamin Franklin's bifocals of wisdom and imagination than view the dusk of other civilizations with the rose-colored glasses of past glories. The American music heritage is very much the college band director's responsibility, and I am confident we shall yet be equal to the task. Let us get on with it.

# The Responsibility of the Musician

James Neilson/1958

We members of the CBDNA have a dual responsibility, as conductors of our college and university bands and as music educators. We must never hold the title "music educator" lightly, or treat it with contempt. Whether acting as conductors or as educators, we always should be musicians. And as musicians we have the responsibility of interpreting our art so that it may be understood by the general public.

In no area is this responsibility more apparent or more misunderstood than in music education. The music educator must teach the young the art of listening to and making good music. Unless this is his guiding philosophy, music education cannot take its rightful place in the total education of the young. Music educators accept as their just due the rights and privileges accorded performing musicians, but are less eager to accept the responsibilities which educational professionalism implies. The responsibilities of the music educator can be summarized in a few simple phrases:
  (1) Encourage young people to become musically literate.
  (2) Increase their capacity to enjoy the best in music.
  (3) Integrate musical literacy with every positive area of life.
Since school choirs, orchestras, and bands offer a valid musical

experience to young people, a faithful discharge of these duties by the music educator involves maintaining standards of performance. Music is not self-perpetuating; it needs the performer no less than the composer or the listener. Since the composer gives only face form to his art, the responsibility of the performer is most important. It is he who invests music with the dignity of discipline and order as he brings the silent symbols of the score to life. The music educator must be truthful to himself and to music. He must have strong convictions concerning music in performance in order to translate a score into meaningful sound. An inept translation robs even the best music of its right to being. The duty of the music educator is completed only when music receives a competent and inspired performance under his hands.

The performances of school musical organizations seem to be waning in style and spontaneity. In what way are we responsible? Is it through inferior, incompetent, and spiritless teaching that we alienate the young from the art of making music, and thereby rob them of an experience through which the soul can be ennobled? Music has no power in the abstract. One may write about it and discuss it learnedly, but unless it is performed it has no influence for good. Nor is this influence valid if the performance is perfunctory. To competency must be added conviction, artistry, and enthusiasm. Only then will music come to life.

Character plays an important part in the performance of music. Sound musicianship is usually supported by strong character and spiritual serenity. How does the music educator conduct himself? What is the state of his spiritual being, the force of his influence? Does he encourage young people to do better, to be better, or does he induce lazy, slothful habits? There is no more to performance than the exercise and control of mental and physical processes. Spiritual discipline must be added if music's expressive and ethical content is to be preserved.

The brotherhood of musicians embraces not only its Bachs and Beethovens, but also music educators and, vastly more important, the young persons they serve. A music educator's ethical code, standards for evaluation, and depth of understanding must be of such high order that they elevate the entire brotherhood. Living as we do in restless, exciting times, the music educator must become a stabilizing influence in the community he serves and, moreover, he must seek to strengthen the moral fiber and deepen the spiritual convictions of the young people he influences. This responsibility has become increasingly important in a time when music has become morally ambiguous. Music is amoral and often used to promote inferior, even diabolical, purposes.

We should oppose, violently if need be, any educational practices and procedures which permit music in the lower grade self-contained classroom to be taught by the room teacher. Teaching music at any grade level is a job for a skilled professional. Quite often the room teacher not only is not a musician, but actively hostile toward music. No amount of in-service training can make these persons musical.

What a sad commentary that we live in a day when a rock 'n roll recording is not considered a success unless it sells well in excess of five hundred thousand copies, most of which end up in the hands of teenagers. The fact that many local radio stations have gone on a steady diet of rock 'n roll should disturb any thinking person.

We wonder at the philosophies, procedures, and practices of music education that have had so little effect on our young that they turn to musical shams. Heaven help us if half a century of teaching music in the schools has brought us to this impasse. We are bothered by the lack of consideration shown the school concert band by music educators. Our efforts to maintain good bands, to strive for perfection in performance, meet either with benign contempt or merciless scorn. Whenever and wherever music educators meet in session, the term "band man" is apt to be used in a most derogatory sense. Yet we of the College Band Directors National Association are not ashamed of bands or the culture we beget. Nor are we afraid for their future.

We live in a world of organization. The general purpose of organized endeavor is to encourage fellowship, promote understanding, and provide a medium for the interchange of ideas. The national organizations through which the programs of music in education are implemented often fail to provide adequate leadership.

Music educators should consider the possibility of adding to the strength of these organizations before multiplying their powers. Nor must these become sounding boards for personal prejudices; that will reduce them to the strength of the weakest member.

There is no royal road to success. One does not achieve outstanding musicianship in a moment. Musical understanding builds gradually, through constant study and preparation and devotion to ethical principles. Musicianship requires that the spirit expand with the intellect. Pity the musician who is only stimulated intellectually by music. Intellectual dogma has little place in true musicianship. Dogma confines the spirit in conforming to the letter of the law. It fails to give a sense of direction. The real musician is never intolerant, except where performance is concerned. He will not allow prejudice to overcome his better judgment. Music educators must discard narrow-mindedness, intolerance, and petty arguments over educational philosophies and procedures. No one person in music education can lay claim to a complete or exclusive understanding of all that is relevant to his domain.

Music education must never become a ritualized expression clothed in ecclesiastical garments. Music makes no demand that we bow before its altar. Music is made for man, not man for music. Educators who assume that practices and procedures are the end and not the means of music education make a big mistake. Many teachers have a way of observing the letter of the law rather than the spirit.

The true musician will not be egocentric. He does not place himself in the center of his musical experience to ask, "What can music do for me?" Rather, he asks, "What can I do for music?" His belief in music will affect his life profoundly. It will call for action, since action accompanies belief. To believe implies having an objective. So far as music education is concerned, the objective must be the enrichment of the soul. Music performed for any other purpose may do incalculable harm to the young and impressionable. The extent of one's belief in the power of music will influence one's thinking and one's spiritual outlook. Rightly considered, correctly adjusted, a belief in the power of good music enables one to live serenely in a world that needs serenity. And it provides a great purpose for living: music for the world, not the world for music. Music educators have at their command the language of the universe, the medium through which heaven and earth may be united. It knows not the bonds of race or creed. It speaks its message to all who will hear—a message of peace everywhere to men of good will. We, music educators all, must understand this language and message thoroughly. Only then are we craftsmen, practitioners of an ancient and noble art, an art with healing for the world.

# Straws in the Winds

Hubert Henderson/1969

There are easier ways of earning a living than conducting a college band program. As a band director dropout, I know. My mistakes as an administrator are rarely as immediately apparent as yours, weather does not affect my performance, and I don't have to worry that next weekend's television show may make me appear overly eclectic.

I have always enjoyed a remark that Mark Twain made when asked his opinion of Wagner's *Tristan und Isolde.* Twain said he thought Wagner's music was better than it sounded. Similarly, I believe bands are more justifiable musically than many of my colleagues would care to admit. However, I do agree with a statement by former CBDNA president Jim Neilson at the Southern Division meeting in 1959: "Gentlemen, unless we join hands with those of the academically elect, unless we become a vital part of our culture through an artistic contribution to its musical life, we are through." Neilson went on to say, "There is one hope for the future of college bands—that college and university administrators begin to view themselves seriously and in doing so find them to be necessary adjuncts to the continued growth of artistic life and influence." The problem may, of course, lie more properly with administrators than with band directors. I personally recognize the importance of the college band from several angles, but I am aware of the devastating negativism of many deans and chairmen.

Such opinions seem related to the fact that many enlightened administrators who do recognize the important role of the arts on campus do not consider the band's activities as artistic. In the April 1967 issue of *Accent*, the dean of my own arts and sciences college at the University of Kentucky, Paul Nagel, wrote: "The presence of the arts (on campus) is a reminder constantly of the precious capacity toward which men may still aspire, the capacity to inspire, to impart vividly ideas and emotions to their fellows. As knowledge retreats deeper into the cavern of obscurity and specialization, and thus grows more remote from men, the arts must of necessity thrive the more. . . . A respect for creativity, and therefore for the artist, should exist nowhere more powerfully than in the academic milieu." I know it would not occur to Dean Nagel that our band program might make even the slightest contribution to such a philosophy unless the possibility were suggested to him. Perhaps many other directors have deans and chairmen who similarly ignore the band as an artistic medium but who do not communicate this attitude to them. Perhaps because you continue to receive larger budgets, you may rationalize that your school is supporting your band. But I suspect the real reasons for support may be athletic rather than artistic. Bands have become associated with athletics in the public and administrative minds, and have prospered because of the general administrative reluctance to oppose public favor.

Beyond unawareness of the band's musical potential and pressures related to athletics there lies an even more critical barrier against administrative acceptance of the band as an artistic medium: its generally appalling literature. With few exceptions, the band has not attracted first-rank creative minds to write for it and it has had less than dramatic appeal for imaginative listeners. Students must not only perform much second-rate music, but rehearse and master it technically. The administrator is probably unaware of these concerns; he knows only that in the world of music the band counts for little. From the college president to the department chairman, many in the administrative hierarchy are aware of these facts:

(1) the pitiful representation of band music in the Schwann catalogue; (2) the lack of a single instance of a foundation grant to a band program of any kind; (3) the absence of bands from the professional concert stage in any form; (4) the avoidance of any mention of bands in historical accounts of twentieth century music; (5) the poor research record of faculty members with band responsibilities; (6) the complete disdain for the band held by musicologists; (7) the failure of a single band conductor to achieve first-rank professional stature; and perhaps the most damning of all, (8) the frequent suggestion that the band is guilty of subverting string teaching.

I could list a few issues that frequently occupy places on the agenda of administrative meetings within and beyond the department of music at any college: (1) should credit be given to students enrolled in musical ensembles, particularly bands; (2) should grades other than passing or failing be given for such work; (3) is the scholarship granted the oboist closer to that granted the chemist or to that given the athlete; (4) should fees be charged for applied music and, if not, would this eliminate the reason for granting scholarships; (5) is it possible to devise some adequate substitute for teaching applied music on a one-to-one student-teacher ratio and, if so, what effect would it have on the present approach to ensembles; and (6) does the idea implicit in the collegium musicum or pro musica reduce the justification for demanding that students devote enormous blocks of time to rehearsing and performing music of the common practice eras?

These problems are confronted and resolved according to the demands of individual situations and predilections. I resist the idea that any group, including the CBDNA, should encourage its members to seek assistance from each other by attempting to apply pressures such as: "Colleges A through Z do so-and-so; therefore our school should be allowed to do it." Something that works at one university may be anathema to another, often with good reason.

The efforts made by some band directors to incorporate into their own programs every idea, gadget, and practice that comes within sight or sound lead to curious contradictions and inanities, not to mention burgeoning budgets. This is particularly unfortunate at a time when colleges are losing money. Over the past ten years, American colleges and universities have doubled enrollments but almost quadrupled total expenditures as well; from 2.8 million students in 1956 to 6 million in 1966 and from $4.2 billion to more than $15 billion. If the ratio between numbers and costs continues to increase, every operation of each department will be subjected to careful scrutiny to determine its value and efficiency. I would guess that almost every institution has at least begun to use the computer to develop cost-accounting data about each course and each staff member. We may well be in for a period of forced retrenchment in order to meet critical exigencies. Though significant savings could be made in many university operations, we all know which area first feels a pinch. I can recall a time when a faculty member hoped to receive a modest salary increment every two or three years; now, most of us expect sizable increases every year. And unless the budget for which we are responsible shows a marked increase over last year's we feel not only slighted but perhaps personally derelict. Many observers suggest we ought to develop priorities, in the event that choices become necessary. We might begin thinking about what level of priority our chairmen might assign to the band, in either a modest cutback or a panic situation. We might be well advised to prepare arguments now for questions that may come sooner than any of us expect.

Even among those chairmen and administrators who have a warm regard for all aspects of the band's program there remains one bothersome question. Is there any logical limit to the size of a band? I suppose some colleges are already faced with the necessity for building auditoriums whose stages can accommodate more people than traditional seating areas can. Perhaps some are even contemplating asking for a change in football rules so that bands can legally have the 200 yards they already seem to need. The historian Pascal wrote, "If Cleopatra's nose had been shorter, this would have changed the face of the world." He meant, of course, that personality plays a role in history, not that the length of her nose was the cause of Mark Antony's defeat at Actium. Perhaps the size of bands projects an image that ultimately works against their best interest. Someone calculated that if all of the bands in America were lined up end to end they would form a column reaching from New York City to San Francisco.

Two other aspects of the relationship between bands and administrators seem to me to be interdependent: first, research, and second, students. As you know, major universities are moving rapidly toward greater emphasis on graduate work, especially at the doctoral level. This trend has implications both for the kinds of band programs we may envision in the future and for the kinds of students we may expect. The band's full glory may be realized by the small college while the large multiuniversity may have to abandon some of the concepts of band programs as we know them. Whatever transpires, it behooves band directors to prepare for situations that on the one hand become more highly selective and specialized and on the other hand must be designed to serve a veritable deluge of students. If American higher education is to improve qualitatively and at the same time accommodate enormous quantitative growth, some experts believe we must develop two distinctly different kinds of institutions: one to serve massive numbers of students and another to serve scholarship. Otherwise, the colleges of 25 years hence will not only closely resemble our contemporary high schools but will be administered by men whose philosophies duplicate those of principals and superintendents.

If the band is to survive at the university level, its proponents will have to don the robes of academic respectability in earnest. Band directors will have to become research-oriented and learn to apply skills which only the musicologist has acquired and practiced, both to protect their own status as college faculty members and wield influence on a generation of students that is better prepared for serious intellectual endeavor. Students will become increasingly disenchanted with bands, band music, and band directors unless they find the same challenges that are available to them in other areas.

We have a new breed of student, one that I believe is for the most part superior to his predecessor. We hear a lot about "student power," but I think many have misinterpreted the meaning of this term. I think students are seeking recognition and means of representation rather than the power of authority, and I am convinced that many of their demands will be realized. Perhaps you noted in the newspapers recently an account of violent student protests at a southern college against what the students termed "mindless athleticism." Is it difficult to imagine such protests being widespread, and involving other than athletics? I am not an alarmist and honestly feel that students can be—and are likely to be—a tremendous power for order, given responsive institutional leadership. But we have much evidence of a changing student body, more intellectually curious and more militant in influencing the college environment. For the first time in the history of this or any country, the U.S. now has a "learning force" (students) that outnumbers the "working force." This situation is of more interest to college presidents than college band directors, but it reflects a change in our socioeconomic structure that inevitably will break down many of our most cherished traditions about the proper role of a college or university. The idea of a college serving in loco parentis has been abandoned by many schools and eventually will disappear. Other doctrinaire practices that have remained unchallenged for decades will soon draw fire. Students are seeking to sit on boards of trustees, to have a voice in the appointment and promotion of faculty, to establish new codes of conduct about such things as room visitations and drinking on campus, and in some instances are attempting to determine curricula. In short, students are vitally interested in the administrative structure of colleges and are no longer content to be concerned about just the academic, social, and pseudopolitical activities that occupied their predecessors almost entirely.

If students do one day turn against, for instance, college athletics as unworthy of their attention and support, after having established the administrative channels to ensure that their views and wishes cannot be dismissed as juvenile or immature, then some changes can be expected. Further, if students draw some rather obvious conclusions about the relationship of bands and music to athletic programs, directors may be in a rather unenviable position. It is not too soon for bands to begin emphasizing their most positive claims to campus legitimacy. I need not even suggest the direction that is clearly indicated in order to establish a secure foundation for the band as a justifiable musical and educational medium.

You can shape the band's future by your own actions as directors, by where you place your primary values, and how you emphasize, by your understanding of the differences between instruction and education, the band's potential for intellectual and creative development. You also can influence your administrators to gain an appreciation of the band's proper role. This might best be done in ways that might not occur to you as being indicative of your convictions, but that might be so interpreted by your chairman. For example, by asking for money to commission new music instead of money for new uniforms, you convey the impression that bands are about something that has to do with music. Most of the bands I have observed over the past twenty years could have survived an additional two years or more without new uniforms; no band, in my opinion, can afford to continue with the same old literature, even though a great portion of it may have a 1969 publication date.

Many of today's most prominent college music people are former band directors. So perhaps the easy answer to all of your problems would be simply to get out of the band business and join the administrators! But since no one cares for the easy way, I think this old proverb may appeal to you, whatever your ambitions and aspirations: an oak tree is the result of a little nut holding its ground, and there are two ways to get to the top of the tree—one, climb it, or two, sit on the acorn.

# The CBDNA in the Future

David Whitwell/1975

I have two concerns regarding the future of the CBDNA. First, I believe the organization needs to be a forum for the most open, free, and wide-ranging discussions. Some of our various philosophies tend to unite us and some divide us into separate camps. Due to the social and fellowship aspects of our organization (which are very important) there is a danger we will concentrate only on ideas that we share. I believe the CBDNA is more important as a forum for ideas we do not share.

The second fear I have is that as the organization becomes more effective there will be a tendency for the organization to become concerned primarily with its own preservation. Then its value would be lost, for its value lies in what it does for the membership. I believe this organization should exist to help each individual member achieve his highest artistic and career ambition. That is not a selfish goal, but rather a democratic one.

My personal debt to the CBDNA is great. In this organization I have found real friends, dependable advice, and unfailing support. I recommend to new and younger members that they take the initiative, be active in the organization, and use it for their own growth. That the organization is responsive to younger members is witnessed by the fact that I was elected to national office after only seven years of teaching experience.

I think the average director does his job rather well and is eager to do it better. The problem is that to do the job well he has almost no time left for the most important obligation every conductor bears: his growth as a musician. Nothing is more critical to the long-range nature of our profession than this problem. The successful college band director who works a hundred hours a week asks, "Where do I find the time?" The college band director who may barely find time to study scores he performs asks, "Where do I find the time to study scores purely for my own musical growth?" The only answer is the one Erica Jong has hung in her studio: "Art doesn't demand much; only everything you have."

The repertoire of the college band has changed dramatically in the last decade. Ten years ago, very few college bands performed programs consisting primarily of original compositions. Today there are very few that do not.

We devote the greatest amount of rehearsal time to the quest for the technically perfect concert. In the future we must devote more time to spiritual qualities. Their discussion lends strength to the quest for technical perfection; their omission robs it of meaning.

The individual college band director is going to have to become more proficient in defining his profession. We are going to have to learn the language of the American educator and to present in that language the ancient beliefs of our profession.

The average college band director has tended to slight his relationships with the rest of music education and ignore the other professional organizations. This diffidence rather reflects the fact that he tends to be a strong, confident, and highly independent musical figure, accustomed to doing things for himself. Again, in the future he will be denied the luxury of privacy. The college band director will have to learn to reach more in his relationships with other music educators—for his own sake.

The college band director could exert much greater influence on the quality of music education in the United States. In a recent interview with *The Instrumentalist*, conductor Georg Solti made the astounding statement that what he misses in America is a basic *music* education for each child. How can he say that? Our schools are frantic with school bands, school orchestras, and so on, of which there are virtually none in Europe! I think where our educators would disagree with Solti is not in the definition of education, but in the definition of music. If you really want to take the pulse of music education in the United States, read the new music reviews in *The Instrumentalist* and *The School Musician*! I am sure Solti would say that whatever all this activity is, it isn't music.

To put this in different words, we have taught performance and how to achieve it—and have done it very well. What we haven't really taught is taste, aesthetics, or how to judge the quality of music itself. As a result our young band directors and the music education entrusted to them fall victim to a problem defined by Weingartner. He said a bad performance can ruin a good piece of music. But one cannot speak of a good performance saving a bad piece of music. A good performance of bad music only brings the weak points of the composition more clearly into focus.

The coming decades will test our profession in many ways; battles fought in the 1930s will have to be refought in the 1980s. It will surely demand the best in each of us. When we take our stand, when we fight those battles, I hope it will be the spiritual power of great music that is our banner and that sustains us. In more than four centuries, it has been the spirit of great music that has produced wind band conductors' finest moments.

In the 1580s, Dalla Casa, filled with the spirit of great music, formed the state wind band in Venice. He desired something more than the expected accompanimental role of the Renaissance. By the way, if there are those of you who feel that the 16th century is a bit remote to have much relevance, there is a Venetian document of 1550 that says, "Those players who refuse to play *canzoni* in procession will no longer be employed in the chamber."

The Mozart wind serenades were written for a society of wind players and conductors who, filled with the spirit of great music, could not accept the social definitions of their time.

The band repertoire for the French Revolution came into existence because a group of conductors, filled with the spirit of great music, wrote symphonies rather than marches for their military bands.

In our century this spirit has produced a number of college band directors who have risen above the didactic necessities to make great performance an accepted goal of music education.

Those of us to whom the college band movement is now entrusted owe to dedicated predecessors and to college band directors yet unborn that our era be judged as one in which the spirit of great music was central to our literature, fundamental to our aesthetic, primary in our teaching, and the common bond of a dynamic society of men—the CBDNA.

# Composers' Analyses of Their Works for Band

# PART 6

# Sinfonietta

Ingolf Dahl/1964

When I received a commission from the Western Division of the CBDNA to write a work for band, there were many things to be considered. First of all, I wanted it to be a piece that was full of size, a long piece, a substantial piece—a piece that, without apologies for its medium, would take its place alongside symphonic works of any other kind. But, in addition, I hoped also to make it a "light" piece. Something in serenade style, serenade tone, and perhaps even form. This was the starting point. You will remember that in many classical serenades the music begins and ends with movements that are idealized marches, as if the musicians were to come to the performance and then, at the end, walk off again. From Haydn's and Mozart's march-enclosed divertimenti to Beethoven's *Serenade for Flute, Violin, and Viola* (and beyond), this was a strong tradition, and it was this tradition that motivated at least the details of the beginning and ending of the *Sinfonietta* (a work in serenade tone but with symphonic proportions, hence the title). The quiet beginning, the backstage trumpets, and at the very end an extremely quiet exit with backstage trumpets—this is the frame of the work. Here is just one of the details in which this music goes contrary to what may be considered certain band music traditions, and even some orchestral traditions. As Richard Strauss said to one of my composition teachers when the latter was a young man: "Fine work, young man, but you should begin every work loudly to get the attention of your audience."

The form of the whole *Sinfonietta* is that of a very large bridge or arch. The sections of the first movement correspond in reverse order and even in some details to the sections of the last. Thus, the opening fanfares are balanced by those of the closing; the thematic material that closes the first movement opens, in varied form, the third. The middle movement, a pastoral nocturne, is also shaped like an arch—it begins with an unaccompanied line in the clarinet section that corresponds to the solo line of the alto clarinet at its end. Thus, the center of the middle movement is the center of the whole work, and this is the gavotte-like section that is the lightest music of the whole *Sinfonietta*, a center stone that does not weigh heavily.

The tonal idiom itself is a simple one. I feel strongly that composers should adjust their intervallic and harmonic attitudes to the special characteristics of overtone structure, blend, and other acoustical properties of different performance media. Thus the overtone-rich instruments of the band, such as tubas, bassoons, and so on, require a harmonic and intervallic approach more concentrated on open (consonant) intervals than would be the case with strings or the piano. A piece of chamber music and a piece for brass choir should reflect their respective media, not only in the thematic material of the work, but also in its form and, most importantly, in its harmonic idiom. The *Sinfonietta* is tonal-consonant, centered around A-flat major. At the same time, it is based in its outer movements on a series of six notes; they, through a considerable variety of manipulations, form the background to the harmonic as well as the melodic patterns. These six notes are half of a twelve-tone row and are used with varying degrees of strictness throughout the first and third movements. This set of six notes is one that permits all kinds of triadic formations, and it may also be of interest that it is one in which the inversion at the interval of the major sixth provides the second group of six notes. In a later work, a piano trio, I used the same set with all the twelve notes. The arrangement of notes here is A♭, E♭, C, G, D, and A. This structure is stated gradually by the backstage trumpets at the beginning, where one by one these notes appear and then form the entire tonal content (including transpositions of the set, of course) of this fanfare. It would lead too far afield here to trace the row deviation of the melodic and harmonic material and the many ramifications of it. The raw material is, on one hand, stated bluntly (as in the opening unison of the last movement) and, on the other hand, disguised so considerably and intentionally as to be quite unrecognizable. It serves as a means of construction that helps the composer and provides unity and direction. To give just one example: the six notes serve as focal points of the march tune that opens the principal rondo section of the first movement, just as they do, in different ways, in connection with most of the melodic material here. Secondly, the set sometimes forms even more basic constructive functions: in the first movement there is a cadenza-like episode for the entire clarinet section (inspired, I do not hesitate to admit, by a wonderful performance that William Schaefer gave of Weber's *Concertino* played by the full clarinet section). Here the entire scheme of modulation derives from the order of the set notes, going through the keys of A♭, E♭, C, and so on, until finally A major is reached, the point farthest removed from A-flat, which is the starting point of the following rondo return.

The first movement starts quietly on the one and only note on which, to my mind, a "band piece" can possibly start—B-flat. Through a set-motivated modulation the main A-flat section is reached: a march rondo. This movement includes kaleidoscopic color interchanges, with the big clarinet cadenza I mentioned (punctuated by percussion and brass staccato) and it ends in full tutti with, as a private joke, the drum pattern that traditionally begins a march.

The second movement, called "Notturno Pastorale," is composed of an alternation and superimposition of several musical forms in a single movement. These musical forms or characters are, first, a fugue; second, a waltz; and third, a gavotte. The fugue subject is first hidden in a lyrical saxophone solo and later slightly varied with each entrance. Its derivation is just a simple tetrachord:

E♭, F, G♭, and A♭. But by octave displacement, rhythmic shifts, and so on, the line of the fugue subject is refracted by slightly different lenses at each entry. Superimposed upon it is the waltz, fading in and out of the texture.

In the second movement I tried to avoid typical band sounds. It is a quiet movement, with no fortes, tuttis, and with dense polyphony.

The tonality of the nocturne is D-flat—the classical key (the subdominant) for the second movement in relation to the first. From D-flat there are always gravitational temptations to go to G-flat, C-flat, and further. The gavotte, which forms the center of the tripartite scheme of this movement, is also the simplest part of the work, consisting of a lightly accompanied oboe tune as a foil for the denser textures of the surrounding music.

The final movement, "Dance Variations," begins with a straightforward presentation of the six-note set, presented as a motto. The "Variations" of the title apply to a passacaglia-like use of the motto in the bass throughout the movement. This passacaglia scheme is not at all obvious to the listener, nor is it meant to be. It is a constructive device, which, like steel rods in reinforced concrete, holds materials together and makes them solid. Over the set-derived variations of the passacaglia bass a great variety of little tunes in shifting colors is played off, over a key scheme that goes through most of the circle of fifths, starting on the A-flat key level. A lyrical section in the center provides contrast, and, after very full rhythmic tutti punctuations, the ending arrives.

Naturally, a composer spends a great deal of time and thought on the consideration of instrumental balances, instrumental varieties, fresh tonal colors, variations of instrumental densities, combinations, and so on. Yet I believe very strongly—and this is just as good a time as any to state this premise firmly, although it has become a controversial one—that there is a hierarchy of musical values, and that it is important for musicians to keep this hierarchy in mind, particularly when so many persuasive forces seem to obscure it. The highest, most important, governing element in music is the element of pitch—that is, of line, of melody, and of melodic-motivic-thematic design. On the next lower level comes the element of harmonic design. And way at the bottom of the value scale in music is the element of tone color, of "dressing up." What makes music great has always been the notes, and never the dressing-up, the glitter, the orchestration, no matter how much it contributes to the effect of the presentation of the musical idea. Therefore I discuss the orchestrational aspects of the *Sinfonietta* last, because I strongly believe that is where they belong.

The attitude of a composer before writing a band work is one of total fear and apprehension. The apprehension is caused, among other things, by the fact that we never know exactly for how many instruments on each single part we are writing. As composers carefully brought up on such textbooks as Rimsky-Korsakov's fine treatise on orchestration, we have been informed that two horns in unison balance a single trombone in certain registers, to give just one example. Having lived with such principles, one is apprehensive about the results when one's calculated two-horn unison will have to balance the third trombone part as played by three, four, or even five players.

My approach is what could properly be called "orchestral;" that is, an approach that sees its ideal in the variety that can be achieved by the opposition of pure colors with mixed colors, and by striving for a considerable amount of such coloristic interplay. Following the example of masters of the past, there are comparatively few tutti passages and subsequently a minimum of doubling in order to preserve the interplay of pure colors. One other detail in an orchestral treatment of band sonority is the combination of similar colors simultaneously occurring in both foreground and background. This combination is what a painter would call *valeurs*—different shadings of the same hue, as, for example, one kind of blue as background for another kind of blue or, in terms of orchestration, half the clarinet section as background to the other half. This approach puts a great burden upon the performer and upon the ear of the conductor, because it is not the kind of orchestration in which balance is "built in," but one in which balance lies in the subtleties of observed dynamics and in the relation of the *valeurs*.

As for the function of the saxophone in the band, having written a whole concerto for it, I am in no position to belittle the instrument. When I told Stravinsky I was writing a saxophone concerto he raised his eyebrows and said, "I don't know; to me a saxophone always sounds like a pink slimy worm." However, these instruments can be nobly played, and if used as a well-defined family that sets up good housekeeping by itself in the middle of the surrounding instruments, they certainly can be a fine family to have around.

Arthur Honegger once was commissioned to write an oratorio (*King David*) for chorus and an ill-assorted group of wind instruments. He asked Stravinsky, "What should I do? I have never before heard of this kind of odd combination of winds." Stravinsky replied, "That is very simple. You must approach this task as if it had always been your greatest wish to write for these instruments, and as if a work for just such a group were the one that you had wanted to write all your life." This is good advice, and I tried to follow it. Only in my own case it was not only before but also after the work was done and the *Sinfonietta* was finished that it turned out to be indeed the piece I had wanted to write all my life.

# Meditation

Gunther Schuller/1964

This piece came into being, as many compositions do these days, in the form of a commission. But in this case it was a very specific commission that determined much of the character of the piece. It was the Edward Benjamin Restful Music Commission, which I had heard about for years but never thought I would be involved with. I was surprised the commission came to me because I know that many people in and out of the music field have an automatic association between dissonance and *non*restfulness. To commission a restful work from a composer who is known as a twelve-tone composer seemed a bit odd. Nevertheless, it challenged and intrigued me, and I therefore decided to accept the commission.

Of course, I don't feel that dissonance is necessarily nonrestful. I don't even accept the whole dichotomy of consonance and dissonance in contemporary music. There is such a thing, of course, in nineteenth- and eighteenth-century music, but we don't think of our harmonies today, our chords, and our melodies as dissonant. They just contain certain pitches that, if you associate them with *earlier* music, would be called dissonant.

In any case, I did want to satisfy the demands of the commission. I knew that I would write a twelve-tone piece and that I would not compromise or "write down" in regard to style. But since I knew this was going to be first played by high school students, I felt I ought to make some compromises in terms of the technical demands made of the players and in the expressivity of the individual parts.

High school students, with some exceptions, are generally at a technical and musical level where one cannot expect from them the highest form of individual expression in their playing. Greater expression comes usually with further musical maturing and with greater mastery of the instrument. I think if the piece had been written for university bands, I would have written it at a slightly different level in that particular respect. And if the language of this piece was going to be new, then the possibility of a student interpreting his particular instrumental line really expressively became even more minimized. So in those two respects I set my sights somewhat modestly.

The piece is written in twelve-tone technique, but it is a rather elementary kind of twelve-tone, technically speaking. This seemed not the place to get involved with some of the most recent manifestations of twelve-tone or serial technique. This lack of emphasis on the more advanced aspects of twelve-tone thinking had another reason. I am very fascinated by the sonoric possibilities of the band medium, possibilities which have gone mostly unrealized for decades. Although recently, within even my own limited experiences in the band field, I have seen a dramatic revolution in this particular respect, both in terms of the programing and the caliber of playing in our country.

I am a composer who is very much involved with the sonority aspects of structure, that is, how timbre and sonority can become structural elements in music. And so, having this marvelous medium—the band—at hand, I knew that I would want to emphasize in this piece the sonoric possibilities, especially when writing for a specific band with, for example, four contrabass clarinets and six bass clarinets.

In earlier band music the assumption was that each individual player was incapable of playing his part alone, and therefore you had to double each part about seventeen different ways. This is no longer the case in most band writing of today.

   I remember being shocked out of my band uniform—in the days when I played with the Goldman Band—when I would get myself all set for a part marked "solo" and to my utter consternation (and dismay) half of the band would come in on top of me: the entire saxophone section, the baritones, one of the trombones, probably the third clarinets, and so on. With this kind of doubling of all the lines you can't really say that you're exploiting the sonority possibilities of the band. For example, one of the most remarkable things about the band is that you have a whole consort or aggregate of clarinets to work with. It seemed to me that this might be something to explore; there is no more remarkable sound than the sound of a whole family of clarinets playing in consort. So this was one thing I also knew I was going to exploit in the piece.

   Previous to our century, there was in music a hierarchy of relationships in which one element of music, namely melody, was in a top priority position. It was the first thing to which a composer turned when he wrote a composition. In a secondary position you had harmony, used either in conjunction with melody or by itself, in strictly homophonic music. Basically harmony was used as a sort of substructure to the melody. Then, in still lesser hierarchical positions, you had the other elements of music, such as rhythm, which we now often refer to as durations; timbre or sonority, that is, the particular instrumentation in which a sound is set; and dynamics. The latter were treated more or less decoratively, in varying degrees, of course, but nonetheless at a tertiary level.

   The musical, stylistic, and conceptual revolution that took place around 1910 brought us into the realm of atonality (I'm not only thinking about Schoenberg, but also about Stravinsky, Bartók, Webern, and Berg), and in effect "democratized" the earlier hierarchy of relationships. In other words, most music that is truly contemporary treats these elements on an equal basis. Timbre is no longer a mere decoration of a particular pitch; timbre and sonority can function as primary and structural elements. They only can do so if they are treated on an equal level with other elements, such as melody, harmony, rhythm, and so on. The result of these changes and innovations was that you might not even have a melody in a contemporary composition or not even necessarily a theme. Thus athematic music came into being, in which by definition there also would be no thematic development, at least in the nineteenth-century sense.

Along with the revolution in melody, harmony, and rhythm, there was also a major revolution in terms of the form and structures of music. The forms associated with diatonic music (the sonata form, for example, and various symphonic forms) became as obsolete as the melodic-harmonic language itself had become. But if you can't use the sonata form or fugal forms or any other classical forms (like the rondo), you have to find new forms. One of the characteristics of new music is that each piece develops its own form. Each composition, especially in twelve-tone and serial technique, is likely to have a form unique unto itself. This concept was almost inevitable once composers did away with the theme as a specifically stated element at the beginning of a piece, a theme that underwent various developments or variations and was probably recapitulated at the end of a piece, making a very neat little formal "package." We now use what is referred to as an "open" form as opposed to a "closed" form. Today a piece may start at a certain point and never return to its opening material or never even refer to it particularly. What we have as a substitute for the theme in twelve-tone music is the twelve-tone row: a precompositional element that undergoes development, variation, invention, and so on.

*Meditation* falls more or less within this category. There is no law, of course, against recapitulation of some kind. A piece can involve various forms of recapitulation, although this is probably somewhat exceptional in orthodox twelve-tone music. In any case, my piece has no theme as such, but it does have a sort of recapitulation of the opening material. There *are* melodies, by the way, although some might disagree with me on that point.

The form of *Meditation* should be, I think, the first concern of the band director who is going to perform the work. The piece breaks down into five major sections. The first of these, while not "thematic," is in some sense expository, and consists of three suc-

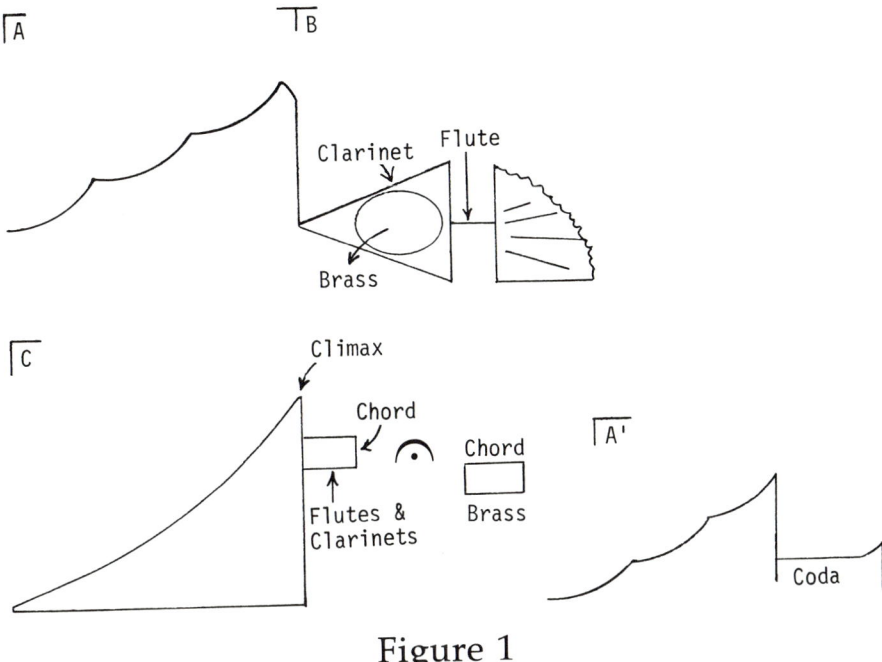

Figure 1

cessively greater climaxes, none of which are the main climax of the piece. The beginning starts with three or four lines in the woodwinds that, although treated polyphonically, take into consideration the harmonic results of this polyphonic texture. The opening and the three subsidiary climaxes can be seen graphically in Figure 1. Once the main musical idea has descended again, I exploit the division of the clarinet section into many individual parts, to the point where there accrues a thirty-two-note chord or "aggregate" with individual clarinet players playing the individual tones. There is no doubling here at all. A single clarinet starts and gradually other clarinets enter in a sort of long, staggered, pyramid chord that fans out in both directions, into the upper register and into the lower register, until finally you have the full thirty-two-note chord. Once this is fully stated I overlay it with two muted brass statements, which have somewhat the same shape: fanned-out shapes treated in very thick clusters.

In effect, I have one music in the clarinets, and another music overlaid on top of that which is distantly related and yet distinct from it. At the point where I have the entire chord going, I have a maximum of pitch distribution. It would be difficult to use many more notes or pitches; thirty-two is already quite a bit. It sounds like a giant "cluster," as a matter of fact. Then I suddenly break that off and go from this *maximum* of sonority, of pitch concentration and density, to its opposite—a single note. That single note is in the flutes with a little oboe line of three or four notes added. Immediately after the note of the flute, the thirty-two-note-chord of clarinets comes back. So you have a kind of formal "incision" in this structure, a formal and conceptual idea which is at least fifty or sixty years old; it is the primary formal structural technique used by Stravinsky in *Le Sacre du printemps*, for example. The interruption of one block of sound by another either totally unrelated, or stated in terms of maximum contrast to the previous structure, is now a fairly common technique. Such structures don't really end; they are merely interrupted at a certain point, and start again at a later point.

Once this thirty-two-note chord had reappeared, I had to think of how to proceed from there. I had an idea to create a symmetrical shape in this B section, but I didn't want to use an *exactly* symmetrical shape—that is, to make the cluster chord disappear in exactly the same way it came up. So I added a melodic line, one of the harder performance aspects of this piece. The line starts in the piccolo, then travels down through the various instruments into the very lowest register, ending with the contrabass clarinet. This line is what is referred to as a *Klangfarbenmelodie*, a word Schoenberg invented, which in German means "tone color melody." It refers to a melodic line stated in a variety of tone colors, usually linked or overlapping, so that the first instrument, very much as in a relay race, leads directly into the second instrument, playing in a different timbre, and then leads from there into the third instrument, and so on, eventually creating a whole "chain" of colors. In my *Meditation* the *Klangfarbenmelodie* goes from piccolo to E♭ clarinet, to the clarinet, then on to the oboe, English horn, alto clarinet, bass clarinet, and finally contrabass clarinet. The problem in performance is to make this whole chain of different instruments sound like *one single melodic line.* This line in turn absorbs each note in the thirty-two-note aggregate as it travels down into the bass register. That is to say, when the melodic line reaches the pitches of the chord, those notes of the chord stop at that point.

There are three ways in which I finish the sustained chord notes. Some of them actually "collide" with certain pitches in the melodic line and are absorbed by the melody. Others that are not necessarily the same pitches as in the melodic line, but are close, end with a slight crescendo and sforzando, like flares shooting off. Still other pitches make a diminuendo and thus disappear. So there are three ways of "liquidating" this thirty-two-note chord. That ends the B section.

In the C section, I start more or less in the manner of the first section. There are melodic lines in the low clarinets and bassoon and eventually in the horn and alto saxophone which group themselves into a polyphonic texture, building up to the utlimate main climax of the piece.

Out of that climax, I extract and sustain an eight-part chord (four flutes and four clarinets) that in turn becomes the link for what turns out to be a "recapitulation." This eight-part chord is made up of two sets of diminished chords, because that is one of the internal characteristics of the twelve-tone row I use which one can break into components that delineate diminished chords.

There is a fermata—a total pause—and then the same eight-part chord in the woodwinds reappears, this time in the muted brass and is used as a liaison to the recapitulation. We can call this A' in our formal scheme, since it is an almost literal recapitulation of the first section. But instead of leading us to what was the B section the first time around, it now leads to a coda, based on a single chord sustained in certain instruments until the end of the piece. It is a very quiet coda, in keeping with the mood of the restful music. It has one tiny little climax just before the end.

Here in the coda I used two other "new" techniques. One is the use of an improvisational procedure, which is perhaps the first time it has been used for the concert band. It is a very limited improvisational procedure since, again, I don't feel that the average sixteen-year-old is going to be a whiz at creating great inventive melodic lines. I give a small number of "soloists" in the band certain notes and they are asked to improvise freely with those pitches in any order they wish to and in any rhythm they wish to, with pauses, where they can breathe, for example, or where they simply can rest. You thus have six players creating an improvised twelve-note structure that I doubt one could notate exactly—aside from the fact that it's going to be different *each* time since it's improvised. The effect is of a sort of "backdrop" of trills in the flutes and clarinets that is going to have an impressionistic, unpredictable quality—almost like leaves rustling in the autumn wind, the precise pattern of which you certainly could not analyze or predict.

Against the trills I have overlaid brass sonorities and harmonies, exploiting the various mutes of the brass and the opposition of nonvibrato sounds with vibrato sounds, so that a kind of *Klangfarbenmelodie* develops out of these brass chords. In other words, all these chords link up in some way and make a kind of "chordal" melody; instead of a single line, they are chords. That is the basic substance of the coda, which progresses very quietly by these means and finally just "evaporates" on the chord, which has served as the harmonic substructure of the entire coda. It's not a terribly "dissonant" chord, and yet it's not an obvious harmonic triad, either. It has as its bottom note the very lowest E of the contrabass clarinet and almost two octaves higher it has a D-natural, which makes the beginning of an $E^7$ chord. I have on top of that two more pitches, an E-flat and a D-flat. Though they do not fit into the $E^7$ chord pattern, the whole chord has a feeling of a piece-ending seventh chord. I have noticed in some performances that the E of the contrabass clarinet tends to be weak—in fact the chord is sort of turned upside down so that the upper notes are much stronger than the lower notes. This of course destroys the particular chordal balance I am trying to achieve. The last chord will have all the more the effect of a final *cadence*, if it is done in a properly balanced way. If it is done in an "upside down" balance, then, of course, it is simply a dissonance that doesn't make much sense.

Incidentally, the piece ends with almost the same chord it started with, only a fifth lower; which is like the dominant resolving to the tonic. But not quite, of course, because what happens in between is not exactly the same as in a diatonic piece.

As far as the twelve-tone technique is concerned, I use one row at a time. There are many composers today who use two or three forms of the row simultaneously. In fact there are now compositions in which multiple versions of the row are used simultaneously. Such music is obviously of much greater internal complexity. But here in my *Meditation* there is a one-to-one relationship between the twelve-tone row and the events in the piece. This is one of the easier and more elementary ways of using the twelve-tone technique. After the row has been stated once—that is to say with the E-natural in the third measure of the bass clarinets—the next form of the row is an inversion. In that way you get the B♭, A, B-natural, and C, and so on. The process consists of going through each of the four forms of a certain transposition of the row: the original, the inversion, the retrograde, and the retrograde inversion. Then I move on to a new transpositional level and I go through all the twelve transpositions with each of these four forms; and at that point I've used forty-eight row forms—at which point the piece ends. So even the duration of the piece is determined to some extent by the twelve-tone row.

One could follow this all the way through the piece. But this kind of analysis is not so important for the player as to delineate the larger structural shapes. It would be of use if one wanted to see how the pitch relationships work in the totality of the piece. Those relationships are of some interest and importance, but I suspect that most bands don't have enough rehearsal time to get around to those more refined and subtle points.

I never found out whether Mr. Benjamin thought this music was restful. Certainly the piece is quiet and slow, and gives an impression of being restful, but I sometimes wonder if he ever was satisfied with my commission.

# Symphonic Requiem

Vaclav Nelhybel/1966

The first movement of the *Symphonic Requiem* starts with a fermata. When you look further, at measure 9, you see another fermata. Turn the page, and at measure 15, there is another fermata. The movement ends, of course, with a fermata. These fermatas must somehow be coordinated.

The piece starts on D and ends on D. It's obviously in some kind of D. And, it's very obviously D minor.

You can count in eighth notes first—nine eighth notes, then eight, then seven, then six and five, closer and closer in a kind of diminution but kind of crescendo toward the sforzato. I would say it's a rhythmical crescendo. The brass start piling up a chord. What is the top note in the chord? F. The chord stops in measure 7 and you see the F, E, F, D, F, and so on, repeated in bells for two measures, and then comes a rest. The next six measures are a repetition of measures 2 through 9. Of course, it's shorter. The piling up is faster and also, if you look exactly, the range of the woodwinds and also of the brass is much closer.

From measure 16 through 21 it is again the same thing. The woodwinds are closely compressed—this time only from F to F#, not exactly two octaves. So are the brass. If you look at the top notes in the woodwinds and in the brass, the first group has F; the second group (beginning in measure 10) has E; and the third group (beginning in measure 16) has F. Finally, in measure 19 it's really on D. F-E-F-D—this is a quotation of the first four notes, from the Requiem Mass: Dies Irae.

Now you know what the Requiem is about. We are starting slowly, and in a complicated way. What are the problems? Problem number one will be to state the content melodically and thematically. Everybody must clearly hear the F on the top of the first cornet when it finally enters, then later on the E, the F, and together on the D. We must hear it because there is so much sound and it's not just a major-minor triad. The more compressed the sound is, the more difficult—because if you have all twelve notes, from F# to F, and fill the whole space of a major seventh, it will be very difficult to still hear the F on the top as the melody.

The first fermata is nothing. It starts from pianissimo, and slowly builds up. The second fermata in measure 9 somehow must be related to the first fermata. It should last about two measures; the third fermata, a little bit less than two measures.

In measure 6, from 6 to 7, no matter how loud your band plays, they still must be able to produce a crescendo. The percussion breaks down into piano and goes through mezzoforte to forte, so the percussion can do it; the brass can do it, too.

Up to measure 21, nothing actually happens aside from stating "Dies Irae." The end is in a kind of unbalanced ABA form. The three measures before the end, 43 through 46, show exactly the same notes, only in chord form, without the piling-up. Here you see very clearly how the compression of sound progresses.

In the center is the statement of the whole verse from "Dies Irae," the original Gregorian chant melody. The clarinets start in measure 22; they repeat it again, and they go a little bit further.

This section is marked pianissimo dolce. At measure 28 the brass take over. They must match the dynamics and tone quality of the clarinets. The low brass choir must sound like a male chorus. You must hear the melody and every entrance must be stressed. If you have a band and this band cannot play subtly or softly, you have to raise the level of the brass. In measure 41 there are clarinets playing those syncopated sforzatos. The brass start a big crescendo.

# Music for Prague 1968

Karel Husa/1971

It was late August 1968 when I decided to write a composition dedicated to the city in which I was born. I thought about writing for Prague for some time because the longer I am away from the city (I left Czechoslovakia in 1946), the more I remember the beauty of it. In my idealization, I see Prague as more beautiful, perhaps, than it really is.

During those tragic and dark moments for Czechoslovakia in August 1968, I suddenly felt the necessity to write this piece so long meditated. My friend and colleague Kenneth Snapp, then director of bands at Ithaca College, had mentioned to me the possibility of commissioning a work for his band to play at the MENC Convention in Washington in January 1969. I was sure the music I would write for Prague would be scored for concert band, a medium I have admired for a long time. The combination of wind and brass instruments with percussion fascinated me and the unexplored possibilities of new sounds and combinations of instruments attracted me. I am not speaking against the orchestra; it is a medium I have written much for and participate in as both conductor and violinist. However, so much great music has been written for orchestra and strings that it is difficult to produce new works in which orchestral musicians would be interested. I had already written one piece for concert band in 1967—a *Concerto for Saxophone and Wind Ensemble*.

As I started to compose, the old Hussite religious song "Ye Warriors of God and His Law" came to my mind. There are several notations of this song; the one I remembered and found in my Czech song book is as follows:

I used only the first four measures (or less). For instance, in the introduction, the timpani constantly develops the first and second measures. E is flatted and C sharped in order to preserve the tension of ascending and descending movements. The following fast fanfare in trumpets (at letter C) also evolves for the song. And of course it is used in many forms: diminution (first movement, two measures before G), augmentation (at T in the last movement), or close to the original speed (last movement, nine measures after M). Although *Music for Prague 1968* is not written in any tonality, the song's use at the beginning and end of the work gives it a strong "center note," which is D, even if the last unison at the end is on E. I have mentioned in the preface a few examples of symbolism. Another can be the ending of the work on the E, which is the highest note in the chorale. This note, together with the A (two measures before V) that I put one octave higher in the trumpets although the line of the song descends, is a gesture of defiance and hope.

Another unifying thread in the work is a chorale-like motif of three notes, always harmonized. It appears at the beginning in flutes, clarinets, and horns (measures 3-4), reappears at A and seven measures after A in clarinets, and at B in horns, trombones, and tubas. Later, in the aria at K and six after K, it shows up in the brass instruments. It appears again in the last movement, nine after Q (in baritones, tubas, contrabassoon, and string bass for the first two chords and in horns for the third), six before R, and at R itself in its strongest form ever, underlying the climax of the work.

Some passages, such as measures 3-9 after E in the first movement and a related passage in the fourth movement around L, are combinations of both the song and the chorale motif.

Shorter and fast figures throughout the whole work also evolve from the song:

These figures appear frequently: seven measures after C in trumpets, one measure after D in woodwinds, at E in saxophones, and two measures after in marimba. They also occur in the second movement three measures before and four measures after K in the woodwinds, in the interlude at O and after in the vibraphone, and again in the fourth movement.

In the first movement, six measures after E, this figure flashes from one instrument to another, first in trumpets, later with added saxophones, and even later with all woodwinds and other brass. It is necessary for the trumpets to play with bells up so that the different sounds of mutes are heard over the ensemble. In the first movement the baritone saxophone melody one measure after B should emerge from the other sound more and more strongly until it dominates, two measures before C. I have added here the bass saxophone and contrabass clarinet, but as these are not always available, the baritone saxophone in this case has to play as loud as possible and then go back just before C into piano.

Other material used in the construction are several rows of twelve tones. They are treated very freely, repeating many notes, sometimes using the twelve notes not in order, not avoiding occasional octaves, and so on. For instance, in the beginning of the introduction, the original sketch of the row was:

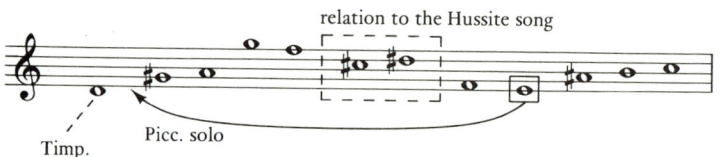

However, in the piccolo the E is used sooner than the G-sharp, and also the Hussite song is used independently from the row in the timpani part. The aria, for instance, has another row:

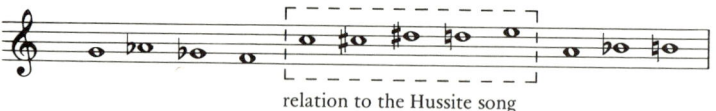

It spreads forward and then backward as "pedal" throughout the piece. The G starts in tubas, followed by A-flat in measure 3; baritones bring out G-flat and three measures later the F comes from tubas; C is played by the second and third trombones five measures before I, and three before I the baritones bring out D-flat. At I the horns play E-flat, followed by a D in the tubas and later E by the trombones. Even later A will sound in the baritones and B in the horns.

Now, as I go backwards in the row, I have decided to eliminate the B-flat in the brass (but it will sound in the vibraphone and marimba at J simultaneously with the B-natural). The B-flat in brass instruments has been reserved for the climaxing section, measure 4 after K, in trombones, tubas, string bass, bassoons, and contrabassoon, and later also in baritones. Then we go backwards in the row: four measures before L, tubas, string bass, and trombones bring in the A; E, D-sharp, and C-sharp are part of the harmony before and after (at L in oboes and first and second trumpet, for instance); D is played at L by all horns, which also play the following note of the row, the C six measures after L; two measures later the F appears in oboes, English horn, and third clarinet; the same instruments, together with all clarinets, will play F-sharp at M.

In the four measures before M, the A-flat will start to sound in flutes, piccolo, and E-flat clarinet. These instruments will play the last note, G; at the end they will be joined by vibraphone and marimba. The row also is used at the beginning of the aria in the vibraphone and marimba; the first tone, G, being in tubas, the vibraphone and marimba play tones two to twelve and start again. Tubas come with their second tone (A-flat), and marimba and vibraphone continue with tones three to twelve and one, two; baritones follow with tone three (G-flat), and so forth.

On the other hand, the saxophones with all clarinets (except the small E-flat) finish with playing note E. This is the same note that the aria started on and derives from the retrograde inversion of the same row started by tubas at the beginning of the aria. It is, in addition, transposed:

I already have mentioned that diminutions of the song are included before and after K, mostly in the woodwinds. There is another important figure that repeats itself in the free middle part of the aria; it is the major third and minor second intervals that start the first movement:

It appears three and five measures after K in the low instruments (brass and woodwinds) and seven after K in saxophones, trombones, horns, and bass clarinet. The role of the percussion instruments is to express anguish or obsession. The title of aria might be a little surprising; it is, of course, not an aria in an operatic sense. I have given it to the saxophones purposely; they have the tremendous ability to sing, sound strong and loud, and yet remain expressive. Their vibrating quality may be close to what we call vox humana on the organ. And this is what this melodic line is about: the anguish, fear, and desolation in awaiting what will come next.

The "next" is prolonged by the interlude: a quiet night, but the sort of quietness before an explosion or storm. I have chosen the metallic percussion instruments to give an impression of bell sounds, and the snare drum to symbolize the occupant. From the point of construction, the interlude takes considerable time: the pitches as well as the rhythm and the dynamics are serialized from the last note in N until the first note in P. I made a few adjustments, but otherwise the structure is rather strict.

The letter O divides the part with cymbals, triangles, and tam-tam (percussion 1, 2, and 3) in half; from the last antique cymbal note the score reads exactly in retrograde inversion backwards to letter O; this is strict mirror rewriting. The only difference is the note before last on antique cymbal (percussion 2), which was added in order to resolve the trill and add one sound I felt was necessary. The vibraphone line has been added later and has an independent, nonrepeating, and nonretrograde line.

Percussion instruments are spread as much as possible around the ensemble for the necessary space effect. If all percussion is put into a small area, the sounds come from one direction and are much too close. I also divided the antique cymbals, triangles, cymbals, and tam-tams among the players rather than give each player the same kind of instrument. The idea was to have these instruments (as well as chimes, vibraphone, and marimba) sound like bells of Prague coming from the city as well as from surrounding hills. I have used the E and B antique cymbals because many orchestras own them for Debussy's *Afternoon of a Faun*. The C has been chosen to match the E and B.

The toccata in the fourth movement is rather straightforward, with contrasting passages: the first in the clarinet solo at A and later in all B♭ clarinets; another in trumpets at C; and still another, a variant of the latter that now sounds more lyrical in clarinets and saxophones at F. All of the toccata is difficult rhythmically; the accents and the rests are placed in a rather intricate way. It may very well remind one of Czech folk dance music. At the end of the toccata at the letter S, my idea of the entrance of the first flute was to wait a long time so that the preceding D of the chime nearly disappears. Then the flutist will try to start as softly as possible without an accent, matching the disappearing sound of the chime in a way to bring it back to us; all instruments should later enter the same way, with no attack on the start but rather sneaking into the existing sound and then extending it by crescendos and decrescendos. Some people have wondered about this passage at S. Why this pianissimo while the timpani is pounding some of the heaviest notes? The symbol was more and more people from afar joining a warrior on the drum and uniting in the song.

The aleatory passage at the end, letter V, as well as before H in the first movement, is to be played fortissimo. The individual players should choose those notes that they play well and that sound strong. Also at letter V there should be two chimes players, each one with two hammers. The sound is much more powerful than with only one, even a strong player.

In regard to baritone mutes, they have been written in as *ad libitum*. Not too many bands have such mutes; however, they are very effective and should be used if possible. There is one passage not marked muted, but the baritones should play with mutes in the beginning introduction, measures 2-6 after B. At letter C they should take off the mutes for the rest of the first movement.

Although we proofread the score and parts several times before publication, there are a few mistakes that escaped us. The most important is the metronome marking of the second movement aria. It should read that a quarter—not an eighth—note equals approximately 60-66.

In the introduction, all flutes should play two measures before B (indication tutti missing there). In the interlude, the indication "not necessarily in tempo" extends to the fourth beat two measures before P. The vibraphonist should be together and in tempo with the conductor on this fourth beat A, as well as on the following ones.

# Transitions

Henk Badings/1973

I belong to those composers who maintain that a composition should produce psychic reverberations in the listener, that the sequence of rhythms, pitches, harmonies, dynamics, timbres, and so on create mental tensions and releases, leaving an image in our minds that we can easily determine and observe, though we are completely unable to explain it adequately in words. So, for instance, after having heard a performance of a Mozart symphony, I feel mentally changed, richer; but any attempt to describe it in words seems to me imperfect if not impossible. Of course we can tell enough about a sonata form, about thematic material and thematic development, about composition techniques or historical aspects, all of them interesting subjects for musicians, but none of them touching the core of the musical experience. I, too, can only touch the outside.

My concerto for wind orchestra is in broad outline a symphonic cycle amalgamated into one unit, consisting of a slow introduction, a main quick movement, a slow middle section, and a lively finale. The title *Transitions* has different references. In the first place it has to do with the transition of thematic contours, the transformation of thematic material. Using the tools, the levers, the crowbars of modern form analysis, it is possible to prove all. Would you like to assert that Beethoven derived the theme for the finale of his "Eroica" from a concertino by Pergolesi? You can! Would you like to assert that Bach derived the theme of the *Fugue No. 1 in C Major* from the third movement of Bruckner's Third Symphony? Musically: why not? It is only hard to maintain in chronology.

I try to avoid such magician's tricks, but I know for myself that I derived the finale theme by several transitions from the main theme of the first allegro section with several intermediate steps in between. The principal part of that main theme occurs three bars after section 6, up to four bars after section 7, in saxophones, brass, and percussion. No egg in the world exists without the hen that laid it. In music no theme exists without motifs or germ-cells that generate them. When you listen to the first germ-cell of my piece, you will hear that such a vague tone-shape can very well originate from the preceding silence, but also it has already the embyronic character of that allegro theme (clarinet III-2, repeated twice).

In the middle of the first and main allegro is a cadenza for percussion. When you listen to the next part of it, you can recognize the relationship with the allegro theme (ten bars from 11, timpani I and II). A following metamorphosis of this theme can be found in the second half of the allegro. Here it has a much more individual character, less vague, less general, with a smaller entropic chaos, more organized. To give chapter and verse about this organization: it becomes a kind of march (tutti, 14 to 15).

Rather far removed from the latter shape seems to be the melodic contour of the beginning of the slow section (five bars at 18, oboe I alone). When I remind you of the very first motif of the piece, however, you will observe the relationship. To me the genealogy seems evident.

The final quick section starts during the last part of the slow section. This beginning has a clear relationship with the first allegro theme (first eight bars at 21; saxophones, brass, and percussion). The march theme from the second part of the first allegro is related to the gay finale theme (eight bars at 21, tutti). Here the thematic material is developed to a still higher level of organization. Or to a lower level of entropy, to use a term of thermodynamics and information theory. The material crystallizes into a more explicit, unmistakably individual character. The transition from the rather grim march theme to this finale theme can be observed in the bars preceding the finale theme, where the tonality with its abundance of semitones is transformed by interval augmentation into an anhemitonic pentatonic arrangement (four allegro bars before 23 until five bars after 24; tutti). The final appearance of this material has a pentatonic arrangement in a different setting (25 to 26, tutti).

All these transformations are surely the most important reason for my choice of title, but not the only one. Another kind of transition takes place from the aleatoric mixture of motifs in the introduction via the rhythmically coinciding but melodically and contrapuntally rather chaotic fabric of motifs to the radiant accompaniment formula of the first allegro theme.

In the view of information theory such procedures provide a maximum of information content—such a maximum that it causes a sharp decline in musical meaning. It is wrong to suppose that a maximum of information content yields a maximum of meaning, as so-called white noise can easily demonstrate. White noise is the acme of acoustical information content: not one fragment of twenty milliseconds is equal to the surrounding time fragments. There are so many differences that we cannot perceive them. Therefore, it is for us one constant grey sound. It has a minimum of musical meaning because for our ears there is no change at all. The human ear cannot catch more than five contrapuntal lines at the same time. In the first measures for woodwinds, up until 1, we have ten motifs together, very close, and this causes a colored-noise-effect. The conductor indicates the beginning of a motif in one instrument, which is repeated *ad libitum*, then the beginning of the next motif and so on, until a whole acoustical layer of motifs is built up. Some people are completely convinced that aleatory is the solution for the dead end they believe modern music has reached. The famous musicologist Curt Sachs warns in his book about meter, rhythm, and tempo that "chaos" (chance structure) was what mankind found on earth and that "order" was a typical human contribution. I would like to add that chaos is only interesting for us as long as we can compare it with order, or with a certain amount of order.

In the woodwind opening to *Transitions*, the instruments play different motifs in different tempo so there is no vertical time correlation. In sections 6 to 7, the vertical time correlation is established. The chaotic motif structure gradually changes into the organized accompaniment formula. Only a twinkling effect is left by means of passing and changing notes. The sound of it is then easily understandable: it is a radiant accompaniment-layer.

Another kind of transition takes place from the loud allegro to the soft lento and later from that lento to the finale. Through the soundgaps of the allegro the lento becomes perceptible (tutti at 17 through six bars). In a similar way the finale appears with the epilogue of the lento still audible in hiatuses between the accents of the finale (tutti, 21 to 22).

Other transitions in the piece are harmonic contrapositions, playing a role like Yang and Yin in Chinese philosophy: Yang the virile, strong, creative element, and Yin the feminine, weak, receptive element, forming together a unity, contrasting but inconsistent without each other. An example of these harmonic contrapositions is to be found in the slow section (tutti, 18 to 20). The first eight bars are circling around harmonic combinations of G#, D, F#, B, F, and B♭, where the next eight bars circle around C#, E♭, G, C, E, and A. A similar harmonic pattern is observable in many other places, though not always as a contraposition of six notes of the chromatic scale against six other notes, as in this case.

What happens in the lower regions of the introduction shows a similar principle (seven measures before 1 to 1). The first combination of tones is, in the order of the entry, D, C#, F#, A♭, G, E♭, and E. The second fragment (one bar after 1 to 2) has F, B, B♭, A, G#, C, and D♭. Apart from the doublings, C#–D♭ and G#–A♭, here is another complement of tone qualities.

This comparison demonstrates that *Transitions* has nothing to do with serial technique. The complementary arrangement of tone qualities is now and then applied in more than two harmonic combinations, so for instance in the next "leitmotiv," where there are three harmonies involved: F#, B, D, G, then F, B♭, E♭, A♭, then C#, A, E, and C (three bars after 21, first quarter note: ♫♩ ). In this and in other cases the motif was exactly twelve notes with the twelve tones of the chromatic scale, but in many other cases this technique is extended over more or less notes.

I don't use forte or any other dynamic grade for all the instruments at the same time. The reason is not only to shade the nuances, to balance the groups, but also to let the direction of the sound source move in the orchestra, to achieve a spatial effect. One of the most striking fragments seems to me to be the cadenza of the two timpanists in opposition. I do not only mean the beats coming antiphonally from the right or from the left, but more specifically the rolls with opposite crescendos and decrescendos. In radio terms this would be called cross-fading. The sound seemingly moves between the two sides of the stage. You also can hear the effect in the tutti from the fourth bar in 9 to 10—a motif wandering from group to group—and in the brass from 3 to 4, where the same harmony moves from two horns and the tubas to the trombones.

That is the outside of my composition. I've already stated that I feel unable to sketch the contents of my piece in words. Perhaps I should demonstrate by trying to do so.

Vague musical shapes arise from silence, mobile in the higher pitches, slow and dark in the lower region. They develop to a higher grade of organization, in the lower part to a rather grim character, in the higher part to a shining, twinkling sound. A dramatic tension develops between two contrasting sound worlds. Later a milder music world becomes audible through the vehemence of the lower sounds; its lyric shapes remain after the grim accents break off. The mild, melodious sound shapes are interrupted by a new violent outburst. This material develops to a less aggressive shape and finally to a gay, playful, pleasant tune.

# Appendixes

# Testimonial to Albert Austin Harding, Honorary Life President

Frederick Fennell/1958

Fortunate is the man who finds work to do that fulfills even the most infinitesimal fragment of his hopes and dreams. More fortunate yet is the man who is born beneath a star of destiny and who, after he becomes aware of the gift from his maker, marshalls the courage, character, and devotion by which this destiny might find its manifestation in service to his fellow men.

Destiny, dreams, and devotion were, indeed, the forces that propelled Austin Harding. The rise of great people from humble beginnings is the story of our country, and the story of Illinois bands and their distinguished founder. That college and university bands today find representation in a national association was made possible only because Dr. Harding and the university he served with undying love created the university band that now exists everywhere in this fabulous land.

I do not believe we are too close to our history to make a just evaluation of those beginnings. Illinois is where it all began. There is where order emerged from turn-of-the-century chaos. There is where the band took a column-right from the street and bandstand to the gridiron. There, too, is where the two-way street was established that allowed the band to countermarch and enter the concert hall. That band was Austin Harding's. There is where the crumbling music economy of the professional touring band found an "institute for advanced studies" that fashioned a program ready and waiting for national adoption when the United States emerged from World War I with a long-overdue awareness of the place of the arts in education. Dr. Harding fashioned that program.

Austin Harding provided the people of America with a single blazing illumination of quiet leadership that may be compared with the life and work of Thomas Jefferson. His uncomplicated philosophy was that the band was good, that he loved it, and that he would give his life to its acceptance and betterment. This he did for forty-three magnificent seasons.

To those who knew Dr. Harding apart from the University of Illinois, as I did at Interlochen, his magic still rubbed off. Dr. Harding gave the country's younger directors and players a leadership that shall long be cherished. But of equal importance to us all are the thousands of university students who, as a result of his life, his work, and his example, have a fine band in which to play while they pursue their preparation for a field in science or art other than music.

It was to the science of engineering that Dr. Harding first addressed his academic interests. But his youthful experiences as a bandsman in his home town and its surrounding area drew him inevitably into the early military band activity of the University of Illinois. He set for himself and for us all the prime example in this choice. Urgent academic and aesthetic questions often center about the resolving of these two same careers. It was as though Austin Harding knew the value of balance in the life of his fellow men and of the urgent necessity of setting the aesthetic gyrocompass whirling while people were in a youthful, formative stage of their development. Why, he must have thought, should they not have both engineering and band music, at least while they are at school? He must have known in 1905 what Howard Hanson has so eloquently expressed in his recent statement:

> More and more we are coming to realize that science does not hold all the answers. Science has proved again and again that while it can

cure, it can kill more quickly; and while it can create, it can more easily destroy. We realize that we must look for something that is above and beyond those things which we see, which we feel, and of which we are sometimes afraid. So we turn from science to religion, and to art, and particularly to music.

Austin Harding turned from science to music and thus both influenced in myriad ways the lives of millions of his fellow men and hastened the day when colleges would rush to the pursuit of things not previously accepted in academic circles. Ours is indeed the time of the university in the field of the arts, other great institutions of professional life having had their time upon its stage. Dr. Harding was among the pioneers in the development of this enormous reservoir for the broad practice of the arts in a democratic society.

He, his staff, and players did all of these things in quarters long borrowed from the decommission list. I never saw them but I know of their glory to the history of bands in our country. I saw a deep affection for those who played in them mirrored in Harding's quiet eyes. We have heard their sounds echoed in the playing of thousands of high school bands all over our land. Judging from the good things they have wrought, they must have been wonderful old rooms.

New rooms have already been dedicated, but we rededicate them to the undying spirit of Albert Austin Harding, whose lifetime devotion to the University of Illinois bands shall forever be remembered in the CBDNA and in the musical life of this nation.

# Citation for William D. Revelli, Honorary Life President

Guy M. Duker/1971

As an energetic, ambitious, and far-sighted young university band director, William D. Revelli saw the need for an organization devoted to the professional concerns of the college band. In 1941 he acted upon this conviction and organized the College Band Directors National Association. In the ensuing years the CBDNA has justified its establishment, flourished, and made countless significant contributions to college band work that have affected every phase of the band field.

Throughout its entire history, the CBDNA has reflected the wisdom and judgment of Dr. Revelli. In its early years he was hyperactive in almost every CBDNA concern. He was president from 1941 through 1945, leading the association through its formative years, whose growing pains were made even more intense by the shackles World War II imposed.

A perusal of CBDNA national books of proceedings will show that his was a voice speaking with authority, prophecy, and rationality on all issues that had a vital effect on the progress of bands. He created an agency for communication and was one of its principal and outstanding spokesmen. Good ideas came from his fertile and facile mind at an astounding rate.

In recent years he has relinquished hyperactive participation in favor of merely active participation. This has been a tacit invitation for younger men to accept leadership and spokesman roles in the CBDNA. While he has given ample evidence throughout his professional career that he is one of the best when it comes to seeing healthy change and adapting to it, he clearly feels that the mood of ever-changing "today" might come through more clearly and properly if younger men were more active, so he deliberately put himself in the background. Through it all, however, he has made available his pragmatic voice of experience.

I recently heard it said that committee work is but the lengthened shadow of the man in charge. This seems to me to aptly sum up the relationship of the CBDNA and William Revelli: the CBDNA is but the lengthened shadow of its founder and honorary life president.

We sincerely hope he will always be proud of his shadow.

We all firmly believe that everyone is entitled to retire from the firing line in order to devote time to the many worthwhile projects that have been put off until the tomorrow that a busy and productive career seems to subvert. But it is our hope that Dr. Revelli will never retire from the position of honorary life president of the CBDNA and that the CBDNA will have many more opportunities to benefit from his sage counsel.

To this brilliant musician and conductor, the CBDNA extends heartfelt thanks for his far-sightedness—without him we would never have come into being—and wishes him the very best of the best for many, many relaxed but productive retirement years.

# *Index*

References to material written by a contributor are printed in italics after his name.

Abato, Vincent, 26
*Accent*, 226
Administrators, and college bands, 225-231
*Afternoon of a Faun* (Debussy), 265
Alexander, Russell, marches of, 38
American Bandmasters Association
   and commissions, 48
   and new arrangements, 41
   and standardized instrumentation, 69, 86, 93
American Federation of Musicians, and broadcasting, 10
American School Band Directors Association, and standardized instrumentation, 69
American Society of Composers, Authors and Publishers (ASCAP), and televising halftime shows, 142

*Apocalyptica* (Rochberg), 56
Arrangements for marching band, 131-132
*Art of Oboe Playing, The* (Sprenkle and Ledet), 198

Bach, Johann Christian, 61
Bach, Johann Sebastian,
   transcriptions by, 27
   transcriptions of works of, 40
Bachman, Harold, *35-44*
   and concert band literature, 1
Bachman Million Dollar Band, 36
Badings, Henk, *267-271*
   *Transitions*, analysis of, 267-271
Bainum, Glenn Cliff, and televising halftime shows, 144
Band audiences, music tastes of, 7
*Band's Music, The* (R. Goldman), 36
Bands, evolution of, 211-217

## 282  INDEX

*Bandwagon*, 51
Barnum and Bailey circus, band music for, 48
Bartók, Béla, 249
Battisti, Frank, and commissions, 48
Beach, Frank, on competitions, 208
*Beautiful Galatea, The* overture (Suppé), 40
Beethoven, Ludwig van
  as innovator, 52
  *Serenade for Flute, Violin, and Viola*, 241
Bell, William, on tuba intonation, 197
Bellini, Vincenzo
  *Norma* overture, 40
  overtures of, 39
Benjamin, Edward, Restful Music Commission, 247, 255
Berg, Alban, 249
  *Four Pieces for Clarinet*, 51
Bernstein, Leonard, on future of symphony orchestra, 55
Bogianchino, Massimo, 66
Boosey & Hawkes, Ltd., and standardized instrumentation, 86
Bowles, Richard, on band adjudication, 201-202
*Boys of the Old Brigade, The* (Chambers), 38
Brasses
  and band sonorities, 71-77
  recommended CIMI scoring for, 96-97
Broadcasting, 10
Bryan, Paul R., *45-50*, *133-134*
Buffalo Philharmonic, and new music programing, 55

Cage, John, and "chance" music, 53
Cailliet, Lucien, arrangements of, 32, 41
California at Davis, University of, and new works, 55

Campbell, William, *147-149*
Carabineri Band, instrumentation of, 216
Carnegie Institute of Technology, 66
Catel, Charles, 59
Cavender, George, *141-145*
Chambers, Parris, *The Boys of the Old Brigade*, 38
Chance, John Barnes, *Variations on a Korean Folk Song*, 169, 170
Chicago Symphony Orchestra
  and new music programing, 55
  under Theodore Thomas, 60
Chicago, University of, grants for new music, 54
Childs, Barney, *Six Events for Fifty-Eight Players*, 55
Clarinets, intonation problems of, 162-165
Cole, William, *123-128*
College band conductors, responsibility of, for training new musicians, 20-23
College Band Directors National Association (CBDNA)
  clinic for composers, 9
  and commissioning process, 48
  Committee on Published Band Music, 33
  Committee on Solos with Manuscript Accompaniment, 33
  and Dahl's *Sinfonietta*, 241
  and eighteenth- and nineteenth-century band music, 62
  founding of, 1
  future of, 233-236
  history of, 31-34
  Instrumentation Committee, 32
  and marching band, 105-107, 133
  Original Compositions Committee, 32-34
  proposed central library for halftime shows, 122

and standardized instrumentation, 69-70, 93, 99-103
and televising halftime shows, 142, 143, 144
College Music Society, and marching bands, 133
Colorado, University of, and instrumentation research, 72
Colwell, Richard, *119-122*
Comité Internationale pour la Musique Instrumentale (CIMI), and standardized instrumentation, 92-93
Commissions for new band works, 28, 47-48
Committee on Published Band Music (CBDNA), 33
Committee on Solos with Manuscript Accompaniment (CBDNA), 33
Competitions, 203-209
Concert band
  instrumentation of, 9
  literature problems of, 1-3, 9, 13-17, 25-29
  purpose of, 19
  relation to athletic department, 6, 16
  relation to service bands, 6
  transcriptions for, 10
*Concert Band, The* (R. Goldman), 36
Concertgebouw Orchestra, and new music programing, 55
*Concertino* (Weber), 243
*Concertino for Marimba and Orchestra* (Creston), 27
*Concerto for Accordion and Orchestra* (Creston), 27
*Concerto for Piano and Winds* (Stravinsky), 65
*Concerto for Saxophone* (Creston), 27
*Concerto for Saxophone and Wind Ensemble* (Husa), 260
Conductor, guest, selection and responsibilities of, 157-159

Conway, Patrick, professional band of, 36
Copland, Aaron
  *Emblems*, 34
  works for band, 73, 75
Cowell, Henry, on Goldman Band, 37
Creatore, Giuseppe, professional band of, 36
Creston, Paul, *25-29*
  *Concertino for Marimba and Orchestra*, 27
  *Concerto for Accordion and Orchestra*, 27
  *Concerto for Saxophone*, 27
  *Fantasy for Trombone and Orchestra*, 27
  *Legend*, 28-29
  *Sonata for Saxophone*, 27
  and standardized instrumentation, 99
  *Suite for Saxophone*, 27
  works for concert band, 4, 73, 75
Czech Philharmonic, 169

Dahl, Ingolf, *241-246*
  *Sinfonietta*, 64-65
  analysis of, 241-246
Dalla Casa, Girolamo, and formation of Venetian state band, 235
Davis, University of California at, and new works, 55
*Death of Custer*, 40-41
Debussy, Claude, *Afternoon of a Faun*, 265
Duker, Guy M., *279-280*
Dvořák, Antonín, "New World" Symphony, 125
Dvorak, Ray, on marching bands, 105

Eastman Wind Ensemble, formation of, 70, 79-84
Effinger, Cecil, and instrumentation research, 72
*Egyptian Ballet* (Luigini), 41

*1812 Overture* (Tchaikovsky), 40, 125
Electronic music, 52-53
*Emblems* (Copland), 34
*Etudes for the Advanced Clarinetist* (Siennicki-McGinnis), 168
Evans, Jack, 166

*Fantasia in F* (Mozart), 65
*Fantasy for Trombone and Orchestra* (Creston), 27
Fennell, Frederick, 9-11, 19-23, 79-84, 211-217, 275-277
  and Eastman Wind Ensemble, 70
Filmore, Henry, marches of, 38
*Finlandia* (Sibelius), 40
Fitzgerald, R. Bernard, 13-17
  and conductor responsibilities, 1
  and standardized instrumentation, 99
*Five Pieces for Orchestra* (Schoenberg), 51
Flotow, Friedrich von, overtures of, 39
Ford Foundation, composers-in-the-schools program, 47
*Four Pieces for Clarinet* (Berg), 51
Fourth Symphony (Ives), 52
Fox, Hugo, and bassoon intonation, 182

Gallodoro, Al, 26
Gaubert, Phillipe, *Taffanel-Gaubert Method for Flute*, 171
Gershwin, George, *Rhapsody in Blue*, 125
Giannini, Vittorio
  and standardized instrumentation, 99
  *Symphony for Band*, 4
  works for concert band, 4
Gilmore Library, editions of standard band transcriptions, 39
Gilmore, Patrick, 35
  and evolution of bands, 214
  professional band of, 38
  programing of, 39
  *Voice of the Departed Soul*, 35
Goldman Band, 249
  and commissions, 48
  Cowell, Henry, on, 37
  programing of, 37, 38
Goldman, Edwin Franko
  and commissions, 48
  marches of, 38
Goldman, Richard Franko
  *The Band's Music*, 36
  and commissions, 48
  *The Concert Band*, 36
  editions of eighteenth- and nineteenth-century music by, 14
  on professional bands, 36
  *The Wind Band*, 36, 133
Gomes, Carlos, *Il Guarany* overture, 40
Gossec, François, *Te Deum*, 59
Gould, Morton
  *Prisms*, 55
  and standardized instrumentation, 99, 100
Gounod, Charles, *Symphony*, 59
Grasso, Benjamin V., and standardized instrumentation, 99
"Great Gate of Kiev" (from Mussorgsky's *Pictures at an Exhibition*), 125
*Il Guarany* overture (Gomes), 40

Halftime shows
  in the future, 137-138
  survey on, 123-128
Hall, R. B., marches of, 38
Handel, George Frideric
  *Royal Fireworks Music*, 65
  works performed by professional bands, 36
Hanson, Howard
  on limitations of science, 276-277

symposiums of new orchestral music, 82
Harding, Albert Austin
 at University of Illinois, 31-32
 testimonial to, 275-277
Harris, Roy, works for band, 75
Hauser, Arthur, 2-3
Haydn, Franz Joseph, divertimenti of, 241
Henderson, Hubert, *135-138, 225-231*
 on clarinet intonation, 164-165
Hérold, Ferdinand, *Zampa* overture, 40
High school bands, preparation for college bands, 6-7
Herbert, Victor
 marches of, 38
 and Pittsburgh Symphony Orchestra, 37
 and Twenty-Second Regiment Band, 37
Hindemith, Paul
 works for concert band, 4
 *Symphony for Band*, 4
 *Symphony in B♭*, 81
 works for military band, 48
Hindsley, Mark, *113-118, 175-199*
Holst, Gustav
 *Suite in E♭*, 4
 *Suite in F*, 4
 works for concert band, 4, 32, 73, 75
 works for military band, 48
Honegger, Arthur, *King David*, 246
Houston, University of, band, 53
Hovhaness, Alan, 51
Husa, Karel, *259-266*
 *Concerto for Saxophone and Wind Ensemble*, 260
 *Music for Prague 1968*, analysis of, 259-266

Illinois, University of
 band under Albert Austin Harding, 31-32, 275-277
 intonation research at, 181
 marching band of, 105
Innes, Frederick, professional band of, 36
Instrument modification, for better intonation, 181-193
*Instrumentalist, The*, 234, 235
Instrumentation
 for concert band, 9
 editing old works, 66-67
 standardized, 32
 and American Bandmasters Association, 86
 and CBDNA, 99-103
 in European countries, compared to America, 85-98
Instrumentation Committee (CBDNA), 32
Interlochen, 276
International Contemporary Ensemble of Europe, 54
*Interpolations* (Jordan), 53, 55
Intonation
 and instrument modification, 181-193
 mechanical adjustments for better, 161-173
 problems and procedures, 175-199
*Intonation Deficiencies in Wind Instrument Performance* (Stauffer), 168
Iowa, University of, grants for new music, 54
Ithaca College, band, 259
Ithaca High School Band, and new works, 48, 55
Ives, Charles
 experimentalism of, 51-52
 Fourth Symphony, 52
 on new music, 57

Jazz, and improvisation, 53

Johnson Intonation Trainer, 194
Jones, L. Bruce, *203-209*
Jordan, Arthur, *Interpolations*, 53, 55
Jordan, Bryce, and bibliography of recorded band music, 2

Kappa Kappa Psi, and commissions, 48
*King David* (Honegger), 246
King, Karl, marches of, 38
Koussevitzky, Sergei Alexandrovich, model for band conductors, 22
Kraft, Robert, and Stravinsky symphonies, 171
Kryl, Bohumir, professional band of, 36

Lang, Philip, and standardized instrumentation, 99
Layton, Billy Jim, on contemporary music, 56-57
League of Composers, and commissions, 48
Ledet, David, *The Art of Oboe Playing*, 198
Leduc, Editions Alphonse, and standardized instrumentation, 86
Leeds Music Corp., and commissions, 49
*Legend* (Creston), 28-29
Leidzen, Erik
  arrangements of, 32, 41
  transcription of Mussorgsky's *Pictures at an Exhibition*, 66
Liberati, Alessandro, professional band of, 36
Liszt, Franz
  *Second Hungarian Rhapsody*, 41
  works performed by professional bands, 36, 60
Literature, concert band, 45-50, 63-67
  and contemporary works, 51-57
  from eighteenth and nineteenth centuries, 59-62
*Lohengrin* (Wagner), introduction to Third Act, 125
Long Beach Municipal Band, programing of, 37
Los Angeles Philharmonic Orchestra, and new works, 64
Luigini, Alexandre, *Egyptian Ballet*, 41
Lunetta, Stanley, *The Word*, 55-56

McGinnis, Donald E., *161-173*
  *Etudes for the Advanced Clarinetist*, 168
McMillen, Hugh
  and instrumentation research, 72
  survey on marching bands, 105-106
Majorettes, drum, 105
Marching band
  and administrators, 147-149
  and CBDNA, 105-107
  and concert band conductors, 113-118
  future of, 135-138
  image of, 105
  instrumentation, 129-130
  large versus small, 119-122
  purpose of, 19-20, 133-134
  at small colleges, 119-122, 151-153
  surveys on, 109-112, 139-140
  and television coverage, 141-145
Marine Band, United States, 213
Marks Music Corporation, E. B., and new works for band, 49
Martino, Daniel, and marching bands, 106-107
Mason, Lowell, and development of music education, 214
Massenet, Jules, *Phèdre* overture, 41
*Meditation* (Schuller), 55

analysis of, 247-255
Messiaen, Olivier, and the avant-
garde, 52
Michigan, University of
concert band clarinet section of, 165
marching band, 105, 120
Milhaud, Darius
*Suite Française*, 4
works for concert band, 73, 75
works for military band, 48
Minelli, Charles, *99-103*
Montclair College, and new works, 56
Mozart, Wolfgang Amadeus
divertimenti of, 241
*Fantasia in F*, 65
wind serenades of, 235
works for wind ensembles, 81
Mule, Marcel, 26
Music educators, responsibilities of, 219-223
Music Educators National Conference (MENC), and Husa's *Music for Prague 1968*, 259
*Music for Prague 1968* (Husa), analysis of, 259-266
*Musical Quarterly*, and reviews of band works, 56
Mussorgsky, Modest
"Great Gate of Kiev" (from *Pictures at an Exhibition*), 125
*Pictures at an Exhibition*, 66
"My Hero" (Straus), 125

Nagel, Paul, on arts in college curriculums, 226
National Association of Broadcasters, and broadcasting bands, 10
National Collegiate Athletic Association (NCAA), and televising halftime shows, 143
National Intercollegiate Band, 27

Neilson, James, *71-77, 219-223*
on future of college bands, 225
and standardized instrumentation, 69-70, 99
Nelhybel, Vaclav, 61, *257-258*
*Symphonic Movement*, 166, 168
*Symphonic Requiem*, analysis of, 257-258
works for band, 36
"New World" Symphony (Dvořák), 125
Ninth Symphony (Shostakovich), 65-66
Nixon, Roger, works for concert band, 4
*Norma* overture (Bellini), 40

*Oberon* overture (Weber), 41
Offenbach, Jacques, *Orpheus* overture, 40
Oregon, University of, and new music, 54
Original Compositions Committee (CBDNA), 32-34
*Orpheus* overture (Offenbach), 40
Ozalid reproduction process, 132

Penderecki, Krzysztof, *Threnody for the Victims of Hiroshima*, 55
Persichetti, Vincent
*Psalm*, 170
and standardized instrumentation, 99
*Symphony for Band*, 4
works for concert band, 4
Petersen Chromatic Tuner, 194
*Phèdre* overture (Massenet), 41
*Pictures at an Exhibition* (Mussorgsky)
"Great Gate of Kiev," 125
transcriptions of, 66
*Pierrot Lunaire* (Stravinsky), 52

288   INDEX

Pittsburgh Symphony Orchestra, and Victor Herbert, 37
Portland State College, grants for new music, 55
Pottle, Ralph
  tuning guides of, 193-194
  *Tuning the School Band and Orchestra*, 168
Poulenc, Francis, 54
Presser, Theodore, Co., 2
Prévost, Arthur, and CIMI, 93
*Principles of Orchestration* (Rimsky-Korsakov), 245
*Prisms* (Gould), 55
Professional bands, repertoire of, 35-44
Pryor, Arthur, professional band of, 36, 38
*Psalm* (Persichetti), 170

*Race of London, The* (Riviere), 40
Ravel, Maurice
  orchestrations of piano works, 27
  transcription of Mussorgsky's *Pictures at an Exhibition*, 66
*Raymond* overture (Thomas), 40
Reed, Alfred, and standardized instrumentation, 99, 100
Reeves, D. W., marches of, 38
Rehearsals
  for halftime shows, 130-131
  importance of, 21
  warmup techniques for, 161-167
Repertory, for future concert band, 25-29
Respighi, Ottorino, works for band, 75
Revelli, William D., *5-7, 85-98, 157-159*
  citation for, 279-280
  clarinet section at University of Michigan, 165
  and founding of CBDNA, 279-280

and standardized instrumentation, 99
*Rhapsody in Blue* (Gershwin), 125
Rhode Island, University of, marching band, 119-122
Ricordi, G., and Company, Inc., and standardized instrumentation, 86
*Rienzi* overture (Wagner), 40, 73
Rimsky-Korsakov, Nikolai, *Principles of Orchestration*, 245
Rochberg, George
  *Apocalyptica*, 56
  on new music, 56
Rosen, Jerome, 53-54
Rossini, Gioacchino
  overtures of, 39
  *Semiramide* overture, 40
ROTC credit for band participation, 122
*Royal Fireworks Music* (Handel), 65

Sachs, Curt, on modern music, 269
*Le Sacre du printemps* (Stravinsky), 252
San Francisco Symphony, new music programing of, 55
Satz, Ralph, and standardized instrumentation, 99
saxophone, as solo concert instrument, 26
scales, differently tempered, 176-178
Schaefer, William A., *63-67*, 243
Schaeffer, Pierre, and the avant-garde, 52
Schirmer, G., Inc., and new works for band, 49
Schoenberg, Arnold, 54, 249
  *Five Pieces for Orchestra*, 51
  and *Klangfarbenmelodie*, 252
School of New Music (Darmstadt, Germany), and contemporary wind ensembles, 54
*School Musician, The*, 235

Schubert, Franz, Unfinished
     Symphony, 73
Schuller, Gunther, 247-255
  *Meditation*, 55
     analysis of, 247-255
  *Symphony for Brass and Percussion*, 65
  *The Visitation*, 53
*Second Hungarian Rhapsody* (Liszt), 41
*Semiramide* overture (Rossini), 40
*Serenade for Flute, Violin, and Viola*, 241
Shostakovich, Dmitri, Ninth
     Symphony, 65-66
Sibelius, Jean, *Finlandia*, 40
Siennicki, Edmund John, *Etudes for the
     Advanced Clarinetist*, 168
*Sinfonietta* (Dahl), 64-65
     analysis of, 241-246
*Six Events for Fifty-Eight Players*
     (Childs), 55
Smith, Hale, *Take a Chance*, 55
Smith, Leonard, Band, programing of,
     37
Snapp, Kenneth, and Husa's *Music for
     Prague 1968*, 259
Solti, Georg, on American music
     education, 234-235
*Sonata for Saxophone* (Creston), 27
Sonorities, band, analysis of, 71-77
Sousa, John Philip, 2
  marches of, 38
  professional band of, 35-36, 37, 38,
     40
  programing of, 60
Southern California, University of,
     Symphonic Band, and new
     works, 64-65
Sperry, Gale L., 129-132
Sprenkle, Robert, *The Art of Oboe
     Playing*, 198
Stauffer, Donald, *Intonation Difficulties
     in Wind Instrument Performance*,
     168

Straus, Oscar, "My Hero," 125
Strauss, Johann, waltz transcriptions,
     40
Strauss, Richard, on composition, 242
Stravinsky, Igor, 249
  and the avant-garde, 52
  and Barnum and Bailey circus, 48
  *Concerto for Piano and Winds*, 65
  *Pierrot Lunaire*, 52
  *Le Sacre du printemps*, 252
  on the saxophone, 246
  *Symphony in Three Movements*, 171
  *Symphony of Psalms*, 171
  on wind instruments, 246
  works for band, 73
Stroboconn, and intonation, 163, 194
Stroboscopes, and intonation, 179,
     181
Stubbins-Kasper mechanism, 184,
     185-186
*Suite for Saxophone* (Creston), 27
Suppé, Franz von
  *The Beautiful Galatea* overture, 40
  overtures of, 39-40
*Symphonic Movement* (Nelhybel), 166,
     168
*Symphonic Requiem* (Nelhybel),
     analysis of, 257-258
*Symphony* (Gounod), 59
*Symphony in B♭* (Hindemith), 81
*Symphony in Three Movements*
     (Stravinsky), 171
*Symphony for Brass and Percussion*
     (Schuller), 65
*Symphony of Psalms* (Stravinsky), 171

*Taffanel-Gaubert Method for Flute*
     (Gaubert), 171
*Take a Chance* (Smith), 55
*Tannhäuser* overture (Wagner), 36
Tchaikovsky, Peter Ilyitch
  *1812 Overture*, 40, 125

works programed by Sousa and
  Thomas, 60
*Te Deum* (Gossec), 59
Television, and marching bands, 141-145
Thomas, Ambroise, *Raymond*
  overture, 40
Thomas, Theodore
  and development of orchestra, 214
  programing of, 37, 60
*Threnody for the Victims of Hiroshima*
  (Penderecki), 55
Toscanini, Arturo, 105
  model for band conductors, 22
*Transitions* (Badings), analysis of, 267-271
Transcriptions for concert band, 10, 14, 27, 41-42, 60, 65-66
*Tristan und Isolde* (Wagner), 21-22
Tross, Ray, and survey of college band directors, 3-4, 201
*Tuning the School Band and Orchestra* (Pottle), 168
Twenty-Second Regiment Band, and Victor Herbert, 37

UNESCO Preparatory Commission for Music, and standardized instrumentation, 92-93
Unfinished Symphony (Schubert), 73
University of California at Davis, and new works, 55
University of Chicago, and grants for new music, 54
University of Colorado, and instrumentation research, 72
University of Houston, band, 53
University of Illinois
  band under Albert Austin Harding, 31-32, 275-277
  intonation research at, 181
  marching band, 105

University of Iowa, and grants for new music, 54
University of Michigan
  concert band, 27
  clarinet section of, 165
  marching band, 105, 120
University of Oregon, and new music, 54
University of Rhode Island, marching band, 119
University of Southern California Symphonic Band, and new works, 64-65
University of Wisconsin, marching band, 105

Vagner, Robert, 51-57
Varèse, Edgard, on the avant-garde, 52
*Variations on a Korean Folk Song* (Chance), 169, 170
Vaughan Williams, Ralph, works for band, 32, 73, 75
Verdi, Giuseppe, overtures of, 39
*Visitation, The* (Schuller), 53
*Voice of the Departed Soul* (Gilmore), 35
Voxman, Himie, on clarinet intonation, 164

Wagner, Richard
  *Lohengrin*, introduction to Third Act, 125
  *Rienzi* overture, 40, 73
  *Tannhäuser* overture, 36
  works programed by Sousa and Thomas, 60
Weber, Carl Maria von
  *Concertino*, 243
  *Oberon* overture, 41
  overtures of, 39
  works performed by professional bands, 36

Webern, Anton, 249
  and the avant-garde, 52
Weingartner, Felix, on performance practice, 235
*Wets and the Drys, The*, 40
Whitcomb, Manley, *139-140*
  on concert band repertoire, 42
Whitwell, David, *59-62, 233-236*
Williams, Arthur, *109-112*
  on brass intonation, 197
Wilson, Keith, *31-34*
  on standard instrumentation, 70
*Wind Band, The* (R. Goldman), 36, 133
Wind instruments, as soloists in contemporary music, 54
Wisconsin, University of, marching band, 105
Woodwinds
  and band sonorities, 71-77
  recommended CIMI scoring for, 94-96
*Word, The* (Lunetta), 55-56

Yale University, concert band, 33
Yarberry, Glen, *151-153*
Yoder, Paul, and televising halftime shows, 144

*Zampa* overture (Hérold), 40
"Zdoz jste bozi bojovnici," and Husa's *Music for Prague 1968*, 260